MR DIAMOND

MR DIAMOND

The Story of Dennis Levine, Wall Street's Most Infamous Insider Trader

DOUGLAS FRANTZ

BLOOMSBURY

Bloomsbury Publishing Ltd, 2 Soho Square, London W1V 5DE
First published in Great Britain 1987
Copyright © 1987 by Douglas Frantz

First published in the United States of America by
Henry Holt & Co., New York in 1987

British Library Cataloguing in Publication Data
Frantz, Douglas
Mr. Diamond, the story of Dennis Levine, Wall Street's most infamous insider trader
1. Levine, Dennis   2. Securities fraud—
United States — Biography
I. Title
364.1'63   HV6697

ISBN 0-7475-0054-1

Printed in Great Britain by
Biddles Ltd, Guildford & King's Lynn

On the day in 1986 when the US Stock Exchange 'watchdog' body, the SEC, finally discovered the identity of the man they called "Moby Dick", his coded Bahamian bank account held $10.5 million. His name was Dennis Levine. He was 33 years old. And for six years, he had masterminded the biggest insider trading ring ever assembled on Wall Street. Among its beneficiaries: arbitrager Ivan Boesky, rumoured to have owed Levine $2.4 million at the time of his arrest. In his five years of active insider trading, Levine had taken a total profit of $11.6 million on which he had earned another million in interest.

As the scandal swept the investment community and more arrests followed, questions mounted. How had a kid from a poor district of New York, with a mediocre education and no connections managed to work his way into the inner circles of investment banking, pull together a network that reached deep into the top law firms, banks and brokerage houses, and contrive a scheme that was so well covered it went undetected for five years? And how had the SEC, once tipped to the ring's existence, managed to pinpoint Levine despite the notorious secrecy of Bahamian banks and without a whistle-blower inside the ring?

Working initially with a contact who was himself a principal player in uncovering the ringleader and whose contacts and reputation opened doors everywhere, Douglas Frantz eventually secured the confidence of key participants on both sides – ring members, bankers, lawyers. The result is an amazing story: rich in detail and anecdote, it is also profoundly revealing of the financial community as it exists and does business today. It is a tale of greed and mendacity and of one man, both arrogant and insecure, cunning, manipulative, and persuasive, for whom more was never enough.

FOR MY WIFE, CATHERINE COLLINS
AND MY CHILDREN, ELIZABETH AND NICHOLAS

Acknowledgments

This is a true story about real events. It would not have been possible without the unselfish assistance of many real people. While it is impractical to list all of those to whom I am indebted, I am most grateful for the invaluable contributions of Harvey Pitt and Michael Rauch, two attorneys who set the right course; to Bruno Pletscher, who told the truth when it counted; and to Robert Wilkis and Ilan Reich, two decent men caught up in a tragedy.

I also wish to thank the many employees of the U.S. Securities and Exchange Commission who answered questions when they could and, when they could not, were unfailingly polite, including John Sturc, Leo Wang, Chiles Larson, and John Heine. Professor Samuel Hayes III of Harvard Business School opened a window on the world of investment banking. Betty Santangelo, an attorney for Merrill Lynch & Company, provided invaluable advice and guidance; Richard Drew of the brokerage firm's compliance division and Robert Romano, a former Merrill Lynch attorney, provided vital information. Ira Lee Sorkin, the former regional commissioner of the SEC in New York, shared his insights into how the system works, as did other lawyers, government officials, and Wall Street professionals.

Finally, I want to thank Marian Wood of Henry Holt and Company, whose enthusiasm, intelligence, and unerring instincts are truly the marks of a fine editor, and my wife Catherine Collins, whose patience and help made it all possible.

Contents

MR DIAMOND

1.

"Mr. Diamond"

Dennis Levine stepped out of the airplane and squinted into the tropical sun. He was twenty-seven years old, six feet tall, overweight, with a roundish baby face and glasses. A straw hat covered his black hair and he wore blue jeans and an open-collared sport shirt, much like the casual clothing of the tourists he followed down the stairs onto the tarmac at Nassau International Airport.

It was May 26, 1980, a Monday, Memorial Day in the United States, a forty-minute plane ride away.

The one-story terminal building was not air-conditioned and offered little relief from the heat. But passing through immigration is a cursory affair for American tourists entering the Bahamas, and Levine, who carried only an overnight bag, moved quickly through the line.

Minutes later, he walked out the front of the terminal and a uniformed airport employee waved his hand to summon a taxi from the waiting ranks fifty feet away. Sliding into the backseat, Levine asked the driver to take him to Nassau's business district.

The drive downtown takes roughly twenty minutes and winds past palm trees and spindly Australian pines, Lake Cunningham and the Ambassador Beach Golf Course, through residential neigh-borhoods and finally along the coastline, where a visitor can catch a first glimpse of the white sand beaches and sparkling azure At-lantic that have made the Bahamas a vacation mecca.

Nassau is the capital of the Bahamas, 700 islands scattered over 100,000 square miles of the Atlantic. Once home port to legendary pirates, modern Nassau is a bustling city of 125,000 where vestiges of British colonial rule mix with the wares of tourism, the nation's leading industry.

But it was the nation's second-ranking industry that had drawn Levine to Nassau.

Favorable tax laws and strict bank secrecy statutes had trans-formed the city into a major offshore financial center over the last decade. By the summer of 1980, banking trailed only tourism as a source of revenue and employment. More than 200 foreign-owned financial institutions maintained offices in the islands, and most were clustered in buildings just off Bay Street, the main shopping avenue.

Tucked in among the tacky souvenir shops, colorful boutiques, and government offices were branches bearing some of the leading names in international banking—Barclays, Chase Manhattan, Credit Suisse—as well as dozens of lesser-known institutions. Those were the places where Levine would spend the next two days, searching for a bank to meet his special financial requirements.

On his second day in Nassau, Levine walked into the modest offices of Bank Leu International Ltd., a subsidiary of Switzerland's oldest private bank. He told the receptionist he was interested in opening an account and asked to see the bank manager.

Jean-Pierre Fraysse, the general manager of Bank Leu, greeted the unexpected visitor and escorted him to his office. Fraysse apol-ogized for the cramped quarters, explaining that the bank would be moving to more suitable space the following month.

Levine told Fraysse that he was calling on all of the Swiss banks in Nassau before selecting the one that he felt could handle his accounts most efficiently. He identified himself as an investment banker from the United States and said he intended to trade actively in the U.S. stock markets. He said he would require fast and efficient service. Discretion was essential.

Fraysse, an experienced international banker, immediately saw Levine as the type of customer who fit into the plans he had for the future of Bank Leu International. He explained to his American visitor that he had joined Bank Leu recently with a mandate to expand business in the Bahamas. He was particularly interested in attracting customers who wanted to take advantage of the bank's stock trading program. Levine left without committing himself, saying he still had other banks to visit. Fraysse was confident he would return.

Jean-Pierre Fraysse had come to Bank Leu on January 4 as general manager after many years in international finance. Most recently, he had been an executive with Guinness Mahon & Co., one of Britain's leading merchant banks. Prior to that he had been an executive in the international division of Lloyds Bank in England and he had worked for investment houses in his native France. At fifty, he was trim and debonair, a wine connoisseur and raconteur whose perfect English was occasionally overcome by a heavy accent, reminding listeners of nothing so much as Peter Sellers playing Inspector Clouseau.

Later that day, Levine returned and told Fraysse he had selected Bank Leu. Levine said he would close his account in Geneva with Pictet & Cie, another Swiss bank, and transfer the funds to Bank Leu. The amount would be small in the beginning, $125,000 or $130,000, but he promised that the account would grow.

Fraysse summoned the bank's vice president and treasurer, Bruno Pletscher, to meet the new customer and handle the details of setting up Levine's account. Pletscher, a tall man whose traditional Swiss reserve was often misinterpreted as dourness, was also new at Bank Leu International. But his background had little in common with that of his superior.

Pletscher had come to the Bahamian subsidiary a few months before, in November 1979, from Bank Leu's home office in Zurich, where he had been a workhorse in the accounting department. Although he was only thirty-one, Pletscher had spent fifteen years in the banking business, beginning with another Zurich bank as an apprentice at the age of sixteen. He had joined Bank Leu in 1967 as a nineteen-year-old junior accounting clerk and earned his accountant's degree at night school. He finished third in the nation on the accountants exam the year he received his certificate.

Since then, Pletscher had risen steadily through the bank's accounting department until he became the head of a division in the home office. He had also managed many special projects for the bank, including designing and implementing the accounting system for Bank Leu International when the subsidiary was opened in Nassau in 1973. The establishment of a subsidiary in the Bahamas was the first foray into international banking by Bank Leu, which built its reputation in Switzerland on more than two centuries as a lender to thrifty Swiss homeowners and small businesses, rather than in the international arena most often associated with its colleagues.

Over the years, the challenges in the accounting aspects of banking had diminished for Pletscher. He wanted to develop a broader range of skills and learn the so-called front-office business of cultivating customers and offering investment advice. In late 1979, Pletscher had happily taken the second-ranking job in the Bahamas and moved his wife and three children halfway around the world.

Fraysse arrived at Bank Leu soon after Pletscher, and the reserved Swiss found a willing and skilled teacher. So when Fraysse summoned him to meet the new American customer on May 27, Pletscher realized it was not only to handle the details of establishing an account. It was another lesson in cultivating clients.

"I'll give you good business, but I want to have top service," Levine said.

Levine was accustomed to dealing with older, powerful men—the heads of corporations and banks. As a young investment banker, he had been on the periphery of some major business deals and he had carefully acquired a patina of professional success, orthodox good manners, and smooth charm that concealed the real man: ambitious, vulgar, deferential only when deference paid. He carried his excess weight with self-assurance and his dark eyes held a knowing gleam. In his few short years in business, Levine had become smooth, likable, amusing, clever at concealing the itch of his ambition.

Levine's instructions to Pletscher and Fraysse were delivered in a polite, demanding tone. He was not rude, but he left no room for misunderstanding. He said he might decide to invest all of the money in his account in a single stock on the spur of the moment. He was not interested in accumulating the traditional diversified stock portfolio. He would not require any investment advice from the bank. He said he knew everything necessary about the American markets. He simply wanted his orders to buy and sell stocks executed efficiently and quickly.

Levine repeated his insistence on maximum secrecy. He would give the bank his trading instructions by calling collect on the telephone. He refused to provide the bank with a telephone number where he could be reached and said that he wanted no communication with the institution, oral or written, unless he initiated it. All account statements and other mail related to the account were to be held at the bank for his inspection on what he said would be regular visits.

Levine then asked which brokerage houses in New York the bank used to execute its trades. When Fraysse replied that the bank sent all of its trading business to EuroPartners Securities Corp., a small firm associated with the bank's home office, Levine said he would feel better if "sensitive" stock transactions were spread among other brokers. He did not press the point.

Fraysse raised the question of whether Levine would open an individual account or create a Bahamian company for an added layer of anonymity. It was an area in which Levine seemed to know little, so Fraysse summoned one of the bank's lawyers, and Levine listened as the attorney ran down the advantages and disadvantages of creating a Bahamian company. Local attorneys could be designated officers of the corporation to shield the owner's identity. The officers could report to the Central Bank of the Bahamas that the corporation was headed by a nonresident and avoid disclosing his name to the authorities. The ownership of the corporation could be held through registered shares, which could be kept by the directors and would not carry the name of the real owner.

Levine said little during the explanation. Fraysse thought he seemed disappointed the bank did not offer to set up the Bahamian company for him that day, but in fact Levine's response was that, at least at the outset, he would operate through an individual account.

Although he had introduced himself to the bankers with his real name, Levine wanted a coded account to protect his identity from outside authorities. He said he would open his account in the name of "Diamond" and that when he called the bank collect with his trading orders, he would identify himself as "Mr. Diamond." That established, Levine repeated his need for perfect service, underlining his insistence by mentioning what he described vaguely as "difficulties" with a prior banking relationship. He said he did not want any problems at Bank Leu, implying that he had terminated the earlier banking relationship because of his dissatisfaction with the service offered.

The truth was that Levine had opened a secret trading account with Pictet & Cie in Geneva in July 1979. He had used the account to start trading on inside information gleaned from his job at Smith Barney, Harris Upham & Co. Eventually, an official at Pictet & Cie had spotted the pattern and stopped Levine's trading. With the inimitable discretion and manners of Swiss bankers, Pictet & Cie suggested that Monsieur Levine close the account and take his business elsewhere.

Fraysse and Pletscher, however, knew nothing of the incident, and they assured Levine that Bank Leu could provide precisely the type of service he sought.

In fact, for Fraysse and Pletscher, Levine's demands were not out of the ordinary. Privacy and secrecy for customers are routine at financial institutions in Switzerland and the Bahamas. Bankers in both countries are trained not to ask too many questions of their customers. As for the coded account, that, too, was routine. Virtually every Swiss bank offered customers the option of holding their accounts in a code name.

Pletscher assisted Levine in completing the forms for the "Diamond" account. He photocopied Levine's passport photo and stapled it into the file so that he could be identified by bank employees when he came to make a transaction. Also attached to the file was the signature card that Levine filled out in his own name and with his home address on Manhattan's East Side. When Levine left the bank promising to wire money from his Swiss account in a matter of days, he seemed satisfied with his coded account.

A coded account may offer a customer a sense of comfort, perhaps a touch of intrigue and glamour. But such an account should not be confused with the harder-to-obtain numbered account. While many accounts at Swiss banks are headed by a code name, the identity of the account holder is known to bank employees and readily available to any employee with access to the file. True numbered accounts are rare and the identity of the holder is a closely guarded secret. A numbered account requires approval from the highest levels of a bank and is offered only to select customers depositing large sums of money, usually a minimum of one million Swiss francs, roughly equivalent to $650,000. The identity of the holder does not appear in the file and is usually known only to two or three top bank officials.

The real protection for foreigners seeking to hide their money or financial transactions in the Bahamas lies less in a code name than in the strict bank secrecy laws. It is a crime for a bank employee to reveal the identity of a customer without an order from a Bahamian court or proper government official.

After Levine left, Fraysse wrote a memo for his files identifying the new customer only as "Mr. Diamond." Never again would Levine be referred to within the bank by his real name. In assessing Mr. Diamond, Fraysse wrote: "He is basically only interested in the

BANK LEU INTERNATIONAL LTD

INFORMATION FOR A NEW ACCOUNT

Client's No.

Surname — *" DIAMOND "*

Christian Name

Type of Account — *C/A — USŁ*

Joint Account — ☐ Yes ☐ No

Mailing Instructions —
☐ To Be Sent to The Client
☒ Hold Mail
☐ To Bank Leu Zurich
☐

Further Instruction

Dennis B. Levine
777,470,11/10

CLIENT'S INFORMATION — ☒ New Client   ☐ Change

☐ Mr.   ☐ Mrs.   ☐ Miss   ☐ Co.   ☐ Bros.   ☐ Doctor

Date of Birth _____ Nationality *USA*

Language *E* Tel. No. _____

Address *225 EAST 57TH STREET*
NEW YORK N.Y. 10022
USA *" HOLD MAIL*

2nd Address

3rd Address

Date *27/5/80*   Signature

Checked:

BANK LEU INTERNATIONAL LTD

NASSAU   BAHAMAS

Application for the opening of **Eröffnungsantrag für** **Solicitud de apertura de** Account/Konto/Cuenta ☐ Securities deposit/Depot/ ☐ Depósito de Títulos	**Account/Konto/Cuenta No.** **Deposit/Depot/Depósito No.** 777,470

Mr./Herr/Sr.
Mrs./Frau/Sra
Miss/Frl./Sta

Complete Name/Name, Vorname usw./Nombre completo

*****DIAMOND******

Dennis B. Levine

Address/Domizil/Domicilio

(HOLD
MAIL)

225 East 57th Street
New York, N.Y. 10022

Nationality/Nationalität/ Nacionalidad

U.S.A.

Activity/Beruf/Profesión

Banker

Line of business/Geschäftszweig/ Ramo

Power of attorney in favour of/Vollmacht zu Gunsten/Poder en favor de

Philip Levine

Correspondence / Korrespondenz / Correspondencia
english ☑
deutsch ☐
français ☐
español ☐

to be sent to
zustellen an
a enviar a

Hold Mail

These documents are confidential and are
supplied pursuant to Agreements with the
Securities and Exchange Commission and
the United States Department of Justice
as to their confidentiality and use.
Neither the documents nor their contents
may be disclosed to any other person or
entity unless pursuant to those Agreements.

U█000005

Safe custody account
For the safekeeping and administration
of all property deposited, the pertaining
regulations of Bank Leu International
Ltd.
are applicable. The account holder
confirms herewith to have received a
copy of these regulations.

Depot
Für die Aufbewahrung und Verwaltung
aller deponierten Vermögenswerte
sind die Bestimmungen des Depot-
reglementes der Bank Leu International
Ltd.
massgebend. Der Depotinhaber
bestätigt, ein Exemplar dieses
Reglementes erhalten zu haben.

Depósito de Títulos
La salvaguarda y la administración
de todos los valores depositados
están sujetas a las condiciones
del Bank Leu International Ltd.

El titular del depósito confirma
haber recibido un ejemplar de
dichas condiciones.

Place and date/Ort und Datum/Lugar y fecha

NASSAU

Signature/Unterschrift/Firma

Dennis Levine

66-01-006-8 93

U.S. market, which he knows extremely well. He will give us his instructions by telephone on a collect call basis. He appeared to be obsessed by security and does not wish to receive any communication from us in a written or oral form." Fraysse concluded the memo by suggesting that careful attention be paid to Mr. Diamond and his trading activity. "He certainly looks a demanding customer," wrote Fraysse.

Later that afternoon, Fraysse took Pletscher aside and told him: "This could really be good business for the bank. The ball is in your court and you should be sure to execute his trades efficiently. This could be very good for us."

Pletscher understood little about the American securities market. He did not even know what Levine meant when he said he was an investment banker, suspecting he worked in a bank and specialized in investment advice for customers. But Pletscher was excited at the prospect of becoming involved in the U.S. markets that handling Levine's trading orders promised. He viewed the American as a "smart guy" who would make money in the stock market, generate substantial trading commissions for the bank, and provide Pletscher with invaluable lessons in the securities business.

Early the following week, two wire transfers brought $128,900 into Mr. Diamond's account at Bank Leu from Pictet & Cie in Geneva. Days later, on June 5, the customer called collect with his first stock purchase order—1,500 shares of Dart Industries. On June 6, the stock was sold after another telephone call. The price had climbed nearly three points a share after the public announcement that Kraft Inc. was planning an offer to merge with Dart. Mr. Diamond made $4,093 on his first stock transaction with Bank Leu.

On August 22, Levine returned to the bank. By now he was a valued customer and Fraysse escorted him to the large conference room in the bank's new quarters at Norfolk House, a pastel green, colonial-style office building downtown. Levine reviewed his accounts and had only one complaint: the $10 charge for each of his collect calls was too high. He then dumped $40,000 in cash onto the table from a plastic shopping bag. It was his second deposit in the "Diamond" account.

Over the next six years, Levine would return to Bank Leu many times. He was always dressed as a tourist and he usually wore a straw hat. He frequently carried a plastic shopping bag. But he would never again need to deposit money.

Instead, Levine would leave with his shopping bag stuffed with cash. Sometimes as much as $200,000, always in $100 bills, always dropped into a shopping bag. By the end, he would withdraw $1.9 million.

The withdrawals were small when compared with the wealth amassed in Levine's account and the magnitude of his stock trading. Over nearly six years of trading at Bank Leu, Levine bought as much as 150,000 shares of stock in a single company. He invested as much as $9 million in a single deal. He bought $99.3 million worth of stock in 114 different companies. He sold that stock for a total of $110.8 million. He picked seventy-one winners and made $13.6 million profit on them. The biggest jackpot was $2.7 million profit on one deal. He lost $2 million on forty-three losers. The worst loser was $274,000. His net profit on all stock transactions was $11.6 million. He added to that nearly one million dollars in interest from the bank.

The numbers are the stark epitaph of Dennis Levine's greed and compulsion, his imperious manipulation of friends and contemptuous betrayal of colleagues. But the numbers are only the cold facts of a story about how the optimism and desperation of one man's thirst for glory destroyed the careers of some of Wall Street's brightest young stars, triggered the greatest scandal since the Great Crash of 1929, and proved that corruption in the era of the global stock market can have global repercussions.

2.

Diamond in the Rough

D ennis Levine was a street-smart kid from a modest home who wound up living in a million-dollar apartment on Park Avenue. But he never forgot what he had learned on the streets, and he used it throughout his career.

For the first twenty-five years of his life, Levine lived with his parents in a small red-brick bungalow, faced with stone, on 208th Street in the Bayside section of Queens. He was the youngest of three sons of Philip and Selma Levine. A daughter, born two years after Dennis, died of a brain tumor at the age of five.

Bayside, tucked between the fashionable neighborhoods of Manhattan and the middle-class suburbs of Long Island, had the look of a small town. Working-class immigrants fleeing decaying neighborhoods in Manhattan had settled there in the 1940s. In the 1950s and 1960s, when Dennis Levine was growing up there, Bayside was much as it remains today: a stable, family-oriented neighborhood with a reputation for good public schools. The houses on the block where the Levines lived all looked alike: they were one-story and rectangular, surrounded by small, well-tended lawns and gardens. Neighbors knew one another, spoke when they met on the sidewalk, watched their children grow up together.

When Dennis was born on August 1, 1952, his father was the office manager for a local construction company and his mother was a homemaker. Philip Levine was a persuasive salesman and astute businessman, and he eventually opened his own small business selling aluminum and vinyl siding to homeowners in Queens and Long Island. He was modestly successful in an extremely competitive business, using his outgoing personality and easy smile to charm new customers.

Even in a neighborhood where families were the focus of most lives, the Levine family was particularly close. The boys got along well with their father and helped out in the family business as they grew up. In exchange, their father passed along to his sons his considerable abilities as a salesman. All three boys would eventually go into sales: Larry would become a real estate salesman in Mission Viejo, California; Robert would take over the family business; and Dennis was destined for the big time.

Selma Levine, a short, plump woman, was devoted to her family, the classic "Jewish mother." She was particularly fond of the baby of the family, Dennis, and it was an affection that Dennis returned. When he opened his secret bank account in the Bahamas, he would use her maiden name of Diamond as his code name.

The house was modest but guests always found it spotless, and the fine crystal and china were brought out for company. Philip Levine had finished the basement himself, installing a wet bar and recreation room, and he spent many hours there with his sons.

Nothing particular distinguished Dennis Levine's childhood. He displayed an interest in sports and was a good swimmer. Although he is remembered by neighbors as friendly and polite, he developed a nickname around the neighborhood—Dennis the Menace. It did not stem from any serious misdeeds, but rather from an overabundance of adolescent prankishness and a tendency to run with a wilder crowd than normally found along the quiet streets of Bayside.

Dennis attended P.S. 74, a public junior high school in Bayside. A classmate remembers him today as a student who hung out with a rough crowd, a follower rather than a leader, who cultivated slick friends and boasted of his successes with girls. He liked to regale his friends with off-color jokes and was viewed by his straitlaced classmates as "a kid with a dirty mouth." He started at Cardoza High School, but in his sophomore year he transferred to Bayside High School. Some said the transfer was because of discipline and truancy problems at Cardoza; the school never disclosed the official reason behind Levine's departure.

Bayside High is a large white-brick building on a quiet block not far from Levine's house. He was one of 4,000 students at Bayside and his academic career was undistinguished. He is not pictured among the members of any of the school's clubs or teams in the 1970 yearbook. The senior photo of Levine shows a baby-faced youth whose neatly combed black hair covers his ears. His full lips curl in a slight smile and his dark eyes look straight at the camera. He did not wear his glasses for the photo session. The list of activities next to the photo is limited to "hall patrol, service aide, tutoring."

In 1970, four out of every five Bayside graduates went on to attend college full-time. Dennis Levine was not among them. The same lack of direction that had marked his years in high school affected him after his graduation. He drifted around Queens for two years, taking occasional classes at a community college, riding a motorcycle that he and brother Robert bought together, helping out in his father's business, where Robert was working full-time. It was salesmanship, not higher education, that put bread on the table in the Levine family.

But in the fall of 1972, Dennis surprised his family and enrolled at Bernard Baruch College, a branch of the City University of New York. He was the first member of the Levine family to attend college, which made him typical of the students at the tuition-free school. Originally called the School of Business and Civic Administration of the City University, the college was founded in 1919.

Since then, it had served as a starting place for the children of New York's working class who were unable to afford private colleges. Many of these students were the children of new immigrants, particularly Jewish immigrants in the early days. Its graduates were trained in accounting and business management, and its alumni frequently combined those skills with the aggressiveness of first-generation Americans to scale the rungs of the business world. In 1968, the name was changed to Bernard Baruch College, in honor of the Jewish financier who had graduated from the school and remained active in its affairs until his death. When Dennis Levine enrolled, many of the 15,000 students reflected the newest wave of immigrants to New York—Hispanics and Orientals.

At the outset, Levine wanted to prepare for a career in business. But once he started to study, he found a fascination and purpose he had never known before, and he applied himself to courses in accounting and finance and business administration. To save money, he continued to live at home, riding his motorcycle back and forth from Queens to the Manhattan campus or taking the Long Island Railroad.

Levine impressed his teachers at Baruch College. In an era of blue jeans and long hair, he was one of the few students who came to class in a suit and tie, with his hair neatly trimmed. In a student body where many had difficulty with English, he was well spoken and occasionally articulate. For a young man who had never lived outside Queens, Levine had a forceful personality that gained him notice in class discussions. He frequently approached professors after class with questions about the lecture or a related topic. The practice would have smacked of bootlicking had not Levine's interest in finance appeared to be so genuine. He was bright and well prepared, serious about his studies and dead set on a career in business.

Toward the end of Levine's senior year, the professor of an advanced business law class asked his students to analyze a law review article the professor had written on regulations covering security for big commercial loans to businesses. Levine had been a standout during the semester, always prepared to answer questions during class and frequently continuing the discussion with his teacher at the end of the session. So the professor, Leonard Lakin, asked Levine to go beyond the regular assignment and prepare an oral presentation on the article for the following week's class.

At the next class, Levine delivered a carefully prepared, insightful thirty-minute lecture. He rarely referred to his notes and was so articulate and confident that Lakin, a lawyer with nearly twenty years of teaching experience, was stunned.

"It was a masterful presentation that revealed enormous self-confidence, aplomb, and absolute familiarity with the subject," Lakin would recall later.

The same self-confidence led Levine to reveal to Lakin a few months later, when seeking a job reference, how determined he was to succeed in business.

"I'm going to be a millionaire by the time I'm thirty," Levine told his professor, who did not doubt his student's zeal but had no inkling of the path Levine would choose to take him to riches.

Levine's college years were marred by the sudden death of his mother from a cerebral hemorrhage. In the neighborhood where everyone knew everyone else, some neighbors said poor Dennis had returned from classes one evening and found his mother lying unconscious on the kitchen floor. Others said Philip Levine had found his wife's body. Nevertheless, the death of Levine's mother affected him deeply and he remained visibly depressed for months. Several months after his mother's death, he and his brothers encouraged their father to begin dating. But when Dennis learned that his father planned to remarry, he told a family friend that he was angered and hurt by what he considered a betrayal of his mother's memory. "It was okay for his dad to go out and date and have a good time, but Dennis could not stand the idea of another woman sleeping in his mother's bed," recalled the friend.

His outlook brightened, however, as his relationship blossomed with a young education major at C. W. Post, a small college near

New York City. Her name was Laurie Skolnick; she was pretty, with long dark blonde hair and a quiet personality that contrasted with that of her jovial, outgoing boyfriend. Despite his schoolboy boastings, Laurie was Levine's first real girlfriend. Her background was similar to Levine's. Her father, a first-generation Jewish immigrant from Europe, owned a thriving string of service stations near Manhattan. Laurie was impressed by Levine's ambition and they shared similar views on the importance of a traditional marriage in which the husband would earn the living and the wife would take care of the home and children. They made plans to marry as soon as Dennis graduated.

Levine was doing well in college. He made the dean's list a handful of times as an undergraduate. He was president of the student finance society. He was majoring in finance, and about midway through his undergraduate studies he had begun to focus on specializing in investment banking. It was a glamorous profession, usually open only to the brightest graduates of the top business schools. It was also a lucrative profession, and Levine set his sights on joining.

Investment bankers had traditionally been the aristocrats of Wall Street, prosperous, venerable, staid, and very much a closed society to all but a few who lacked Ivy League educations and a proper social pedigree. Corporations had an investment banker much the way individuals had a family doctor. While it has become something of a joke in recent years, the most important hour of an investment banker's day was lunch, when relationships were nourished and deals were sealed on a handshake. In the middle of the 1970s, recruiters for investment banks were still limiting their interview sessions to the campuses that tradition dictated—Harvard, Yale, Columbia, Wharton, Stanford, the University of Chicago, and a handful of others.

In the simplest terms, investment bankers match people who need money with those who have it. Investment banking firms offer a wide array of services to accomplish that match. They assist companies that want to merge, arranging financing and evaluating the soundness of the transaction. They offer advice and help raise money for companies that want to take over another business. Similarly, they develop strategies for companies that want to avert a takeover. But in the 1970s, before the frenzy of mergers and takeovers that hit Wall Street in the next decade, investment banks earned much of their lucrative fees by underwriting and selling corporate and government bonds, advising governments and businesses on their finances, and managing private and public pension funds. In addition, they gambled their own money by investing in stocks or taking other financial risks.

Although the work was often routine and rather prosaic, the fees were substantial and a respectable level of prosperity was a virtual guarantee. Plus, investment bankers could always look down their noses at the helter-skelter world of their brethren in the retail brokerage houses who served the mass of small investors. While a broker at E. F. Hutton & Company is perfectly happy to buy $1,000 worth of IBM stock for a schoolteacher in Indiana, an investment banker deals with the chairman of the board of IBM and its top corporate finance executives in multimillion-dollar transactions.

Jack Francis, a professor of economics and finance at Baruch, had taken an instant liking to Levine early in Levine's studies. Francis was not particularly impressed by the young student's intellectual abilities and considered him only slightly above average as a student. What did impress him, however, was Levine's intense interest in finance and his single-minded focus on making money. The professor and the student, with only a dozen years separating their ages, developed a friendship.

For Dennis Levine, it was a friendship that would leave a greater mark on him than any other relationship in those crucial college years, when he was soaking up everything he could learn about finance and Wall Street.

Francis was well dressed, given to the gray pinstriped suits of Wall Street. He had developed a cynical attitude about New York and the business world since arriving there, a Hoosier with a doctorate in economics from Indiana University.

For Levine, the young student who still lived at home in Queens, Francis represented the first window on the world of high finance and dealmaking. He was someone to admire and learn from, someone whose opinions helped shape those of his admiring student.

The professor and the student engaged in many long conversations about finance and Wall Street during bull sessions in Francis's small office or while commuting home on the Long Island Railroad. Francis found his student to be driven by a desire to make money, as much of it as possible, as soon as possible. It was a philosophy that Francis understood and expressed in blunt terms during one of their conversations in his office.

"Greed is a nice religion," Francis told Levine. "If you are really greedy, you are going to keep your shoes polished, you won't run around on your wife or get drunk. You will do whatever it takes to maximize your lifetime income, and that doesn't leave time for messing up."

Levine agreed and repeated what he had often told Francis: "I only want to make money."

An aspect of Francis that most dazzled Levine was the professor's outside consulting work. Levine loved to listen to Francis talk about the business deals he arranged and the small corporate mergers for which he provided advice—and collected handsome fees.

During Levine's senior year, Francis asked if he would like to help him find a merger partner or buyer for a small furniture company whose owner was nearing retirement. Francis said he could use Levine to prepare financial studies for the transaction.

Although Francis would pay him only a small sum, Levine went right to work, asking endless questions of his professor and handling the financial calculations well. Eventually, the student got involved in some shuttle diplomacy between the elderly furniture company owner and the executives of a prospective purchaser. Levine told Francis he was amazed to find that he could actually deal with business executives. It was a glimpse of the real world— and of the potential fees for arranging even a small transaction. Levine's determination to enter investment banking was solidified.

As graduation neared, Levine sidetracked his plans to get a job in investment banking and marry Laurie Skolnick. After matching his job prospects with his ambition, he recognized his naiveté and decided he would have to postpone marriage and obtain a master's degree in business administration. The MBA, he told Francis, was a ticket that had to get stamped before he could land the kind of job he wanted in investment banking.

Levine wanted to enter Baruch's MBA program, but Francis encouraged his young protégé to broaden his educational background by applying to other schools.

"Look, Dennis, you ought to try to get into an Ivy League school," Francis said, explaining that Baruch graduates often weren't viewed on their merits, that its degree carried a working-class stigma he might have difficulty shaking, particularly in the world of investment banking. "An Ivy League school gives you a hook, a way in the door."

Levine stubbornly refused to consider switching schools, telling Francis: "No, I like it here. I like Baruch."

Levine was accepted into Baruch's MBA program and received his degree on June 18, 1976, in ceremonies at Carnegie Hall. His master's thesis had been about the factors that determine compensation for underwriting bond issues in investment banking. The thesis, which was dedicated to the memory of his late mother, contained the following passage: "The investment banker's reputation is an essential part of his business. The leaders, for many years, were referred to as a 'closed club' based on long-established family ties. What may appear to be snobbishness among leading investment bankers is essentially nothing more than an attempt to maintain a reputation for quality."

Jack Francis was sitting in his office at Baruch College in the summer of 1976 when Dennis Levine stopped by. As Francis had predicted, the Baruch MBA had not secured a job for Levine and he was having difficulty even getting interviews at most investment banks. This particular day, however, Levine had an interview and he was wearing a new suit for the occasion. He wanted to show the suit to Francis before heading off to his interview.

"What do you think of this?" Levine asked as he stood before his former professor in a $300 Italian designer suit, nipped at the waist.

Francis surveyed his young friend and shook his head. "Dennis, it looks like a suit a pimp would wear," he said bluntly.

"But it cost three hundred dollars," protested Levine.

"You look like a pimp," Francis said. "It's not what people on Wall Street wear. And it's not going to get you a job there."

Levine sat down, surprised and dejected, and Francis explained the importance of proper dress. "Sure, you stood out as a student partly because you wore a suit and tie to class. But it isn't enough just to wear any suit now. You have to wear the right one. An interview depends on first impressions, particularly when you come from Queens and went to Baruch. You have to look right. Go to Brooks Brothers and look at what they sell there. You don't have to buy it there. It's too expensive. But that's what people on Wall Street wear and you should go out and find a suit like that."

Soon Levine returned to the office in the somber gray pinstriped uniform of Wall Street and the banking world. Francis nodded approvingly.

Even the new suit did not help. Levine continued to live at home and send out dozens of résumés through the summer, fall, and winter of 1976. He wasn't a quitter, though. He had his dream and he pursued it relentlessly, telling Francis and his family that he would find a job, that it was tougher because he didn't have a fancy Ivy League MBA, but that he was just as smart and someone would notice.

Nine months after receiving his MBA, after hundreds of letters and résumés, dozens of interviews, and two new suits, Levine got a job with Citibank Corp. in Manhattan. But it was not the coveted spot in investment banking. Rather, Levine signed up with Citibank in March 1977 as a $365-a-week management trainee in the corporate foreign exchange department on Park Avenue in midtown Manhattan.

He was bitter about his failure to obtain a position with an investment banking firm. He complained to friends that he had not gotten a fair shake because he was from Baruch College, not Harvard. But Levine, who was almost twenty-five years old, had a foot in the door and he promised his mentor Francis, "As soon as I make officer I'm going to get my résumé typed and send it to all the other places again. This will make the difference."

Levine profited in many ways from his tenure at Citibank. He had been unhappy living at home since his father's remarriage and he was finally able to begin saving money so that he could move out on his own and marry Laurie Skolnick, who had been waiting patiently. In December 1977, Levine moved out of his childhood home for the first time. He rented a $379-a-month apartment on Yellowstone Boulevard in the Forest Hills section of Queens, a step up as far as neighborhoods go. On December 17, 1977, at Congregation Beth Sholom in Lawrence, Long Island, Dennis and Laurie were married. Her father, the service station owner, threw a lavish reception. Guests received yarmulkes as souvenirs.

At about the same time, Levine was developing another important relationship.

Robert Wilkis had come to Citibank a few months before Levine and was an account officer in the lending department that dealt with multinational corporations, which put him well above Levine. Some elements of his background were similar to Levine's: he had grown up in a modest home and gone through the painful death of a parent; also, he was something of an outsider in the financial world.

But there were sharp contrasts with Levine, too. Wilkis, who was four years older than Levine, was an emotionally intense, extremely intelligent man. Where Levine was jovial and outgoing, Wilkis could be thoughtful and brooding. Levine was plump and unathletic; Wilkis was lean, a runner of marathons.

Wilkis had been an outstanding student and leader in high school in Baltimore. After graduation in 1967, he entered Harvard on a scholarship. It was a time of social ferment as America's college campuses were engulfed by protests. Students from Boston to Berkeley spilled out of their classrooms and into the streets to demonstrate. At Harvard, the intellectual heart of America's education system, Secretary of Defense Robert McNamara was surrounded by a mob of students and forced to explain the war in Vietnam from the roof of a car, and Students for a Democratic Society held almost daily protests in Harvard Yard.

But Robert Wilkis suffered another form of disillusionment. Shortly before he entered Harvard, his father died of cancer. The loss devastated Wilkis, who developed extreme depression and eventually took a leave from Harvard, returning to Baltimore, where he got employment driving a truck. His emotional problems grew more severe and he sought professional help to cope with his depression. His father had been the core of a close and warm family, and the loss left Wilkis exposed. It would make him vulnerable to the later manipulations of Levine.

After a year of working on an archaeological dig in Israel and living on a kibbutz, Wilkis returned to Harvard and graduated magna cum laude in 1973. His major was Near Eastern and Western European studies; he spoke five languages; and his senior honors thesis was the result of a fellowship in Paris.

His first year after graduation was spent teaching handicapped students in the Boston public schools. It was a very happy year for Wilkis. He met and married another young teacher, who had recently received her master's degree from Harvard. The idea of public service was appealing to Wilkis. In the fall of 1974, he enrolled in the MBA program at Stanford University in Palo Alto, California, taking coursework with an emphasis on public management. He intended to pursue a career in government after finishing the two-year program. During the summer of 1975, Wilkis worked as an intern at the U.S. Treasury Department in Washington, D.C. When he received his MBA in 1976, he applied for a post with the World Bank in Washington, but was told he needed a year or two of experience in the international division of a major bank first. Taking the advice to heart, Wilkis got a job in the international lending division of Citibank, and he and his wife moved to an apartment on the Upper West Side of Manhattan.

Wilkis, whose intensity made him something of a loner, saw in Levine qualities that he admired—the easygoing charm, the sharply focused ambition—and he responded to Levine's overtures of friendship. They began going to lunch together, walking the streets of midtown Manhattan, grabbing a piece of pizza as they compared dreams. Wilkis was not motivated by money and he talked about his desire to go into government work. His goal, he said, was to become an assistant secretary at the State Department or the Treasury Department. Levine unabashedly told Wilkis he wanted to make money, get into investment banking, go to the top on Wall Street. Wilkis was surprised by the amount of investment banking knowledge and lore possessed by Levine, even down to knowing about the scoundrels in Wall Street's closet.

Shortly after they became friends, Wilkis was promoted to junior officer and given a sticker for his Citibank identification card that allowed him to eat in the officers' dining room. It was a privilege denied Levine, who pestered Wilkis to tell the bank he had lost his identification so he could get a new one, peel off the dining sticker, and give it to Levine.

"I'm your friend," said Levine. "You don't want to eat alone."

Neither man was to stay long at Citibank, but Dennis Levine and Robert Wilkis forged a friendship in 1977 that would become important to both of them as the years went on.

At Citibank, Levine learned the intricacies of foreign currency exchange. He gained valuable experience working with big corporate clients in complex currency transactions. But he found a special camaraderie with the department's traders, who spent their days on the telephone in a near frenzy, buying and selling currencies on markets around the world. While Levine aspired to greater heights, he was a natural salesman and he relished the excitement of the traders' world.

At Citibank, Levine also gained a measure of sophistication and polish from his regular dealings with corporate leaders. It smoothed over some of the rough edges of the young man from Queens. Gone was the motorcycle and a tendency to tell crude jokes at the wrong moment. The Italian suits had been replaced by more conventional business wear, although he retained a bit of dash by developing a fashion trademark—he wore a monogrammed silk handkerchief in the breast pocket of his suit coat.

In early 1978, before the end of his first year there, he was rewarded with a promotion to senior corporate adviser, an impressive-sounding though relatively insignificant title. His $19,000 annual salary did not increase, but he had the title he wanted. True to his promise to Francis, Levine sent out another flurry of letters and résumés to investment banking firms. This time, Levine emphasized his experience with Citibank and downplayed his education. The letter that accompanied his updated résumé showed care and education.

In early February 1978, a copy of Levine's résumé arrived on the desk of Bruce Wesson, first vice president at Smith Barney, Harris Upham & Co., a brokerage and investment house known as an enclave for men of proper Protestant lineage. (Few on Wall Street were aware that Nelson Schaenen, the president of Smith Barney in the 1960s, was Jewish.) Throughout its history, in keeping with its founding in Philadelphia in the nineteenth century, the firm's image had been steadfastly old-line WASP. It was the brokerage house that would use the stentorian voice of actor John Houseman to advertise itself as a place that made money "the old-fashioned way—we earn it."

The traditional American investment banks had been created out of the great expansion of capitalism that followed the Civil War. Their founding father was J. P. Morgan, *primus inter pares* of the so-called Robber Barons, the ruthless tycoons who built the nation's great industrial and banking empires. These Yankee Gentiles—

Morgan, the Brown brothers, the Harrimans—looked down their noses at the creative German-Jewish merchants who followed hard on their heels to establish more speculative financial houses. Over the years, however, the reputations of the Jewish bankers grew and their investment houses became some of Wall Street's most powerful institutions—Lehman Brothers; Goldman, Sachs; and Kuhn Loeb.

By the late 1970s, many of the rigid social and ethnic barriers on Wall Street were gone or vanishing. A few women and minorities were appearing among the ranks of investment bankers and account executives. Jews and Gentiles could be found at every big firm. But vestiges of the old system remained and, in 1978, Smith Barney still had a reputation as a conservative, straitlaced Gentile house.

In those days, the typical new investment banking associate at Smith Barney still came from one of the nation's leading business schools. Successful applicants had to pass muster in at least two on-campus interviews followed by a full-day session at the firm's offices in New York. Because so much of the business involved dealing with executives of leading corporations, an applicant had to be polished and physically presentable. Image was important in the securities business because even the most junior associate was regarded as a proxy for a firm's intangible product.

All this meant that for a Jew from Bernard Baruch College to win a place at Smith Barney, he would have to present an impressive and convincing case to those interviewing him. There were, however, forces working in Levine's favor, both on Wall Street in general and at Smith Barney in particular.

In the late 1970s, Wall Street was emerging from a period of turmoil that had started in May 1975 when brokerage commissions were deregulated and, almost overnight, commission revenues dropped 40 percent. Many firms, unable to withstand the losses, folded or were merged into healthier companies.

Smith Barney, a leader in investment banking during the 1930s and 1940s, had steadily lost market share over the previous two decades and dropped from the first rung of investment houses. The firm still maintained a strong institutional investment portfolio, but the company was undercapitalized and the fallout from 1975 threatened its survival. So Smith Barney was forced to search for a merger partner. A proposed merger in 1975, with Hornblower & Weeks had fallen through at the last minute. But in 1976, Smith Barney merged with Harris, Upham & Co., a less prestigious firm, but one that offered an element Smith Barney lacked—a large, nationwide network for stock sales to individual investors.

Even this merger did not ensure survival, and the firm's search for new revenues led to plans for expansion of the mergers and acquisitions division of the corporate finance department. M&A, as the field was called, was a narrow specialty within corporate finance. It advised clients on financing and strategies for carrying out or averting a merger or takeover. The full corporate finance department offered a much broader range of financial services to corporate clients, but many investment houses and retail firms had found M&A to be a profitable arena for recouping revenue lost through the deregulation of commissions.

Smith Barney had recently hired J. Tomilson Hill III to head its fledgling M&A division, luring him away from the far more prestigious First Boston Corporation with the promise that he could run his own expanded department. At the same time, Smith Barney's partners had begun to wonder if the firm needed a new, aggressive image to regain its place in the market, new blood with a different way of seeing things.

From his letter and résumé, Dennis Levine appeared to have the potential to fit in with the strategy, both in the expanding M&A division and in line with an aggressive strategy.

On the morning of March 7, 1978, Levine arrived at Smith Barney's offices on Sixth Avenue for the first round of interviews. The following week, he returned for a second round. Over the two sessions, he was interviewed by a mix of partners and young associates. Among those who interviewed him was Robert Hodakowski, a thoughtful young associate about Levine's age, who took the prospective employee to lunch during the second round of interviews. As they chatted over lunch at a steak house near Smith Barney's offices, Levine talked about his job at Citibank and his dealings with corporate executives and traders in currency transactions. He talked as well about his ambition to become an investment banker and to concentrate on mergers and acquisitions.

To Hodakowski, Levine seemed to be clever enough, with a broad knowledge of the financial world. He exhibited what Hodakowski described to himself as "street smarts" and he certainly appeared more self-assured and aggressive than the candidates the young associate had been meeting in interviews on college campuses. But Hodakowski had reservations about the depth of Levine's knowledge of finance, questions about whether Levine would be able to handle the technical aspects of the job. He seemed the sort of person who would sit back and examine "the big picture," leaving the less exciting and more exacting technical work to others.

Hodakowski left the lunch with mixed emotions about Dennis Levine. His reservations, however, were mild and they were not shared by others who had been at Smith Barney longer than Bob Hodakowski and had more stature than the young associate. Any concerns these men had about the candidate's technical abilities were overshadowed by Levine's personal charm and ability to sell himself in his interviews. In their written critiques of him, the Smith Barney recruiters zeroed in on the qualities that would later help Levine become a successful investment banker.

"An attractive and highly motivated candidate. Dennis is aggressive yet polished—he exhibits good natural selling skills. I found him to be like successful new business developers I have known," wrote one recruiter who recommended hiring.

The same qualities were evident to a Smith Barney partner who said: "He is very self-assured but pleasant. He seems very well grounded in finance, has a smattering of excellent experience. He represents diversification of our personnel." Another recommendation to hire.

The notion that Levine represented a change at Smith Barney was also noted by another interviewer: "Dennis is very aggressive and self-assured. He seems to have done a good job at Citibank. He comes across as a hard worker and a bright fellow. His style is a little different than most SBHU people, but I liked him."

So, with good timing and personal charm, Levine moved a step closer to becoming an investment banker. He was hired as an associate in the corporate finance department at Smith Barney. He started work on April 3, 1978, at a salary of $23,000 a year.

Among the various forms handed to Levine that first day on the job at Smith Barney was a routine, four-paragraph notice to all new employees that dealt with regulations governing stock trading. It required Levine's signature acknowledging that he was aware of the requirement to notify the firm's compliance division if he held or opened a trading account for himself or a family member. It was a standard memo and Levine signed it, just as he would sign similar notices at other places as he moved up the ladder on Wall Street.

The economic health of Wall Street depends on its integrity in the eyes of the public. Any perception that the playing field is not level, that the professionals at the brokerage houses and investment banks use information unavailable to the public, damages that integrity and threatens the economic stability of the Street. While Wall Street's efforts at policing itself had never been much better than those of other professions, most big firms had in-house compliance departments by the end of the 1970s. Their effectiveness varied dramatically from firm to firm, but most maintained them at least for window dressing.

In addition to requiring Levine to notify Smith Barney's compliance division if he opened a trading account, the form stipulated that he should familiarize himself with the firm's regulations intended to safeguard against abuses of the information that its employees acquired through their jobs. These regulations stipulated that, among other things, employees were not allowed to maintain a stock trading account anyplace other than at Smith Barney, where it could presumably be monitored to ensure there were no conflicts between business and trading.

The Paris office of Smith Barney traditionally maintained a spot for a junior associate from the corporate finance department. Shortly after Levine was hired, the position became vacant. The post was out of the corporate mainstream and the work tended to be more clerical than the associate spots in New York, so the job was not coveted, particularly by ambitious young bankers. With his experience in foreign currency and his lack of seniority, Levine was the likely choice to fill the spot.

When Tomilson Hill told Levine he wanted him to accept the job, Levine resisted. He complained to Hill and other employees that he had cooled his heels long enough at Citibank. He wanted to make his mark in New York right away. In the end, he had little choice but to take the Paris position. He was able, however, to extract a promise from his superiors that he could move into the mergers and acquisitions division of corporate finance if he performed well during his tenure abroad.

So Levine and his wife went through a crash course in French, and in June 1978 they packed their belongings and crossed the Atlantic. The young couple moved into an apartment maintained by Smith Barney on the fashionable Avenue Foch, a dramatic change from their small apartment in Forest Hills. Levine, who had never lived anywhere except in his parents' house until seven months before, was wide-eyed in Paris. He and his wife visited museums and traveled frequently on weekends. A colleague remembered Levine being "like a kid in a candy store." Indeed, Levine developed a taste for French cooking and he began to put on weight, going from 180 to almost 200 pounds during his thirteen months in Paris. Another colleague recalls, however, that Levine remained anxious to return to the "action" in New York, and his wife was unhappy about being out of the country and was frequently ill.

In the beginning, the work was not particularly challenging. His position in the Paris office was very junior, and he spent much of his time handling routine details of bond financings and providing advice to corporate clients of Smith Barney. Toward the end of his year in Paris, Levine's responsibilities increased and he got involved in some mergers and acquisitions involving U.S. and foreign companies.

By the summer of 1979, he had gained enough experience and performed well enough that Smith Barney decided to move him back to New York and give him a crack at its mergers and acquisitions department. When he returned, the street-smart kid from Queens had acquired a new layer of sophistication. Underneath it, he was as determined as ever to become a star on Wall Street. He would prove to everyone that he could make more money than any Harvard Business School graduate.

In many ways, the world of investment banking was ripe for Dennis Levine. Mergers and acquisitions specialists, once relegated to routine business deals, were about to become celebrities, commandos dropped behind enemy lines to pull off hostile takeovers. Ambition and drive were suddenly going to be prerequisites for success. The big money would be grabbed by those who moved the fastest.

3.

Cracks and Faults

Shortly after taking office as President of the United States in 1801, Thomas Jefferson started trying to buy the Port of New Orleans from the French government. Jefferson wanted to move the foreign power out of the strategic port and ensure that it did not fall into the hands of England in the event of a war between France and England. So the new President instructed his minister to France, Robert Livingston, to try to purchase New Orleans and Jefferson obtained a $2 million appropriation from Congress to pay for it. Negotiations faltered for months because the one man in France who could make the decision to sell, Napoleon Bonaparte, was unwilling to part with his foothold in the New World.

However, in April 1803, the French leader changed his mind and decided that he would sell the new republic not only New Orleans, but the entire Louisiana colony. On April 8, Livingston was told he could buy the entire French holdings for 100 million francs, or about $15 million. The offer represented one of the best real estate deals in history. The United States could double its land size and obtain the most important outlet to the Gulf of Mexico for about four cents an acre.

But the Congress had only appropriated $2 million for the purchase and the treasury of the new country was virtually empty. In a step he later acknowledged exceeded his constitutional authority, Jefferson decided to borrow the extra $13 million in the name of the government. To raise the funds, he sought the services of a financial middleman, Alexander Baring, an Englishman. Baring's family was engaged in the relatively new practice of raising vast sums of money for governments by drawing on pools of capital from partnerships and private banks. Baring traveled to the United States and, drawing on his resources in England and Europe, put together financing for the Louisiana Purchase.

Professional middlemen, such as Baring, were the predecessors of today's investment banker, and the origins of the profession in America can be traced to Europe and the beginning of the nineteenth century. Until that time, governments relied largely on wealthy individuals to provide the loans required to finance public projects. In return for such loans, governments issued interest-bearing securities, which could later be redeemed at full value.

By the beginning of the 1800s, however, the financial requirements of governments had grown to a point where the assets of even the wealthiest individuals were not sufficient. In response, middlemen emerged who were able to tap into large pools of capital raised from many different sources through the creation of underwriting syndicates. These middlemen often cooperated with one another in putting together confidential lists to allocate the sale of government-backed securities, then as now considered a sound investment when issued by most developed countries. They also negotiated the terms of the loans, guaranteed that the money would be delivered to the borrower on time, and assisted in the secondary sales of loan securities in much the same way investment banks act today. The result was enormous financial power, and certain families—the Rothschilds, the Warbugs, the Barings—came to dominate English finance by means of their role in financing the government through the sale of such securities. This in turn led the families to create private investment banks, which sought to maintain their dominance over time by carefully controlling the supply and distribution of securities.

Developments in the United States lagged several decades behind those in Europe, which was one reason Jefferson had turned to Alexander Baring for help with the Louisiana Purchase. America did not develop the need for homegrown investment banking until the Civil War and railroad building of the mid-nineteenth century created an increased demand for capital.

A number of the firms that would rise to prominence in the investment banking profession trace their origins to the great railroad financings of the last half of the nineteenth century. These firms served as intermediaries between the capital raised by the established European houses and the privately owned railroad systems that were spreading across the United States. This railroad financing was followed by a wave of industrial consolidations and mergers from 1900 to 1902 in which investment houses served as both catalysts and promoters.

During this period, investment bankers expanded their influence through membership on corporate boards. These involvements became extensive, and the natural result was the creation of long-term loyalties between the banker and the client. For instance, in 1913, officers of five New York banks, led by the powerful J. P. Morgan, held 118 directorships in thirty-four banks and trust companies, thirty directorships in ten insurance companies, 105 directorships in thirty-two transportation companies, sixty-three directorships in twenty-four producing and trading companies, and twenty-five directorships in twelve public utility companies. As a result of these relationships, investment houses became principal banks for corporate America and expanded their services to offer more general financial advice.

For the bankers, these long-term relationships ensured access to substantial fees, which helped attract the talented people who were necessary to provide an expanding list of services to clients. The relationship also created new ways for the banks to earn income. There were the traditional fees for underwriting the sale of government and corporate securities, or debt; fees for financial consulting and for investing the client's deposited funds; and fees for overseeing the reorganization, consolidation, and sale of a corporation's assets.

There was a troubling side to the new coziness, however, because it meant that bankers sitting on corporate boards were suddenly in the position of offering advice on the need to expand or reorganize the corporation's business—activities that would themselves generate income for the bank. But in an era of growing prosperity, the potential conflict of interest was largely overlooked and the relationship thrived.

While some investment houses also maintained small retail distribution arms, most derived the bulk of their business from these corporate client relationships, with their accompanying issuing of securities and other services. By the 1920s, the underwriting of corporate securities, particularly debt offerings, had become as important a revenue producer as government underwriting, and the basic mechanism for an offering was much as it is today.

In the simplest terms, here is what happens: company XYZ wants to raise $10 million to finance an expansion of its plant. XYZ could dip into its limited cash reserves or take out a commercial loan from a bank. But it will probably be cheaper to issue securities because the interest the company will pay on the securities is less than interest on a commercial loan.

These securities are essentially promises to the buyers, or creditors, that are secured with the corporation's assets or cash flow. The promise is that XYZ will pay a set interest rate and then redeem the securities at a specific date. To arrange the offering, XYZ approaches its investment banker. The banker works out the details with the corporation, including its management fees and the terms of the offering. The banker then arranges for a group of securities firms to organize into a syndicate for the specific purpose of offering and distributing $10 million worth of XYZ securities. The firms that join the syndicate are called the underwriters. In signing the underwriting agreement, they commit themselves to selling a certain portion of the issue to investors or, if that fails, to buying it for their own account. The underwriters earn fees based largely on their sales of securities and so the larger the portion, the greater the fees. In addition, the lead investment bank, called the manager, gets fees for managing the transaction and guaranteeing the soundness of the securities.

The process, as it had in Europe in the previous century, offered the means to raise enormous amounts of capital and spread the risk among many participants by bringing together a number of securities firms to participate in the sales.

The sale of securities was the chief way that investment banks earned money. Commercial banks were also involved in underwritings and maintained large corporate finance departments to handle the transactions. The commercial banks, however, generated most of their financing from upstart companies or riskier businesses, which were less attractive to the dominant investment houses. The investment houses were able to control the competition and create an unchallenged hierarchy that determined which firms would take the lead position on underwritings and collect the lion's share of the fees. This hierarchy took the form of a pyramid that placed enormous power in the hands of a few firms at the pinnacle. Though there were no formal written rules, it was broadly understood that these dominant firms would determine the participation in the major underwritings of securities by the rest of the industry.

At the apex of the pyramid in the early 1900s stood a few dominant private banks, such as J. P. Morgan and its Philadelphia affiliate, Drexel & Co., and Kuhn, Loeb & Company. Below them were the less powerful investment houses and the commercial banks.

As the United States changed from a net importer of capital to an exporter following World War I, the dominance and wealth of these institutions expanded dramatically. European governments came to New York to seek financing, while the needs of succeeding American administrations and of corporations grew dramatically. The postwar prosperity created an almost insatiable appetite for investments in the United States, and the private banks and their commercial counterparts were more than willing to feed those appetites. The industry seemed to be driven not by the desire to earn a fair commission by issuing sound, well-grounded securities but by the need to continue supplying products to a ravenous public without undue concern for the underlying value.

With the public engaged in a speculative orgy, the banks became extremely innovative in creating devices to absorb the money. One of the most imaginative creations was the investment trust, which existed with no practical operation except to hold securities from other corporations.

The most dramatic example of these trusts, which were popping up almost daily by 1928 and 1929, may have been the Goldman Sachs Trading Corporation, created by Goldman Sachs & Co. in December 1928. The corporation issued one million shares of stock, which were all purchased at $100 a share by Goldman Sachs & Co. Ninety percent of the stock was then sold to the public at $104. When the stock market crashed on Tuesday, October 29, 1929, the assets of the corporation were wiped out and the price plummeted to $1.75 a share.

While the private and commercial banks at the top of the investment banking pyramid survived the economic destruction that engulfed many of their less fortunate colleagues, the public demanded a reckoning. Out of that accounting came New Deal legislation that imposed regulation on the banking and securities industry for the first time. The Securities Act of 1933 established laws to regulate the public offering and sale of securities, and the Securities Exchange Act of the following year created a new federal agency to police the area. The Glass-Steagall Act of 1933 created a barrier between investment and commercial banking in an attempt to discourage speculation, limit conflicts of interest, and promote bank soundness.

While Glass-Steagall was intended as a reform and did succeed in improving the soundness of commercial banking, an unintended side effect was to reinforce the hierarchy of investment banking. Glass-Steagall required private bankers to choose whether they wanted to give up their business as underwriters or their role as a depository for savings. At the same time, commercial banks had to dispose of their securities units and scale down their bond departments to handle only government securities. Investment banks were forced out of the commercial arena and commercial banks were prohibited from engaging in the activities associated with investment banking. In abandoning one or the other aspect of their business, some firms merged and created new entities. Others disappeared entirely. Morgan decided to remain in commercial banking, but several partners left and formed the investment house of Morgan Stanley & Co. And the First Boston Corporation was created from the cast-off securities departments of several commercial banks.

The unintended result was the elimination of a significant element of competition from the arena of investment banking—namely the commercial banks. Indeed, the services required of an investment bank remained the same, but the business itself was safeguarded from outsiders, and those that remained in the business were able to strengthen their dominance.

In 1949, the federal government attempted to dismantle the hierarchy of investment banking by filing an antitrust suit against seventeen leading underwriting houses. The suit failed, however, and the federal judge who dismissed it, Harold R. Medina, said he found a "pattern of no pattern."

It remained for a young business professor at Columbia University to lay bare the dominant power structure in investment banking and the way its members did business.

In an influential article in the *Harvard Business Review* in 1971, Samuel Hayes III, who would later become professor of investment banking at the Harvard Business School, provided a detailed breakdown of precisely where each investment banking firm fit into the hierarchy. Hayes divided the underwriting firms into distinct levels, based on their share of the market and traditional dominance. The brackets were so firm, he pointed out, that they determined not only how much business a house received, but also its place in the "tombstone" advertisements that accompanied all public solicitations for securities offerings.

In the blue-chip division, or "special bracket," were four firms whose clients represented the highest quality of underwriting and who dominated every major public offering. Those firms were Morgan Stanley & Co.; First Boston Corporation; Dillon, Read & Co.; and Kuhn, Loeb & Company. Dillon, Read and Kuhn, Loeb were descendants of the traditional partnerships that had dominated the business for nearly a century. Morgan Stanley and First Boston had been created following Glass-Steagall.

Listed just below the traditional "special bracket" firms were Merrill Lynch & Company and Salomon Brothers Inc., two firms that had recently begun to play a major role in underwriting because of special competitive strengths they had developed.

Merrill Lynch was the nation's largest brokerage house, with a vast network of offices and brokers to serve its constituency of individual stock investors. Like most big brokerage houses, however, Merrill Lynch also had a small investment banking department. Merrill Lynch was then on the brink of moving into the top rank of investment banking because the muscle of its vast retail network facilitated the quick sale of securities, particularly corporate stocks.

Salomon Brothers was also mainly viewed as a brokerage firm. But Salomon Brothers specialized in serving big institutional clients who bought stocks and bonds in large amounts. The firm earned its position in underwriting because its unrivaled stable of institutional clients also provided a ready source of customers for securities.

The second division was the "major bracket," and it covered seventeen firms that wielded great power on Wall Street without quite reaching the highest tier of investment banking. This category included Goldman Sachs & Co.; Kidder, Peabody & Co.; Lehman Brothers; Smith Barney & Co.; and Lazard Frères & Co.

Next came the "submajors," a twenty-three-member group dominated by brokerage firms known for their ability to distribute securities through vast networks of retail customers. While these companies were not as large as Merrill Lynch, the group included familiar names in the retail business, such as E. F. Hutton & Company; Bear, Stearns & Co.; and Harris, Upham & Co., which would later merge with Smith Barney.

Hayes found that a firm's position in the underwriting syndicate determined the firm's immediate and long-term profitability and competitiveness. Advancement to a higher and more profitable bracket was carefully governed by the members of the higher level, with the bluest of the blue chips, Morgan Stanley and First Boston, designated as the chief social arbiters. Advancement depended not only on performance in selling securities, but on the personalities and backgrounds of the leading partners of the firm. There was also a concern with good form, which included, among other things, not raiding the client list of another firm. Wall Street could quickly close ranks and punish inappropriate behavior by refusing to include the offender in future offerings.

In the 1971 article, Hayes observed that some ripples of change were beginning to appear on the placid, staid surface of the investment banking industry. Competition was becoming more visible. The rise of Merrill Lynch, based not on its pedigree but on its vast retail distribution network, was evidence that the traditional "special bracket" firms could be challenged successfully.

By the middle of the decade, a combination of regulatory and economic factors had swelled the ripples into a wave, and the transformation of investment banking began in earnest. Two landmarks stand out as evidence of those changes.

In 1974, International Nickel Company made a hostile takeover bid for Electric Storage Battery Company, and both firms employed investment bankers as strategists. International Nickel won an extended bidding war, but the real legacy of the deal was that blue-chip investment banks had gotten involved in a hostile takeover for the first time. Prior to that deal, the bankers and most companies considered hostile takeovers unethical.

The other landmark was known simply as "May Day."

On May 1, 1975, the Securities and Exchange Commission decreed that commissions paid in stock transactions would no longer be based on fixed rates. The commissions would now be negotiated. Virtually overnight, the amount paid for the sale or purchase of securities dropped 40 percent.

The effects were immediate. Revenues on Wall Street plunged $600 million. The large wholesale houses, with their reliance on sales to institutional clients, sustained the most damage. More than one hundred firms went out of business or were forced to merge with other companies. The dominant investment banks suffered, too, because they served as brokers for large block transactions with institutional clients, and the revenues from these deals declined.

Coupled with May Day was a surge in inflation and an increase in the worldwide price of oil. The impact of these two economic trends left stock prices depressed and unattractive to many investors and sent interest rates soaring into double digits. Simply stated, the credibility of the product sold by investment firms—bonds and stocks—was lousy. At the same time, the cost of overhead in investment banking was rising, fueled by the high interest rates, capital expenditures (including computerization in order to tap into the almost instant global information network that was percolating), and increased salaries for personnel.

The investment banks responded by searching for other sources of revenue and found their economic salvation in a product that was created by the same forces that had threatened them—inflation and high interest rates.

What came along was a tremendous increase in mergers and acquisitions activity in corporate America. Inflation and high interest rates had greatly increased the cost of starting a new business or expanding into new areas and product lines. At the same time, double-digit inflation had swelled the value of corporate assets faster than stock prices. The result was that many companies were undervalued in the stock market; a business bent on expansion might find it cheaper to acquire an existing company, rather than to start a new one from scratch or even to pump capital into its own expansion.

Investment bankers always had provided advice and assistance in mergers and acquisitions. Indeed, there were flurries of M&A activity dating back to the turn of the century. But, faced with their declining fortunes in other areas, the investment banks found they could become midwives to this unprecedented wave of takeovers and mergers and earn the sizable fees necessary to pay their overhead and retain their level of prosperity.

In the aftermath of May Day, many blue-chip firms, such as Morgan Stanley and First Boston, lived off the fees earned by their M&A departments. Up and down the ranks, investment firms began to expand in that area. Hiring increased and so did competition for the brightest young business school graduates. The retail firms expanded their investment banking departments and started their own mergers and acquisitions divisions to compete with the investment houses. This new competition brought its own changes. With more banks to choose from and fees open to negotiation, traditional corporate relationships between banks and clients were tested, challenged, and, in some cases, broken.

As Samuel Hayes pointed out in a 1979 update on the state of investment banking for the *Harvard Business Review*, corporate managers were also less dependent on their investment bankers than they had been in the past, and the personal ties between the investment banks and their corporate clients were weaker. Once awed by the mystique of Wall Street and lacking the investment banker's sophistication, corporate financial leaders had relied heavily on their investment bankers. But in the late 1970s, these corporate leaders were better educated and more adept at dealing with the financial community themselves.

These factors came together in 1979 in a transaction that forever changed the rules of the investment banking game. The impact of the event was felt across Wall Street because of the eminence of the participants, IBM and its longtime investment banker, Morgan Stanley.

As the preeminent investment house in America, Morgan Stanley had enjoyed the luxury of refusing to co-manage an underwriting transaction with any other house. Other firms were brought into the syndicate to sell the securities, but Morgan Stanley retained the sole role as manager—and 100 percent of the lucrative management fees.

In 1979, IBM's financial managers asked Morgan Stanley to break with tradition and sign up Salomon Brothers as co-manager of the company's new debt offering. IBM felt that Salomon Brothers would provide a ready pool of institutional investors in the securities. When Morgan Stanley refused, IBM turned to Merrill Lynch, which agreed to co-manage the deal with Salomon Brothers, excluding Morgan Stanley. While it was just one deal, the stature of IBM and the blow to Morgan Stanley's image made it a landmark in the transformation of the profession.

Suddenly, it was acceptable for corporations to shop around for the best deal on management and underwriting fees in a transaction. And if this was now the case, why should investment banks refrain any longer from raiding one another's client lists?

The new competition sent fees down for corporate underwritings, and the established investment houses found that the rigid syndicate system was no longer as effective in deflecting challenges from upstart firms, particularly among the retailers. Some firms responded by underwriting entire deals without using a syndicate at all. This kept all the money in-house, but it also concentrated the risk and further fractured the unwritten rules that had sustained the pyramid structure of the profession for decades.

A parallel movement was occurring on the personnel side of investment banking among the hundreds of young people who were being hired to expand the mergers and acquisitions departments.

In the old days, a young investment banker worked for a small salary as an associate for many years because of the prospect of someday becoming a partner, which meant genuine wealth. The investment banks were relatively small operations, so they could easily absorb most of the young men who remained long enough to merit promotion to partner. This created a strong bond of loyalty and, before the 1970s, almost no one switched from one investment firm to another. It simply wasn't done.

But with the expansion in the 1970s, the growing number of young men and, eventually, women needed to perform the services in the investment banking houses meant that the chances of making partner were diminishing. The number of associates increased at a pace that far outstripped the number of partnerships that would be there for the associates to fill. The bright business school graduates flooding into investment banking saw what was happening. They were no longer content to work for meager wages on the basis of a future payoff because the partnership carrot was now only a long shot. So investment banks had to pay their associates more up front to keep them. This increased overhead at the banks, which in turn increased the pressure to complete more deals to pay the overhead.

The diminished opportunity to become a partner also decreased the loyalty of these young bankers. They no longer had the long-term stake in the firm that had kept their predecessors working at the same house year after year. Many found that they could earn more money by switching jobs and firms every two or three years. The new investment banker became, in Professor Hayes's analogy, the equivalent of a free agent in baseball, willing to sell his or her services to the highest bidder.

The profile of the most desirable young professional was also changing during this tempestuous period as the major investment firms and the retail companies aggressively recruited the top MBA students from the leading business schools. It was a phenomenon that Professor Hayes described in his 1979 study: "An earlier interest in social and family background has given way to searches for the brightest, most articulate, and most attractive candidates available, regardless of background." For instance, in 1965 almost half of Morgan Stanley's partners were listed in the Social Register; over the next eleven years, only six of the thirty-two new partners admitted carried that stamp of blue-blood background. Women and minorities also began to penetrate the once exclusively white male ranks, although their numbers were modest.

As the new recruits had changed, so had the game they were signing on to play. By the late 1970s, the assurances of substantial fees and long-term clients had given way to a competitive scramble for business. The hustle was on. The pressure was greater. The pace was more frenzied. The old rules were abandoned, and with those old rules went some of the ethics and standards that had guided the nation's investment bankers for decades. The long-term relationship gave way to the short-term transaction.

There is no reason to romanticize the Wall Street of the 1920s and before. The men who built New York into the nation's financial center were not called Robber Barons for nothing. And the blame for the devastating Great Crash could be placed squarely on the shoulders of the Wall Street power brokers who preached that the prosperity would be never-ending.

Yet for all of its faults, the old oligarchy had imposed a certain gentlemanly veneer, and the ironclad unwritten rules checked the elemental forces of power and money that drove Wall Street. A banker did not go after another firm's clients. No one could engage in sharp practices and corner cutting without the risk of professional censure. Loyalty was rewarded and consideration was given to long-term relationships with employees and with clients. The social pedigrees of the old investment bankers often carried with them a sense of responsibility and ethics.

The old system also stifled competition and restricted the entry of outsiders. It allowed the few to dominate the many. But when that structure collapsed under an onslaught of competition and change on Wall Street, there was nothing to take its place. The same forces were present, the lure of money and attraction of power. In addition, there were now newer forces: the desire for fame, for a stake in reshaping corporate America, for an opportunity to rise to riches and power far faster. The basic composition of the institutions was much the same as fifty years earlier, but as with many other institutions at the end of the 1970s, the fabric was ripped.

All of these factors were present at the close of the 1970s, and they would all be multiplied many times in the next decade as a wave of mergers and acquisitions swept Wall Street, swelling the stakes dramatically and creating unprecedented pressure on the fragmented profession of investment banking. The cracks and faults that had developed in the previous decade would widen and break open, swallowing lives and shaking the foundations of the nation's financial center.

It was on the eve of this tumult that Dennis Levine, with his freshly minted Swiss bank account and his unbridled ambition, returned from Paris to New York City in the summer of 1979.

4.

Making Friends

The first time he saw Dennis Levine, Ilan Reich was standing in Conference Room 1 in the thirty-sixth-floor offices of Wachtell, Lipton, Rosen & Katz, one of Wall Street's best-regarded law firms. A huge table constructed of stone slabs was between them, and twenty to twenty-five men in business suits and white shirts milled about the large room.

Levine, who had returned from Paris a few months earlier, was a twenty-seven-year-old member of the mergers and acquisitions department at Smith Barney, Harris Upham & Co. He was dressed in a pinstriped suit, with a silk handkerchief tucked in the breast pocket, and he was chatting amiably with a small group of investment bankers and businessmen. Reich, who had joined Wachtell, Lipton the previous month, was impressed that someone so close to his age seemed to fit in so well. Even from across the room, Levine's cool charm was something that Reich envied because it was a quality he knew he lacked.

Reich, a May 1979 graduate of Columbia University Law School, was twenty-five years old. He was tall, slender, and handsome, with prematurely gray hair and wide-set, intelligent eyes. He was also well mannered, soft-spoken, and articulate, but he was a loner, instinctively withdrawn and slow to make friends.

He had grown up in a well-to-do Orthodox Jewish family. He had also grown up in the shadow of his brother, Yaron, who was a year older. Ilan had tagged a year behind his brother at Columbia as an undergraduate and in law school. A Columbia professor would one day explain to *American Lawyer* magazine: "If Ilan was considered one of the best, Yaron was always considered one of the very best." Some who knew him believed Ilan's difficulty in building friendships was somehow tied to his relationship with his brother.

Whatever the reason, Ilan Reich had difficulty making friends. Although his professors viewed him as one of the smartest members of his law school class, he rarely spoke up in groups to voice his opinions. More often, he kept his thoughts to himself and doodled on a legal pad, both habits he kept up long after leaving school.

The firm he joined after law school was powerful and its partners were the best-paid lawyers in New York City, averaging over $500,000 a year. The section that Reich joined was mergers and acquisitions, one of the most demanding and rewarding at the firm. It was led by senior partner Martin Lipton, the creator of the poison-pill defense against hostile takeovers and a recognized genius in the complex field. Wachtell, Lipton also was less formal than the white-shoe Wall Street law firms, and a precocious lawyer stood a chance of making partner before the standard seven-year tenure. Reich would later come to be viewed as one of the most brilliant and creative lawyers in the history of the firm. But in the fall of 1979, he was new at Wachtell, Lipton, and had met only a few of his fellow associates and partners. The transaction that brought him to Conference Room 1 that day was only his second deal at the law firm.

The meeting that morning involved the friendly merger of two large cement companies. A company called Gifford Hill was acquiring a company called Amcord. Smith Barney was serving as investment banker for Gifford Hill, and Wachtell, Lipton was legal counsel to Gifford Hill. Along with four or five representatives each from Smith Barney and Wachtell, Lipton, the meeting was attended by equal numbers of lawyers and investment bankers representing Amcord, as well as executives from the merging corporations.

Preliminary talks had already been conducted between the two cement companies, but this was the first face-to-face meeting between the principals of the two firms. Soon after the meeting started at 10:00 A.M., Martin Lipton had taken the chairmen of both companies and their principal advisers to a smaller conference room across the hall to discuss the proposed merger in a more intimate setting. Their departure left those remaining with nothing to do except stand around and chat, not an unfamiliar situation at that point in a transaction.

Smith Barney's fledgling M&A department was located on the forty-eighth floor of the company's corporate headquarters. When Levine joined it, he was assigned a desk in an open area known as the bullpen, which was home to the young associates in the department. The bullpen was in the middle of a large room, and the offices of the department's senior members were along the walls.

His colleagues at Smith Barney soon discovered that Dennis Levine cared little for the technical aspects of the mergers and acquisitions business. He hated the drudge financing work that was a part of any deal and he showed little talent for it. He saw himself as a "big picture" strategist and a dealmaker. Levine's attitude created friction in the small department and the young newcomer frequently clashed with the department's head, Tomilson Hill, an intense, straitlaced investment banker whose opinion of Levine was never high.

Information has always been a commodity of enormous value on Wall Street. Among mergers and acquisitions departments in the changed world of investment banking, information was essential in the search for new clients. Employees were constantly on the prowl for new business, and most firms designated a senior partner as the person in charge of soliciting new business.

There are many legitimate ways that a smart banker can spot a potential merger target or a company in the market to expand. One means is to monitor stock prices carefully, watching for increases that might signal a takeover attempt or low stock prices that could make an undervalued company ripe for takeover. Stockwatchers supplement their observations with research on the financial status of companies and reports on trends in the various industrial sectors. If a company appears vulnerable, a discreet inquiry can be made to one of its executives.

Another way to get new business is to tap into the vast network of rumors in the financial world. Advance word that a company might be looking for a merger partner or that a firm might be a target for takeover—or "in play," in the parlance of the Street— can result in the investment bank signing up one side or the other as a client.

Levine gravitated to the rumor-mill side of the business, where his skills as a salesman and his natural aggressiveness proved useful. One of his superiors in the mergers and acquisitions department grudgingly conceded that Levine had a very good way with people, a certain chutzpah that helped him feel comfortable making the types of calls that might drum up new business.

Indeed, Levine was already cultivating a network of contacts on Wall Street, ranging from colleagues at other investment houses and young lawyers to members of the arbitrage community who played a central role in many mergers and acquisitions. Levine seemed most comfortable in his dealings with the arbitragers. Like the currency traders back at Citibank, the arbitragers were a better match to Levine's aggressive style and gregarious personality than the patrician investment bankers.

Arbitragers are investors who speculate on the stocks of companies involved in takeovers. They frequently deal with millions of dollars' worth of stock and usually operate for the account of a brokerage firm or investment bank or on behalf of a limited partnership.

Classic risk arbitrage, which has existed since the last century, involves purchasing stocks of takeover targets that the arbitrager believes are undervalued in their marketplace. The arbitrager waits until a transaction is announced before taking a position in a stock. When he buys the stock of a company targeted for takeover or acquisition, he is betting that the value of the stock will increase as a result of the outcome of the transaction. An arbitrager will assess a variety of factors that may affect the outcome of the deal. When all goes well, the arbitrager sells his stock at or near the completion of the deal and turns a healthy profit on his risk. If the deal collapses, the stock of the target company may tumble and the arbitrager may lose big.

It is a business of balancing the risks, and accurate information on the prospects of a transaction is essential to a successful evaluation of those risks. As a result, arbitragers try to communicate with all sides involved in a pending deal. Good arbitragers are on the telephone constantly, trying to obtain as much information as possible from the lawyers and investment bankers and corporate executives.

A newer version of arbitrage gained tremendous attention in the late 1970s. It involved detecting trading patterns that signaled a takeover in the offing. Detection could involve careful analysis of stock prices and buying patterns. And detection could involve collecting rumors and betting on them.

Betting on rumors is riskier than buying into transactions that have been announced. But the potential rewards are far greater. An arbitrager who can buy stock before a deal is announced will get it at a lower price than those who invest after the deal is revealed and the stock has begun to rise. An advance tip of as little as an hour can give an arbitrager an edge. He may sell out as soon as the proposal becomes public, taking the easy profits of a few hours' worth of increase in the price. Among the favorite sources of advance information are investment bankers, who are involved in transactions long before deals become public.

For their part, investment bankers often are willing players in this game. They know that arbitragers can also be accurate sources of information. Often an arbitrager gets advance word that a company is searching for a merger partner or that a company is a likely target for takeover because of internal financial troubles not yet made public. The savvy investment banker realizes he may be able to capitalize on the information by lining up the company as a client.

Investment bankers not uncommonly clue in arbitragers in hostile takeover attempts if they think their buying will be so huge that it might well destabilize a company that, because of its size, was once thought immune to takeover threats. Moreover, stock in the hands of arbitragers is readily available to the acquiring company because an arbitrager can be counted on to sell to the highest bidders; the arbitrager is looking for short-term profit, not long-term investment.

The stakes create an enormous temptation among the members of the network to trade confidential information, which is commonly known as "inside information."

For an arbitrager, a solid tip could be worth millions and, for an investment banker, signing up a new client could mean millions in fees. The information network operates on the frontier of legality in its best moments, with the participants often caught between the powerful forces of greed and ambition and their ethical and legal obligations.

Investment bankers have a clear legal obligation not to divulge information about a merger or acquisition before it is announced to the public. They also have an ethical obligation to protect the information, since premature disclosure of a deal can send the stock of a target company soaring and make the acquisition more expensive or even impossible for the bank's client corporation.

Similar legal restrictions apply to lawyers, corporate officials, and almost anyone else who receives such information in the course of working on the transaction. Arbitragers who come into possession of such information are prohibited from trading on it. The restrictions also extend beyond Wall Street professionals and corporate employees.

But it is the Wall Street professionals, particularly those involved in mergers and acquisitions, who deal with this type of confidential information daily. And it is among them that the temptation is greatest to abuse it.

Elaborate security measures are taken to restrict access to inside information among Wall Street's law firms and investment banks. Some of the steps are effective; others are window dressing; none can protect against someone intent on using the information for his or her own enrichment.

Agreements signed with clients pledge that the employees of the investment bank or law firm will not divulge any inside information or trade on it. Transactions are given code names, although most Wall Street professionals believe the code names are more to comfort the company involved than actually to conceal its identity. Documents related to the deal are restricted to a limited number of people and papers are often shredded. Mergers and acquisitions departments are safeguarded by special locks. Department offices and telephones are swept routinely for electronic listening devices, although no one on Wall Street has ever reported finding a "bug."

Investment houses and many law firms have explicit policies prohibiting trading in securities while employees possess inside information. Lists of restricted stocks are circulated among personnel, although this can sometimes serve simply as a tip sheet for someone intent on breaking the law by selling or trading the information or by purchasing stocks on the basis of it. Nonetheless along with violating the firm's ethical obligation to its clients and jeopardizing its integrity, such actions would violate federal securities laws.

The regulations prohibiting dispensing or trading on inside information are administered by the Securities and Exchange Commission. The SEC, which is based in Washington, D.C., can impose civil fines and bar offenders from the securities business. Criminal violations can also be involved in insider trading, which means that the Justice Department has some jurisdiction, and insider trading can lead to prison.

During the 1970s, the New York Stock Exchange and the Amer-

ican Stock Exchange improved their surveillance programs designed to pick up evidence of potential insider trading. The exchanges
monitor every trade for price and share volume. Each time a transaction exceeds preset limits for price and volume, a computer kicks
out the trade. Hundreds of trades a day are flagged and exchange
investigators examine the most suspicious, calling the company
involved to check on whether there are any pending corporate developments that have been leaked, such as an earnings report or
a merger announcement.

The exchange will identify the brokerage firm that booked the
suspicious order, and the firm must identify the account holder
who made the trade. Investigators then check to see if the investor
is an officer in the target company or the acquiring corporation or
if any other links can be established. At any of a number of points
along the way, the exchange is likely to pass on its information to
the SEC, which may join the inquiry.

As the SEC and two major exchanges became more effective in
detecting suspicious trading, sophisticated traders moved their activities offshore. Financial institutions in various secrecy havens,
such as Switzerland, the Bahamas, and the Cayman Islands, cannot
be compelled to divulge the identity of their clients to U.S. authorities. But as more and more insiders routed their trades through
foreign banks, the SEC and Justice Department began an effort in
the early 1980s to reach agreements with foreign governments that
would allow U.S. authorities access to bank records in certain instances.

At the same time, the courts and the SEC were broadening the
interpretation of what constitutes inside information. The result
has been some legal confusion, but a useful rule of thumb for
defining illegal insider trading is this: if an investor has reason to
suspect that a stock tip is based on private, nonpublic corporate
information and that the stock price would be affected if the public
knew about it, the tip is probably considered insider information
and trading on it would be illegal. An investor is in violation of
insider laws even if he or she doesn't get the information from an

insider. The investor merely has to "know or have reason to know" that it came from an insider.

A New York cabdriver was charged with insider trading after the SEC tracked purchases in takeover stocks to his Swiss account. He had bought on the basis of tips from passengers, including a proofreader at Skadden Arps Slate Meagher & Flom, a leading takeover law firm. A Connecticut psychiatrist caught by the SEC was forced to return profits from trading on information he obtained from a corporate executive during a counseling session. The executive had confided that he was concerned about the effects on his wife of his corporation's pending sale.

Illegal insider trading can also involve the misappropriation, or stealing, of confidential information. An employee who learns that his company has entered into takeover negotiations would violate the law if he bought its stock; an investment banker or lawyer involved in merger or takeover talks would violate the law if he bought the stock. In effect, the SEC has said, the employee or banker is stealing profits from shareholders that they might otherwise earn.

An employee also has a legal responsibility to his corporation and could be charged with breaching that duty by simply giving away information about a pending deal. For instance, an investment banker who provided inside information to investors about a planned takeover would violate this duty, even if the banker did not trade in the stock himself. He would not even have to receive anything in return.

But in 1979, the SEC was not regarded by the financial community as an aggressive enforcement agency when it came to insider trading. In its forty-five-year history, the SEC had brought fewer than fifty cases of insider trading. Insider trading seemed to be a crime where the potential rewards far outweighed the per-' ceived risks.

As Ilan Reich watched Dennis Levine that day in the fall of 1979, the young investment banker appeared to be working the room, making a point of introducing himself as he moved from group to group, engaging in small talk as he went. Eventually, Levine introduced himself to Reich and they chatted for several minutes.

There was nothing memorable about the conversation from Reich's point of view—how do you think the deal's going, have you heard about this transaction, how do you like the weather. But Reich was surprised to find that Levine was as low in the pecking order as Reich was, despite his well-tailored look of power and success. He also had the vague sense that Levine was working hard at getting to know the lawyers from Wachtell, Lipton who were in Reich's age group and on his experience level.

Negotiations between the chairmen of the two cement companies took six hours that day. Over the next two months, there were several more meetings to finish details for the merger, which was completed in late December. The sessions often drew Reich and Levine together and sometimes they chatted briefly.

In late February or early March 1980, Reich was sitting in his office at Wachtell, Lipton when he received a surprising telephone call.

"Hey, Ilan, it's Dennis Levine," the caller announced cheerfully. "Let's get together for lunch."

Although Reich had been at the law firm for several months, he had no real friends there and no regular lunch partners. He happily arranged to meet the young investment banker. Later that week, over lunch at a restaurant near Levine's office in mid-Manhattan, the two men talked about their families and careers. It would have been a routine business lunch for most people, but Reich was pleased to have made a friend and he enjoyed the chitchat immensely.

Toward the end of the lunch, Levine steered the conversation away from the mundane subjects and into the area that was his real reason for seeing Reich. Levine told Reich that he liked his job but he was tired of being an adviser to people who weren't as smart as he was. He wanted to earn $10 million or $20 million in the next few years and then become a principal himself. Levine, who was then earning less than $30,000 a year, said he would hire the lawyers and bankers and he would cash in at the end of the deal and walk away with the big money.

When Reich asked how he intended to accomplish it, Levine brought up the subject of insider trading.

"There's a lot of money to be made by trading on inside information," Levine said in a knowledgeable tone. "Everybody does it. It's all over the Street. The arbitragers live off of it. Investment banking guys do it and lawyers do it and corporate types do it. Wachtell, Lipton is a big clearinghouse for inside information."

Reich protested. "That can't be. That's not right. Besides, the risk is much too great."

The response from the young lawyer gave Levine his cue and he launched into a long discussion of how easy it would be to trade on inside information without being detected. He said he had spent time in Europe and had learned all about setting up a secret foreign bank account. He knew about international wire transfers of money and using collect telephone calls to place trading orders with foreign banks. Levine gave his luncheon partner the impression that he knew all about how to hide vast sums of money abroad.

Reich had the feeling that Levine already was involved in insider trading. It was nothing specific that the investment banker said, just the knowing manner in which he outlined how the scheme could succeed, the tone he employed in describing how to set up the bank accounts.

Levine explained that using only information he obtained through his job at Smith Barney could create a trail that might eventually lead back to him, if his scheme were ever discovered. He wanted to develop several sources for information, and he needed a guy inside one of the big law firms, such as Wachtell, Lipton, to provide information about deals that couldn't be connected to the investment bank.

Levine asked Reich to become that source. The lawyer protested again.

"I'm not high enough to know intimately what is going on," said Reich. "We'd be shooting in the dark."

Levine said he wasn't looking for one certain source whose information could be easily traced by the SEC. That was the beauty of his plan, to gather several sources and trade on information from more than one place. That, he vowed confidently, would camouflage the scheme. He explained that the key to his success would be getting word on a deal early enough that he could buy several weeks before the transaction was announced. By doing that, he could avoid the last-minute purchase that might attract the attention of the SEC or the stock exchanges.

Also, Levine said, with many different sources, he could make enough by purchasing stocks or options in several companies in small-enough amounts to pass under the level that might trigger an inquiry.

"I'm going to buy quietly, over a long time," Levine said. "That way I won't create a stir. It's risk-free. Only the guys who are dumb enough to get greedy and make big buys are going to get caught."

Reich was well aware that what was being proposed was illegal. But he did not leave the restaurant. He did not upbraid Levine for trying to take advantage of their friendship. He didn't even say no. He said he would think about it.

Perhaps Ilan Reich was merely a lonely young man who didn't want to lose a potential friend and lunch partner. Perhaps he was naive and unsophisticated enough to buy the sales pitch that the scheme was risk-free. Perhaps the $41,500 a year he was earning didn't seem enough money. Perhaps he was concerned that he wasn't going to fit in at Wachtell, Lipton, that he wouldn't make partner and he needed a nest egg for the future. Perhaps he was tired of living in the shadow of his brother, who had joined an equally prestigious Wall Street firm, Cleary, Gottlieb, Steen & Hamilton, where he was already considered a superstar of the tax department.

Later, Reich would have time to mull over these and other reasons for not rejecting Levine's proposal outright. He would find some truth in all of them. He would also tell himself that he was not thinking clearly that day because of emotional problems.

About mid-March, Reich and Levine met again for lunch. They began with the same talk about family and business, but Levine again applied pressure on his friend to join the scheme. He repeated the arguments he had made at the previous lunch and urged Reich to join him, promising the lawyer's involvement would be secret. There would be no paper to connect him to the scheme. The foreign account would be in Levine's name alone.

Later that week, Reich telephoned Levine. He said he would pass confidential information to Levine. In fact, he said, he had some information on a deal under way right now.

In what would become a pattern for their exchanges of information, Levine and Reich did not discuss the deal over the telephone. Instead, they arranged to meet at 10:00 A.M. on the following Saturday in front of the Plaza Hotel at the corner of Fifth Avenue and Central Park South. It was, Reich thought, a sufficiently anonymous public place for the very intimate conversation that was about to take place. It was also near Wachtell, Lipton's offices and, as a first-year associate, Reich had plenty of work to do that day in the law office.

The weather that Saturday, March 22, 1980, was unseasonably warm. Levine and Reich met in front of the Plaza and walked across Central Park South into the park. They strolled for a while, chatting about families and the weather. Neither man was in a hurry to go to his office on such a pleasant day, and Reich was in no hurry to take the final step into Levine's scheme. Finally, they sat down on a bench overlooking the skating rink.

Reich was nervous, tentative. Despite his decision to go through with the scheme, he was nagged by doubts. He was troubled that he was violating the trust of his firm. He was afraid of being caught and punished. And he was not sure Levine was smart enough to pull off this elaborate, risky scheme, despite the assurances.

At one of their earlier meetings during the cement deal, Reich had been explaining the legal intricacies of a transaction to Levine when he realized that the investment banker was completely lost and did not understand what Reich was talking about. Reich concluded that Levine was charming and friendly, but not particularly intelligent. But, Reich told himself, no one had to be a rocket scientist to succeed in investment banking.

As they sat next to each other on the park bench, Levine confidently repeated his assurances that Reich would be protected in the scheme. He said it was foolproof. He repeated his own plans to earn $10 million to $20 million and launch his new career as a power on Wall Street. As for his new partner, Levine said that he would start Reich off with $20,000 in his secret trading account. He said he would make the trades on Reich's behalf in tandem with Levine's own larger trades through the foreign bank account. Reich's name would never appear on a piece of paper or be revealed to anyone. Levine would keep track of Reich's profits and the young lawyer could "draw" from the account whenever he wanted cash.

Despite his reservations and tentativeness, Reich had come to the meeting that morning committed to the scheme and he plunged ahead. He told Levine that there was general talk in the firm involving an attempt by a French company to make a hostile takeover bid for Kerr-McGee Corp., the mining and refining conglomerate with headquarters in Oklahoma City.

In a hostile takeover, secrecy is paramount because the target company is expected to resist the attempt. The acquiring company tries to retain as much surprise as possible while lining up financing for the transaction, assuring that the legalities are met, and developing a strategy that will result in buying enough stock to gain control of the target. If word of the plans leaks, the target company can trigger its own defenses before the transaction gets under way and diminish the chances of success.

The effect of leaks on stock prices is another important factor in maintaining secrecy. An acquiring company expects to pay a premium price when buying enough stock to take control of another firm, particularly in a hostile deal. Depending on the size of the transaction and other factors, the premium may be 20 to 25 percent of the price at which the stock is trading on the day the proposal is announced. So, when inside information leaks out, the stock price of the target company can be driven up as arbitragers and other speculators make large purchases with the expectation of later selling at a premium. The effect on a stock can be cumulative; as the volume of buying goes up, others jump on the bandwagon and the price goes higher and higher. Every dollar that the stock goes up is another dollar the company must raise to finance the transaction.

Although Reich said he was not involved in the Kerr-McGee proposal, he told Levine that he knew from office gossip that several lawyers at Wachtell, Lipton were working on a deal with Lazard Frères & Co., a prominent Wall Street investment bank that would be advising the French firm Elf Acquitaine. Reich told Levine the transaction was going to be the first hostile takeover attempt in the history of Wall Street to top the $1 billion mark. He expected Kerr-McGee's stock to rise dramatically once the attempt was unveiled—the perfect opportunity for making a killing by purchasing Kerr-McGee now on the basis of this inside information.

Levine, who had been listening carefully, turned to Reich and smiled and shook his head knowingly.

"I already know," said Levine and he proceeded to provide enough additional detail to convince Reich that he was not bluffing, that he was indeed aware of the pending transaction.

The lawyer was stunned. He had doubted whether Levine had the intelligence to carry out the scheme. Yet he already knew about the deal. Reich felt stupid. He had brought what he considered a major prize to the park meeting and he had been told it was worthless. The revelation shook Reich's confidence, which was never too steady in one-on-one relationships anyway. It gave Levine a psychological lever over his new partner, and Levine pulled it subtly and surely.

Levine implied that Reich would have to work harder to get useful information if he was to be of value to their scheme. Reich would have to listen carefully to the conversations of his partners,

observe who was visiting the lawyers involved in mergers and acquisitions.

What Levine did not reveal was the source of his information
about the French proposal to take over Kerr-McGee. Reich knew
that Smith Barney was not involved in the transaction, so Levine
had gotten his tip elsewhere. It meant that at least one other person
was feeding information to Levine. Reich assumed that the other
source was at Lazard Frères, but Levine was silent on the subject.

Reich was chastened, not so much by Levine's admonition as by
his own failure. He was a proud young man and he had determined
that if he were going to participate in this scheme, he would do it
well. That was how Ilan Reich did everything.

After urging him to work harder to obtain information, Levine
cautioned Reich that he must not be too obvious in digging it out.
Secrecy was essential, he said, and the authorities must never get
wind of their scheme because of a mistake on Reich's part.

It was after 11:00 A.M. when the meeting drew to a close. As
they walked out of Central Park, past joggers, laughing young cou-
ples, and mothers pushing prams, Levine turned to Reich. The
charming smile was gone and a look that Reich had never seen
before swept across Levine's face. It was mean, almost ugly. Just
as fast, the smile returned. But his voice was flat and the words
were ice cold as Levine told Reich:

"If you ever talk to the SEC, I'll cut your balls off."

5.

The Company

I lan Reich's instincts were on target.

Levine was trading on inside information. He had been doing so for eighteen months. And he had a source at Lazard Frères who was feeding him information.

On July 20, 1979, just before leaving Paris, Levine had made his secret trip to Geneva to open his trading account at Pictet & Cie. His initial deposit was $39,750. Merely opening the account was a violation of Smith Barney regulations and could have resulted in his dismissal.

A month after his return, on August 29, 1979, Levine made his first insider trade in the account and collected a few hundred dollars in profits. The start was small because of Levine's limited capital. He had to choose his stocks carefully and avoid any big risks that might wipe out his account. He was also cautious because he was testing the system, finding out how far he could go with his Swiss bankers.

Levine kept his scheme secret from everyone except his old friend from his days at Citibank, Robert Wilkis.

Wilkis had also left Citibank and was now working in the international banking department at Lazard Frères.

He and Levine had kept in touch during Levine's tour abroad, and they had lunch together soon after Levine's return. After lunch they took a walk, and Levine boasted about how easy it had been to open a secret bank account and place his trades through collect telephone calls. There were millions to be made and they could share the wealth. Wilkis would make enough to leave Wall Street, launch the career in government he had confided to Levine was his dream.

All Wilkis had to do was listen for information on pending deals at Lazard Frères and pass the information on to Levine. Levine would do the same at Smith Barney. They could pool the information and make themselves rich.

"You gotta do it," Levine told Wilkis. "Everybody else is. Insider trading is part of the business. It's no different from working in a department store. You get a discount on clothes you buy. You work at a deli. You take home pastrami every night for free. It's the same thing as information on Wall Street."

"I'm scared," Wilkis replied.

"Look," said Levine, "it's foolproof. And I'd love to give you tips. But you gotta get set up like the big guys. You gotta open a foreign bank account so that it will all be confidential."

When Wilkis continued to balk, Levine said: "I know you want to help your mother and provide for your family. This is the way to do it. Don't be a schmuck. Nobody gets hurt."

The appeal hit Wilkis's most vulnerable spot. A few years after his father died, his mother had remarried a man who had swindled her out of her savings before they were divorced. Wilkis had often told Levine his mother was financially dependent on him. If he could amass a significant amount of money in a secret bank account, he wouldn't have to worry about providing for her or for his own family, Wilkis thought. He could also give serious consideration to leaving Wall Street.

Wilkis had never been at home in the transactional atmosphere of Wall Street. He viewed himself as an outsider, someone who was far more introspective and intellectual than his colleagues, people Wilkis believed rarely saw beyond the next deal. He felt that Wall Street was a place where people got ahead by self-promotion and glad-handing, with little regard for real talent or intelligence. It was, in his mind, an environment that rewarded superficial traits and ignored true intelligence.

Wilkis and Levine had variations of that first conversation on insider trading for three months before Wilkis flew to Nassau in November 1979 and visited a number of Swiss bank branches. Using the code name "Mr. Green," he opened a trading account at Credit Suisse with an initial deposit of $40,000, which represented his entire life savings along with money he borrowed from banks. Following Levine's instructions, Wilkis told the bankers that he would place his orders through collect telephone calls, and he asked that all correspondence related to the account be held for him at the bank.

Over the next few months, Levine and Wilkis talked on the telephone regularly and met frequently for lunch to exchange information on pending deals at their respective investment houses. In order to throw off any nosy secretaries or colleagues who might pick up the telephone, they created a code name for their conversations. Whenever either man telephoned the other and had to leave a message, he would leave the name Alan Darby, an alias Levine dreamed up.

The partnership with Wilkis was mildly profitable, and Levine's account at Pictet & Cie grew gradually as he traded stocks on the New York Stock Exchange through the Swiss bank's brokers in New York. But Levine was far from satisfied and he realized that, if two people could dig out twice as much information as one, the possibilities were unlimited if he could enlist the help of others in the financial world. He told Wilkis he wanted to create a giant ring of insider traders, with sources at every major investment house and the two biggest takeover law firms, Wachtell, Lipton and Skadden Arps.

Before his success with Reich, Levine had made cautious approaches to at least one other investment banker and two other lawyers, a young associate at Wachtell, Lipton, and another at Skadden Arps. The pitches were subtle and withdrawn at the first suggestion the person wasn't interested. It was not until his encounter with Reich in the spring of 1980 that Levine succeeded in adding another conspirator.

As Levine's ring expanded, Wilkis remained his only real confidant. Wilkis knew Levine had recruited a young associate at Wachtell, Lipton, although Levine refused to tell Wilkis the name of their new partner, referring to him only as "Wally," a reference to his law firm's name. And later in the summer of 1980, Levine told Wilkis of a candidate for the ring, a summer intern at Smith Barney who was destined to return to Wall Street after finishing up at Harvard.

Often during their lunchtime walks, Levine described the importance of secrecy to their growing operation.

"A chain is only as strong as its weakest link," Levine was fond of saying. Part of the strength of his chain was that nobody knew anyone else's name. If any individual were caught, the investigation would stop with that person. Only Levine, the master of the operation, was aware of everyone's identity. Levine even picked up the nomenclature of the spy world, referring to the insider trading operation as "the company," and assigning code names to many of the people in his life. In addition to referring to the lawyer at Wachtell, Lipton as "Wally" and using "Alan Darby" in telephone calls with Wilkis, Levine called Wilkis "Liz" because he worked at Lazard Frères. J. Tomilson Hill III, Levine's boss at Smith Barney, was dubbed "Three Sticks" because of the three IIIs behind his name. The Securities and Exchange Commission was "the air conditioner" because its enforcement chief at the time, John Fedders, shared his last name with a major manufacturer of the devices. In the parlance of their game, the arbitragers with whom Levine was in increasing contact were "field agents." Insider information was known as "I Squared," and the amount of money in a secret bank account was "P Squared," for purchasing power.

It was all part of the excitement and fun that hooked Robert Wilkis. And it became a way to compensate for his growing dissatisfaction at Lazard Frères.

Wilkis knew far more than Ilan Reich about the extent of Levine's operation. Reich did not even know, because Levine had refused to tell him, where the trading account that supposedly contained Reich's profits was held. And he certainly was unaware of the setback Levine had suffered in the spring of 1980, soon after Reich had signed on as a new recruit. The disclosure might well have frightened off the skittish lawyer.

Since his return from Paris, Levine had gradually increased the pace of his insider trading. In the spring of 1980, an employee at Pictet & Cie, reviewing Levine's account, discovered that Levine had bought a large block of stock in a company the day before a takeover announcement. Further examination disclosed that the American routinely picked stocks just before they were involved in merger or takeover attempts.

Pictet & Cie became concerned about Levine's trading. Switzerland's insider trading laws are different from American regulations. The principal difference is that it is not illegal for an actual insider, such as a corporate executive, to buy stock on the basis of confidential information. It is illegal, however, for the executive to provide inside information to others. Several other Swiss criminal statutes can be applied to some insider trading situations. As a result of the bank's concerns, Levine was asked to stop his trading and find another bank for his account.

Swiss banking laws made it highly unlikely that the bank would report that such a trading pattern had been detected in Levine's account. Yet a less emboldened crook might have been frightened by the discovery, taken his profits, and gone straight.

But Levine had accumulated only a fraction of the wealth he craved. He viewed the incident as a temporary setback, an annoyance which meant that he could not trade until he found a new bank. As Jack Francis had discovered when Levine was trying desperately to find his first job in investment banking, "Dennis was no quitter."

Wilkis had been trading smoothly through Credit Suisse in Nassau. His trades were never as large as Levine's, which meant that the chance of attracting attention was always less. In fact, Wilkis was barely breaking even and had recently deposited another $30,000 in his account to keep it going. Levine decided to look to the Bahamas. He and Wilkis recognized the folly of Levine opening an account at Credit Suisse. Two Americans trading in the same stocks would be bound to create a stir at the bank. So Levine decided to take an exploratory trip to Nassau.

May 26, 1980, was a holiday on Wall Street, the Monday of Memorial Day weekend. Levine went to Nassau, where the businesses were open. He visited several Swiss and Canadian banks before deciding on Bank Leu International, where he took an immediate liking to the French manager of the bank, Jean-Pierre Fraysse.

By the start of the following week, Levine had wired $128,900 to his new account from Pictet & Cie. It represented his entire earnings on the $39,750 he had deposited in Geneva ten months earlier. On Thursday, June 5, during his lunch hour, he called Bank Leu collect from a pay phone near the Smith Barney offices.

Bruno Pletscher accepted the call from "Mr. Diamond," who was checking on the safe arrival of his money and the precise amount. Levine then instructed Pletscher to invest half that amount in a single stock. Pletscher would soon learn that this would be the client's pattern: he would check the amount in his account, for he never knew the exact balance, and then he would instruct the bank to invest half of it or sometimes all of it in a single stock.

The first transaction involved the stock of Dart Industries Inc. Levine had learned that Kraft Inc., the big foodmaker based outside Chicago, was about to make a merger offer for Dart, a manufacturer of consumer products, such as Tupperware and West Bend home appliances. On Levine's orders, Bank Leu purchased 1,500 shares of Dart Industries at a total cost of slightly over $61,000.

Levine was purposely starting slowly with Bank Leu, not investing the entire amount in his account. He wanted to see how smoothly the bank would execute his trades, whether any questions would be asked. He was also trading very close to the expected announcement of the merger offer and he wanted to avoid creating a stir in the market.

Late on the afternoon of Friday, June 6, after the markets closed for the weekend, Kraft announced the planned merger. When trading opened on Monday, Dart stock jumped three points and Levine telephoned Bank Leu with a sell order. He collected more than $4,000 profit on his weekend investment.

Levine continued to trade cautiously at Bank Leu in the first weeks. He had not been scared off by the Pictet & Cie incident. He was too driven for that. But he had learned a lesson about moving slowly, and it would stick with him, at least for a while.

He was also slowed by the imprecision of the inside information he was obtaining at Smith Barney and from Wilkis and Reich. None of the ring members was at a senior level, which meant that they saw only portions of most transactions and lacked a definite sense of whether a deal was going to go through or not. In the case of Wilkis, the information was even less accurate because he was not involved in mergers and acquisitions; he had to rely on office gossip or tips he picked up peeking on the desks of colleagues in M&A. Indeed, Levine complained frequently to Wilkis that his information from Lazard Frères was resulting in more losers than winners. The hostile takeover planned for Kerr-McGee had been an expensive lesson in the limitations of Levine's ring in the early days.

Through his position in the international division at Lazard Frères, Wilkis had gotten wind of the bid that Elf Acquitaine, a company owned in part by the French government, was planning for control of Kerr-McGee. Wilkis had passed it on to Levine, and Reich had confirmed it during their meeting in Central Park. Levine bought heavily in Kerr-McGee through his Pictet & Cie account. But the French had been worried from the outset about the success of a $1 billion hostile takeover attempt and, before a public announcement could drive up the price of Kerr-McGee, they withdrew the proposal. Levine lost money, though not for the last time.

After opening his Bank Leu account, Levine sustained other losses in 1980: $60,000 betting on a takeover of Tesoro Petroleum; $13,000 when a deal involving American District Telegraph collapsed. But the losses were more than offset by the wins.

On August 22, Levine returned to the Bahamas and deposited an additional $40,000 in his Bank Leu account. A month later, he hit his first jackpot.

In mid-September, Reich telephoned Levine and suggested that they get together for lunch, a signal that Reich had information to pass on a deal that was brewing. Reich told Levine that Wachtell, Lipton had been hired by Jefferson National Insurance to provide legal advice on a possible acquisition by a larger firm, the Zurich Insurance Company. The deal was a sure thing and the Zurich offer was going to be well over the current price of stock in Jefferson National.

By then, Levine's total deposit of $168,000 had more than doubled, and he telephoned Bank Leu on September 24 with an order to use virtually every penny in his account to buy stock in Jefferson National.

Despite Levine's concerns, Bank Leu was still using only one broker to handle its securities trading and so the order for 8,000 shares of Jefferson National was placed with EuroPartners Securities in New York. Levine's investment totaled $383,063, the biggest bet of his short career as an insider. If the deal went sour, he would have to start over from nothing.

Two days later, Zurich Insurance and Jefferson National announced that acquisition talks had begun and Jefferson National stock jumped. Levine sold immediately and made a profit of $155,734.

Under their arrangement, Reich telephoned Levine and set up a lunch date whenever he came across worthwhile information. They ate at a variety of restaurants around their offices or sometimes bought pizza by the slice to eat while they walked.

Levine was always careful to place the lunch in the context of his friendship with Reich. They would discuss their families, business associates, sports. They never began by talking about sensitive matters and they never discussed inside information while at a restaurant.

But after they ate, or while they walked with their pizza, Reich told Levine about various deals under way at Wachtell, Lipton. Usually, he had a specific transaction in mind to tell Levine about.

As it did with Wilkis, the excitement of the game appealed to Reich. He liked the sense of secrecy, of being in the know. The lonely young man enjoyed the camaraderie of conspiracy. In addition, the rebellious intellectual in Reich relished breaking the rules, and he assauged his troubled conscience by telling himself no one was getting hurt. After all, he never gave legal advice based on Levine's stock positions.

Much as Reich enjoyed the game and liked Levine, he made it a rule to confine their business dealings to office hours. He was therefore angered on the one occasion when Levine called his home. Levine, surprised by Reich's anger, told him he was sometimes called out late at night to talk to one of his other sources. Reich asked how Levine explained his sudden exits to his wife.

"I just tell her it's business," Levine said. "She doesn't ask any questions."

Levine went on to say that, if his insider scheme were ever detected and he had to choose between a fast escape by himself and remaining in the United States with his wife, he would flee.

"I don't know about your relationship with your wife, but I'd pick up and leave if I had to," Levine said.

Reich interpreted Levine's words in the context of a conversation between friends and did not analyze their significance to their business association. He not only overlooked the strength of Levine's instinct for survival. He also failed to see that the same instinct might apply to his own relationship with Levine if their interests did not coincide at some future date.

In addition to keeping the scheme secret from their wives, one of the cardinal rules Levine stressed was that they were never to live outside their legitimate means. In the early days, he left his money safely in the Bahamas and resisted the impulse to spend it on a fancy car or to move out of his modest apartment on East Fifty-seventh Street.

"I'm not going to do anything stupid," Levine told Reich on numerous occasions. And indeed, in the matter of material display, he managed to control his appetites. Yet early in 1981 Levine did something that struck Reich as incredibly stupid: he invited Reich to a dinner party at his apartment on a Saturday night. Despite their frequent lunches and what Reich viewed as a genuine friendship, the two men had never socialized with their wives. The dinner party seemed like a good way to break the ice. Reich accepted happily.

"Great," responded Levine. "There will be a bunch of people there and you'll get to meet some others from the insider business."

Reich was stunned. One of his fears from the start had been that he might be linked to the insider scheme in some way, that it might become more than his word against Levine's. Here was Levine proposing that he actually go to a party and meet others involved in the most secret part of his life.

"No fucking way I'm going to find out who those people are or that they're going to find out who I am," Reich shouted at Levine.

Levine tried to soothe his friend, telling him no one would actually know who there was involved in the scheme. He wouldn't risk exposing Reich or anyone else who was involved. But Reich was unconvinced and did not attend the dinner party.

Psychiatrists say that some people keep their secret lives so separate from their everyday activities that, for a time at least, the two do not intersect. It is akin to having an affair on a business trip. It doesn't really have anything to do with life at home. Or so it appears.

A secret life can also provide excitement and a rush of victory that compensates for a sense of inferiority. The hidden triumphs can ease temporarily the boredom of a mundane job or erase the feeling that you have not received proper recognition for normal activities.

Psychiatrists warn that this secret, compartmentalized life will eventually fail to satisfy most people precisely because of the secrecy. For the victories to mean anything, someone has to find out about them.

By the middle of 1981, Levine's insider scheme was moving along smoothly, and his account at Bank Leu was growing steadily. Life at Smith Barney was less satisfying.

Since returning from Paris nearly two years before, Levine felt he had been performing the job of a vice president without the title. He complained to friends that he was being denied promotion because he wasn't a blue blood or a Harvard man. He said Smith Barney was too old-fashioned and straitlaced to jump him ahead of other associates with more seniority but less ability. Yet to others, Levine boasted that he would be promoted soon and that he was amassing a great fortune from salary and bonuses.

The truth was that Tomilson Hill, the head of mergers and acquisitions, was no fan of Levine's. The chemistry between the men was wrong from the start. Hill had come to Smith Barney from First Boston Corporation. He was conservative and straitlaced, and Levine's bluster and aggressive joviality annoyed him almost as much as Levine's obvious inattention to the technical side of the business.

So Hill blocked the promotion that Levine thought he deserved, and Levine began thinking about finding another job.

That summer Levine also began considering ways to add more secrecy to his trading operation. He had planned to transfer his Diamond account to a Panamanian company nearly a year before, but he had never gotten around to it. With the press of his job and the tension of his insider trading, he had put it off.

Toward the end of the summer, Levine and Reich were walking along Third Avenue after lunch at a Chinese restaurant. Levine began giving the lawyer an update of Reich's trading profits.

The bargain struck in the spring of 1980 was that Levine would start Reich off with $20,000 and trade on Reich's behalf within Levine's own account. He would trade for Reich only on the tips that Reich provided. Reich, who had kept a running estimate of his account in his head, was not surprised when Levine informed him of the size of his balance.

"Look," Levine said as they walked, "you've got $100,000 in there and you might want to set up some mechanism to get your money in case something happens to me."

"What do you suggest?" asked Reich.

"A Panamanian company and your own account," replied Levine.

He went on to explain that he intended to transfer ownership of his trading account to a Panamanian company set up by his lawyers. The beauty of the plan was that it virtually eliminated the possibility of tracing ownership.

Levine told Reich that a lawyer would incorporate a company for Levine in Panama. The lawyer and two associates would serve as the company's directors. The ownership of the company, however, would be represented in the form of a single bearer share, which would convey ownership rights to whoever possessed the paper. Without the share, the authorities would not be able to identify the owner of the corporation.

Panama had become a favorite location for money laundering by drug kingpins from South America and the United States. Certain intelligence services also used Panamanian companies to conceal their activities. Panama had 150,000 companies that consisted of no more than a few typed pages in a manila folder, which enabled their foreign owners to do business anywhere in the world, anonymously and tax-free.

But Reich was unconvinced and he rejected the proposal.

"Dennis, somewhere there would be a piece of paper with my

name on it," he said. "It's bad enough that you know my name. I'd just as soon close the circle at that."

Levine then told Reich that he would be making a trip to his bank soon and asked if he could withdraw some money for Reich from his "account."

Reich refused the offer, as he had once before. He had yet to take a penny in the scheme. It was one of the things that helped him live with himself in the dark moments when he questioned his judgment for dealing with Levine.

It was one of the things that disturbed Levine about his lawyer friend. Complaining later to Wilkis that "Wally" refused to take any money, Levine said he wanted the lawyer to accept some money so that he would get a "taste" of what it could buy and start working harder to develop more inside information. A couple of times, Levine told Wilkis he was considering throwing a wad of $100 bills on the table in front of Reich during lunch to force him to take money. He never carried out the threat.

On October 30, 1981, Levine arrived at Bank Leu for a meeting with Pletscher and Christian Schlatter, the bank officer who was handling most of the Levine trades.

Schlatter and Levine first reviewed Levine's trading activities and account balance. When Pletscher joined them in the bank's conference room, Levine said that he wanted to transfer the money in the Diamond account to another account. The new account would be in the name of a Panamanian company that Levine had created. Pletscher provided Levine with the forms to open the new account and Levine left the bank, saying he would have his lawyers fill them out and sign them.

Levine returned a short time later with the completed forms. The name of the new company was Diamond Holdings and it was registered in Panama. The president was Hartis Pinder, a Nassau lawyer. One of Pinder's partners, Richard Lightbourn, was vice president, and an employee of their law firm, Maris Taylor, was secretary. Levine's name was gone.

Before the money was transferred, however, Levine wanted to make a withdrawal. He asked Pletscher for $30,000 in $100 bills. Pletscher got the cash and handed it to Levine, who put it inside a plastic shopping bag and left the bank.

It was only the second time Levine had withdrawn cash from his account. In the middle of May 1981, he had withdrawn $4,000 during one of his routine visits to the bank to check on his account. The $30,000 figure did not surprise Pletscher. Rich customers frequently made large withdrawals from the bank and many went directly to one of Nassau's casinos to throw the money away on the gambling tables.

But Pletscher didn't think that was what Levine had in mind because he always seemed to be in a hurry to leave the Bahamas. Part of his obsession with security, he had once explained to Pletscher, was that he had never stayed overnight in Nassau since his first visit. In fact, that was one of many lies Levine told the bank. He and his brother Robert frequently spent weekends in Nassau, although they always stayed at a new hotel each time and paid their bills in cash to lessen the chance of attracting attention.

In the course of time, Levine also told Pletscher and others at Bank Leu that he varied his itinerary to the Bahamas. In an attempt to make his travels impossible to track, he sometimes flew to Montreal and came down on one of the many direct flights filled with Canadian tourists. Other times, he flew to Miami from different American cities at the end of business trips. On some occasions, he told Pletscher, he leased a jet for a portion of his trip.

Levine said no one knew of his trips to Nassau, not even his wife. He said he always paid cash for his airplane tickets, although in the fall of 1981 Levine placed the cost of tickets on a credit card and turned in the receipt as a business expense for reimbursement by Smith Barney.

The man who was always referred to as "Diamond" at the bank also boasted that he used false identification to enter the Bahamas so his frequent trips would not be noticed. Americans are supposed to provide proof of citizenship when entering the Bahamas, but a passport is not required. A birth certificate or voter's registration card is an acceptable substitute. But the Bahamian authorities are reluctant to discourage any tourists and, with a little persuasion, a driver's license can be sufficient identification for entry.

Despite his boasts, Levine actually entered the islands by presenting his own birth certificate, which did not have his current address or other identifying information. He did not use his passport, however, because he did not want it to be filled with stamps noting his frequent trips to Nassau.

On October 30, however, Levine's primary concern was not in laying a false trail but in carrying cash out of the Bahamas. U.S. Customs Service agents are stationed inside the Nassau terminal, and Americans leaving the country are required to fill out a declaration form that includes disclosing whether they are carrying more than $10,000 in cash.

On October 30, Levine was going to attempt to pass through U.S. Customs in Nassau carrying more than $10,000 for the first time. Luggage and carry-on packages are almost never checked exiting the Bahamas. Nonetheless, Levine was nervous, a little frightened.

As time went on, Levine would withdraw larger and larger amounts from Bank Leu, always in cash, preferably $100 bills, always carried away in a plastic shopping bag. And on that first exit, as on all those subsequent occasions, Levine passed through Customs without a problem and boarded a plane to return to the United States with his $30,000.

He had made his first significant withdrawal to pay for a vacation with his wife, Laurie. The vacation was to celebrate his new job as a vice president in the mergers and acquisitions department of Lehman Brothers Kuhn Loeb, one of the oldest and most respected investment houses on Wall Street.

6.

Win Some, Lose Some

When Henry, Emanuel, and Mayer Lehman left the family cattle trade in Bavaria in the middle of the nineteenth century, they bypassed the traditional immigrant city of New York and settled in Montgomery, Alabama, the hub of the cotton trade. In 1850, they established a dry goods and trading business called Lehman Brothers.

The Lehman brothers were Southern partisans in the Civil War, but soon after its end they moved their headquarters to lower Manhattan and helped found the New York Cotton Exchange. In response to the nation's postwar expansion, they branched out into sugar, grains, oil, and, eventually, stocks and bonds.

The traditional Yankee investment banks were offering conservative financing to established companies. They left it to the Lehman brothers and a group of innovative German-Jewish merchants to invent riskier ways to finance fledgling companies. Among those creative merchants were Jacob Schiff and Solomon Loeb, who would later join efforts to found Kuhn, Loeb & Company, and Marcus Goldman, a founder of Goldman, Sachs & Co.

The reputations of these and other German-Jewish investment

bankers grew on Wall Street, and eventually they were accepted and honored. None was more prestigious than the house of Lehman Brothers, where the partners were men of stature, members of the business aristocracy.

But the firm never shed the speculative and entrepreneurial flavor of its origins.

At Smith Barney, when Levine was again passed over for promotion in the summer of 1981, he responded by quietly starting the search for a position in another investment firm. By the beginning of October, he reached an agreement with Lehman Brothers, which had merged with Kuhn, Loeb in 1977 to become Lehman Brothers Kuhn Loeb.

At the time Levine submitted his resignation, he had spent three and a half years at Smith Barney but was only a second vice president with a salary of less than $40,000 a year. But whatever the animosity between him and his boss there, on the form recording Levine's departure, Tomilson Hill indicated that he would rehire the employee if the opportunity arose.

In November 1981, Levine joined Lehman Brothers Kuhn Loeb as a vice president at a substantial increase in salary. He had been hired by Eric Gleacher, the head of the mergers and acquisitions department. Gleacher was impressed by Levine's modest origins, which were similar to his own, and by Levine's unbridled ambition.

The ambience at Lehman Brothers was sharply different from that at staid Smith Barney. The celebrated entrepreneurial spirit was thriving. Lehman Brothers was managed loosely and the premium was on individual accomplishments, not team play and partnership.

Nowhere was this premium more evident than in the firm's bonus system. Wall Street professionals traditionally receive their annual bonus about Christmastime. The tradition goes back to the era when Wall Street firms were partnerships with limited resources. They conserved their funds through the year by paying modest salaries, which were then supplemented handsomely each December. For top partners and executives in an investment banking firm, the bonuses can be $1 million or more a year. Typically, the amount is based on a fixed percentage of the firm's overall profits plus seniority.

At Lehman Brothers, seniority and the firm's profits served as guidelines for determining a bonus, but individual factors, such as the amount of fees generated by a particular banker, were also considered. The system created enormous disparities between men with the same seniority and contributed to the almost constant tension at the firm, even in the enormously profitable years of the early 1980s.

Michael Thomas, a successful author, former Lehman Brothers banker, and the son of onetime Lehman chairman Joseph Thomas, once described the firm this way: "Lehman Brothers was a culture of the virtuoso. Lehman Brothers was like the New York Philharmonic: great musicians who are impossible to conduct."

It was an atmosphere that also has been described as attracting "great talent and great problems."

Lehman Brothers was a respected, highly profitable house when Levine joined in the fall of 1981, and he quickly found the emphasis on individuality to his liking. His talent for generating new business from his contacts with arbitragers, lawyers, and bankers at other firms made Levine a valuable employee with a promising career.

A Lehman colleague later described Levine this way to the *Wall Street Journal*: "Dennis's day consisted of sitting in his office, looking at the [stock quote] screen, talking on the phone, occasionally jumping up, looking for a partner to chase a rumor with. His information seemed to be impeccable. He was very protective of his sources. If he found out from one arb [arbitrager] about a deal some other firm was working on, he would trade information to another arb. He basically spent his day looking for information and looking for ways to use it to make a fee."

Unknown to his Lehman Brothers colleagues, Levine was also looking for a way to make a profit through his insider trading scheme. He was on the job at Lehman Brothers less than a month before he traded on inside information from a deal he was working on involving two electronics firms. His profit on the trade was $60,000.

At Lehman Brothers, Levine was twice-blessed. His aggressive talents were recognized and rewarded by involvement in bigger deals, and he renewed his friendship with Ira Sokolow, the young Smith Barney summer intern he had befriended the year before.

Sokolow was twenty-six in the summer of 1980. A graduate of the Wharton School at the University of Pennsylvania, he had spent that summer at Smith Barney between his first and second years in Harvard's two-year MBA program. His desk was near Levine's in the bullpen on the forty-eighth floor at Smith Barney.

Levine had immediately recognized Sokolow's intelligence. Sokolow, who had worked in business after graduating from Wharton, was quick to grasp the significant details of a transaction. With Sokolow's education and intelligence, Levine had been sure he would return to some investment firm on Wall Street after Harvard.

The summer of 1980 had been a busy time in the investment banking profession. The wave of mergers and acquisitions that would eventually engulf Wall Street was beginning. Few of the ambitious young associates or overworked partners at Smith Barney had time for the summer intern—few except Levine. He invited Sokolow to lunch and regaled him with inflated tales of his successes as an investment banker.

Sokolow was reserved and impressionable. An acquaintance described him as "a sweet kid." He responded to Levine's overtures of friendship. He listened intently to Levine's stories of successes in Paris and on Wall Street.

Now Sokolow was a beginning associate at Lehman Brothers, but the intelligence and skills Levine had spotted a year before marked Sokolow as an important participant in mergers and acquisitions. Occasionally, he and Levine worked on the same deal. More often, they worked on separate transactions, which offered Levine the opportunity to expand his pool of inside information.

Levine employed the same techniques he had used with Reich and Wilkis. He and Sokolow went to lunch together frequently. Levine talked about his ambition to become an independent player.

He described his foolproof scheme for trading on inside information. He said everybody was doing it. He offered to provide a $20,000 stake for Sokolow and said he would make trades on Sokolow's behalf in tandem with his own larger trades.

By the end of 1981, less than two months after Levine's arrival at Lehman Brothers, Sokolow had agreed to provide confidential information to Levine. He was less than four months into a promising career as one of Wall Street's brightest young investment bankers.

Just as Sokolow signed on, Levine was having to cope with trouble from Reich, who had never resolved his doubts about the invincibility of Levine's scheme, never shaken his deeper anxiety over betraying his law firm. Reich had rationalized his participation. He had never taken any money. He had never allowed his role in Levine's scheme to affect the legal advice he offered a client. But he remained troubled by his involvement and had been searching for a way out.

In early 1981, Reich became aware that Levine had bought the stock of a company he was certain was the target of a takeover attempt by a client of Wachtell, Lipton. On a Friday, Levine telephoned Reich to check whether he had any information for him. Reich knew the takeover deal had collapsed. He knew that information would allow Levine to sell his stock in time to avoid a major loss. But he kept quiet.

"I want him to lose a lot of money," Reich told himself. "Maybe that way he'll stop and this will all end."

Levine lost a substantial amount on the deal, but it was not enough to halt his insider trading. Reich wasn't off the hook.

Reich remained in Levine's ring at least in part because he was afraid of what Levine might do if he tried to withdraw. After all, he had provided him with inside information. There was always the possibility that Levine might attempt blackmail.

Reich failed to see that Levine could not blackmail him without the risk of revealing his own participation, but it was a failure that probably stemmed from another sort of blackmail he feared subconsciously, which was far more subtle, although equally intimidating: Levine might have no further need for his friendship with Reich, their lunches might be over. It was an important consideration for the troubled young lawyer because, despite his reservations and even his betrayal, he valued his special relationship with Levine.

Reich was progressing well at Wachtell, Lipton, where he had been recognized as that rare lawyer who understands the technical aspects of a financial transaction and can simultaneously develop startling creative innovations for sorting out the inevitable legal tangles.

Marty Lipton, the senior partner who was largely responsible for the transformation of Wachtell, Lipton into the most sought-after takeover law firm on Wall Street, was known for his ability to come up with solutions that were so complicated only the most sophisticated lawyers and bankers could understand them. In Reich, Lipton found his intellectual match. Lipton often had to ask his young associate to write down his complicated ideas so Lipton could follow them.

Yet Reich encountered difficulties at Wachtell, Lipton. He was not viewed as a team player and made no secret of his dislike for the drudgery that inevitably accompanied any transaction. Once, he read a newspaper while other lawyers briefed a client on a point Reich considered too mundane for his concern.

Reich was aware of his personality problems, and they were part of what robbed him of the confidence to extricate himself from Levine's scheme, despite his repeated attempts.

About two months after Levine told Reich his account was up to $100,000 and suggested he create a Panamanian company, they bought options in a company Reich heard was going to be involved in a merger.

Options are essentially the right to buy a stock at a given date in the future at a specified price. A "call" is an option to buy at a higher price, and a "put" is an option to sell at a lower price.

The attraction of an option is that, simply stated, it offers more bang for the buck. An options investor pays a "premium" that amounts to only a small fraction of the actual selling price of a stock. But the premium represents only the right to buy the stock, not the stock itself, and the risk is that the stock price will not move in the predicted direction and the options will expire, wiping out the entire investment.

Yet the possibilities for huge returns on a small investment make options a lure for the most adventurous speculators—and for people with inside information. For example, a Kuwaiti businessman named Faisal al Massoud al Fuhaid parlayed $50,000 into $1.1 million by buying options on Santa Fe International Corporation in September 1981, shortly before the company was acquired by Kuwait Petroleum Corp. Faisal and seven other foreign investors accused of insider trading by the SEC eventually gave up $7.8 million in profits.

Early in his trading at Bank Leu, while he was trying to build his account rapidly, Levine used call options frequently to magnify his purchasing power. He was on fairly solid ground because his inside information told him that the stock would be going up as a result of a pending merger or acquisition.

However, the deal that Reich had heard about never materialized. The stock price did not climb and Levine lost all of his investment. Because the tip had come from Reich, he told Reich he had invested most of the money he was holding for Reich in the options. Reich's account had been nearly wiped out, Levine told him.

It was the motivation Reich needed to act.

"This may be risk-free, but it's also return-free," he told Levine after lunch shortly following the options fiasco.

"You're right," Levine conceded. "We've been foolish. We got involved in every deal. We have to be more careful. We've learned now and we're going to do well."

Reich went several weeks without telephoning Levine and triggering a lunch, although he could have passed on information about several deals. When Levine telephoned him, Reich put off his friend. He was too busy to talk. Reich would promise to call back later and then never call. He would schedule a meeting with Levine and purposely show up half an hour late, missing his friend.

Reich told himself, "I'm not going to do anything. He'll just go away."

But Levine persisted. He never eased the subtle pressure and eventually Reich resumed passing on information.

In the fall of 1982, however, Reich told Levine he was quitting for good. Reich had managed to separate his arrangement with Levine from the rest of his life. He thought of it as a closet and kept the door shut as much as possible. But the psychological wall had begun to break down, and Reich felt Levine was taking advantage of him.

"This is the wrong thing to do," he told Levine after lunch one day. "I don't like this anymore."

Levine tried to convince Reich to remain. He repeated his promises that the scheme was foolproof, that everybody was doing it, that they could make millions. Finally, Levine gave up. As he walked away, Reich thought Levine looked sad and unhappy. Levine never attempted to blackmail Reich and they continued to meet for lunch regularly.

In all, Reich had tipped Levine on eight deals.

Unknown to Reich, Levine had developed problems in the Bahamas that were potentially far more serious than the loss of a participant in his scheme.

Jean-Pierre Fraysse, who earned about $140,000 a year in salary and bonuses as general manager of Bank Leu International, was as adept at handling his own finances as those of his customers.

He had left England in late 1979 to avoid the heavy taxation imposed on foreign residents who stayed there more than nine years. When he arrived in the Bahamas, he sought to minimize the English taxes by establishing a corporation to dispose of the assets he and his wife, English painter Madeleine Rampling, retained in England.

"The scheme is expensive but worthwhile," Fraysse wrote to a business associate in London in a 1982 letter to which he added a postscript: "It would be safer if all the correspondence related to this matter was destroyed."

The first time he met Dennis Levine, in May 1980, Fraysse recognized that the American possessed extensive knowledge of the U.S. securities market and, as he kept an eye on "Mr. Diamond's" account, a pattern emerged: Levine demonstrated uncanny skill at buying stocks just before major price increases.

Using the account at Bank Leu he had created for his English assets, Fraysse began copying some of Levine's trading for his own benefit. Christian Schlatter, the young accountant who handled most of Levine's telephone orders, also noticed that Levine picked a lot of winners and he copied trades for his personal account, too.

The practice of copying a client's trades, known as "piggybacking," is not illegal, and Fraysse and Schlatter kept their own stock purchases at fairly low levels. The practice, however, placed the two bank employees and the institution itself in a gray area of the law. Investing on the basis of inside information violates U.S. securities laws if the investor has reason to know that the information should have been kept confidential.

Schlatter was far less sophisticated than Fraysse and once confided to Bruno Pletscher that he was copying the trades of "Diamond" because the American appeared to be a smart and successful trader.

Fraysse, however, was alarmed in the spring of 1981 when he learned that the U.S. Securities and Exchange Commission was cracking down on people using foreign bank accounts to conceal trading on inside information on the American markets.

The Bank Leu official who had warned Fraysse of the crackdown had given him an article from the March 30, 1981, edition of the *Wall Street Journal*, which discussed an attempt by the SEC to discover the identity of suspected insiders who used a branch of Switzerland's Banca della Svizzera Italiana to conceal their trading.

The case marked the start of a long battle by the SEC to penetrate foreign bank accounts.

Fraysse attached photocopies of the newspaper article to a memo that he sent to Schlatter, Pletscher, and a Bank Leu administrator, D. A. Benjamin.

"Mr. J. P. Gabriel said in Miami that the SEC was getting very tough on insiders and that we had to be quite careful if we had clients sailing a bit too close to the wind. We have one," Fraysse wrote in his April 10 memo.

The reference was clearly to Levine, and Fraysse suggested several precautions. He said the bank should warn potential clients of the risks of insider trading, and he said stock orders that appeared to be "excessive" should be reduced by the bank. He also said consideration should be given to avoiding the use of EuroPartners because the New York brokerage firm was owned by foreign institutions, including Bank Leu in Zurich, which meant that it might attract additional attention from American authorities wary of foreign-based trading.

Perhaps because Schlatter knew virtually nothing about the American securities market and how to go about finding another brokerage firm, he ignored the suggestion to stop using Euro-Partners. It was for much the same reason that Bruno Pletscher had ignored Levine's suggestion back in May 1980 that the bank spread trades among many brokers. It was an omission that led Bank Leu International and "Mr. Diamond" to their first brush with the SEC.

In mid-June 1982, Fraysse received word from EuroPartners Securities that the SEC was investigating the possibility of insider trading in at least two stocks that had been purchased by Bank Leu. While the inquiry was viewed as routine, Fraysse suggested to Pletscher and Schlatter in a memo that the time had come to divide their stock orders between two or three brokers.

He said he had mentioned the SEC inquiry to "Diamond" twice the previous week and that he had asked the American to stop

trading for a brief period. Fraysse said Levine understood the situation and had called back at the end of the week to say his lawyer
had told him there was nothing abnormal about the SEC inquiries.

Levine had tried to calm the nervous bank manager by explaining
that the inquiries were simply the result of SEC monitoring of all
trading activity in a stock for a certain time period before and after
the announcement of a merger or takeover transaction.

"Nevertheless," Fraysse wrote in the memo, "I gave him again
the advice not to deal in too big numbers close to an acquisition
date, for his own sake. I furthermore indicated that if more caution
was not exercised in the dealings, we would have to review the
situation of the account."

Schlatter responded by opening trading accounts in the bank's
name at two other New York brokerage houses to avoid concen-
trating Levine's trades with EuroPartners.

Levine slowed his trading briefly, but he was picking up information from his ring that was too valuable to avoid trading for long.
Within a month he was again purchasing large blocks of stock
through Bank Leu.

On July 13, he placed an order for 12,000 shares of stock in
Thiokol Corp., an electronics company. The announcement of an
acquisition proposal six days later resulted in a profit of $116,205
for Levine. On August 17, he bought 27,000 shares of stock in
Criton Corporation and sold it a week later for a profit of $212,628
after a tender offer was announced by another company.

A portion of each purchase had been placed through Euro-
Partners, and both transactions came under the scrutiny of the
SEC.

In September 1982, Pletscher flew to Zurich for a vacation. As
he always did on his trips to Switzerland, he stopped in for talks
with executives at the bank's home office. On September 9, he met
with Hans Peter Schaad, the bank's general counsel, and the topics
included the stock purchases by the bank that were under SEC
scrutiny.

When he returned to Nassau, Pletscher found a letter waiting for him from John Lademann, a member of the executive board of the parent Bank Leu and a board member of EuroPartners. The letter listed the stocks under SEC scrutiny and asked, "Could you please check these transactions and inform me whether or not any irregularities have been noted?"

Across the bottom of the letter, Pletscher typed a note which explained that he had telephoned Lademann on September 16 and given him the details of the questioned transactions.

"He expressed his concern about dealings which might trigger some SEC inquiries," Pletscher wrote of Lademann's reaction. "He said that it is advisable to be very careful in placing stock orders in large numbers."

Four days later, a New York broker who had handled a portion of the bank's Thiokol stock purchase telephoned Schlatter and alerted him to the SEC inquiry. The call was the first indication that the SEC inquiry had spread beyond EuroPartners, but when Levine telephoned Schlatter that same day he downplayed the accountant's concerns. He said the inquiry was routine and would amount to nothing.

Fraysse, however, was worried. He wrote a terse memo to Schlatter: "This is becoming dangerous—Bank Leu International on SEC list of insider dealings."

In the end, Levine was right. The SEC inquiries had been little more than routine. Computerized monitoring of trades by the New York Stock Exchange and the American Stock Exchange had picked up surges in stock purchases involving several companies. The surges preceded the public announcement of merger transactions in each case, so the exchanges had reported the information to the SEC.

Despite inquiries from SEC headquarters in Washington and at least two regional offices, no hard evidence was discovered of insider trading. For the SEC, it was one of many frustrating dead-end investigations into possible insider trading, a crime that is extraordinarily difficult to detect.

There are no bloodstains in insider trading. The use of foreign bank accounts provides an effective means of concealing the identity of the person behind the trading, as well as the trading profits. Court fights to force a foreign bank to divulge the name of a customer could take years. For instance, the SEC was in court for more than five years before resolving the insider trading case involving clients of Banca della Svizzera Italiana, the case mentioned in Fraysse's 1981 "sailing a bit too close to the wind" memo.

But Fraysse was concerned by the SEC inquiries and insisted that precautions be taken to avoid a repetition. He ordered the opening of several new brokerage accounts for the bank in New York so Levine's stock orders could be divided among brokers to avoid the concentrated buying that had attracted the SEC.

7.

Piggybacking

Bernhard Meier was one of the leading experts on the American securities market at the Bank Leu home office in Zurich. He had started at the bank in 1978 as a personal assistant to Hans Knopfli, the executive vice president. Two years later, Meier had been sent to the United States to learn the American investment business. He had attended seminars and professional courses at six major U.S. banks and management programs at New York University and the Wharton School. In June 1981 he passed the New York Stock Exchange examination for a broker's license.

A native of Switzerland and a graduate of its finest business school, the University for Economics and Social Sciences at St. Gallen, Meier was a small, fair man of sophistication and charm, his outgoing personality more in line with the gregarious Americans he had met in New York than his reserved fellow Swiss.

Driven by Levine's torrent of buying and selling, the investment activity at Bank Leu had grown rapidly since Fraysse took the helm, and by 1982 it had become a major source of revenue for the bank. The load had gotten too heavy for Schlatter, which was one reason he had been slow to open the extra accounts necessary to spread out Levine's purchases.

Well before the EuroPartners scare, however, Fraysse had appealed to the home office for a more experienced person to handle the bank's investment business. In July 1982, Meier arrived to fill the post.

Meier was thirty-one years old when he came to the Bahamas as a $36,000-a-year assistant vice president. Accompanying him was Helene Sarasin, a tall, beautiful twenty-five-year-old from Basel, Switzerland, whom he later married. They moved into an apartment at the exclusive Lyford Cay Club, where Fraysse rented a three-bedroom home on the ocean. The bank bought the Meiers a $5,000 membership in the club, and Fraysse encouraged the young couple to develop friends, and potential clients, among the wealthy foreigners at the resort.

After settling in over the summer and gradually learning the bank operations, Meier assumed Schlatter's duties and Schlatter eventually left the bank for another job. One of Meier's first tasks was expanding the bank's network of trading accounts in New York to nearly a dozen brokerage houses to spread out "Mr. Diamond's" trades.

As he reviewed the Diamond account, Meier quickly recognized the trading pattern. He compared the successful trades with the stories he read in American newspapers and with the research reports sent to him by New York brokers. And soon after taking charge of the investment division at the bank, Meier began to piggyback Levine's trades, placing orders for 200 or 300 extra shares of stock for his personal account, code-named "Ascona."

It wasn't long, however, before Meier, succumbing to the lure of Levine's success, increased the volume of his piggybacking.

For instance, on November 12, 1982, Levine telephoned Meier with instructions to invest his entire account in Itek Corporation stock. Levine cautioned Meier that the purchases should be made over a period of several weeks and be scattered among several brokers to avoid attracting the attention of the SEC.

Over the next five weeks, Meier bought 50,000 shares of Itek stock for Levine's account. The total investment was more than $1.5 million. Meier also purchased 1,300 shares of Itek for his own account over the same time period.

Meier watched the stock closely during December and the first two weeks of 1983. The price rose steadily. He fought the urge to sell out ahead of Levine at a sizable profit. If Meier had known what Levine knew, he would have been content to wait.

Itek was the perfect transaction for Levine, an insider's dream come true.

He had learned of the deal early enough to make a major purchase well in advance of any public announcement, greatly reducing the chance that his purchases would attract the attention of the SEC or the stock-monitoring program at the New York Stock Exchange. His source of information was impeccable, yet Levine was insulated because he himself was not personally involved in the transaction.

The perfect insider deal began when Litton Industries, a major defense contractor based in Beverly Hills, California, hired Lehman Brothers in September 1982 to serve as financial adviser for Litton's attempt to acquire Itek, a manufacturer of defense and graphics equipment based in Lexington, Massachusetts. The acquisition was unsolicited and Litton stressed the need for confidentiality.

One of the mergers and acquisitions experts Lehman Brothers assigned to help arrange financing for the transaction was Ira Sokolow. It was Sokolow who kept Levine abreast of the deal and who told him in November that the acquisition attempt was a certainty for early 1983.

On January 17, 1983, Litton announced its intention to acquire Itek Corporation at a premium price of $48 a share. Levine had bought some shares as low as $22 in November; when he sold his entire holdings on January 18, he collected a profit of $805,000. Meier sold his 1,300 shares at a profit of $21,761.

After that experience, Meier bought anywhere from 1,000 to

3,500 shares of stock in concert with almost every purchase made by Levine.

Meier also copied Levine's trades in some of the client accounts he managed at Bank Leu. In these accounts, investors rely on the bank's expertise in investment decisions. While Meier did not profit personally through the managed accounts, he generated commissions for the bank and made himself look like a smart trader by following Levine.

Bruno Pletscher expected a great deal from Meier when the securities expert arrived at Bank Leu. Pletscher had handled Levine's stock orders in the first months of his trading. But as the bank expanded, Pletscher had assigned those duties to Schlatter and spent his time on other areas. As the investment side of the bank grew into a major profit center, Pletscher agreed with Fraysse that an expert was required, and he was pleased when Meier arrived and moved into the job smoothly.

Meier's presence was timely. Levine began stepping up his trading activity in mid-1982 and reached the point where he was telephoning with instructions involving a new stock almost once a week.

The method for dealing with the Diamond account remained unchanged: Levine telephoned Meier collect from a pay phone in New York, usually during Levine's lunch hour, and placed his stock orders. The orders frequently involved thousands of shares of stock, and Meier would spend hours on the telephone spreading the purchases among various brokers.

One afternoon in the late fall of 1982, Pletscher stopped by Meier's office for a word with him and Meier said curtly: "Do not interrupt me. I have to execute a large order for Diamond as quickly as possible."

One element that changed, however, was Levine's withdrawals. At the start, he had left his account almost untouched as he built his capital for larger and larger purchases. But in late 1982, with his profits finally topping $2 million, Levine began to withdraw larger sums. On February 21, 1983, he walked out of Bank Leu with $100,000 in cash, his first six-figure withdrawal.

Levine always insisted on $100 bills. He always packed the money in a plastic shopping bag. He never objected when Meier or Pletscher required him to sign his real name to the withdrawal form because bank regulations prohibited the use of code names for cash withdrawals. They never asked what he did with the money. It was none of their business.

Levine was a valued customer, and his demand for huge numbers of $100 bills sometimes sent bank employees scurrying to various banks to come up with enough U.S. cash. Occasionally, Meier or Pletscher opened the bank on a Saturday or Sunday to accommodate the schedule of their American client.

At one point, Levine inquired about the possibility of the bank delivering cash to him in New York. When told regulations would require the bank to declare the cash to the U.S. Customs Service and probably disclose his name as the ultimate recipient, Levine dropped the idea. He rejected a counterproposal by Pletscher that the bank send him money from the account via wire transfer or check.

In 1983, Pletscher and his wife separated. She took their three children and returned to Switzerland. Pletscher agreed to provide a substantial amount for child support and maintenance during the divorce proceedings. Although he was earning in excess of $60,000 a year in a country without income tax, Pletscher was strapped for cash.

Meier was aware of Pletscher's financial problems and he offered the bank vice president some advice. Meier said he was involved in some stock trading through his account. Pletscher might want to open an account of his own and earn extra money by doing the same thing.

"Bernie, how risky is it?" Pletscher asked. "You know my private situation."

"There's little risk," Meier replied. "There are certain new issues of stocks in the market that are very safe. You can buy them before the general public and then, when they go on the general market and the price is higher, you can sell them for a profit."

Pletscher opened his first account at Bank Leu in late 1983 under the code name "Yellow Bird" and began to make small purchases, always on the advice of Meier or occasionally Jean-Pierre Fraysse.

In late March 1984, Meier suggested that Pletscher purchase 200 shares of Jewel Companies, a giant chain of supermarkets and drugstores based in Chicago. A couple of weeks later, Meier told Pletscher that he should buy another 400 shares of Jewel because the price was going to go up soon. When Pletscher complained that he disliked holding stocks for such a long period, Meier said he had information from Diamond that something was going to happen to boost the price of Jewel soon. It might involve an attempt by another company to take over Jewel. Pletscher agreed to buy another 400 shares. At the same time, Meier expanded his own holdings in Jewel to 3,400 shares.

Their investments paled in comparison with Levine's. After an initial purchase of several thousand shares on March 22, Levine had increased his holdings in Jewel to 75,000 shares at a total cost of $3.7 million on April 2. Levine was certain of his information because his employer, Lehman Brothers, represented American Stores Inc., the Salt Lake City–based food and retail store operation that was quietly preparing an attempt to acquire Jewel. But Levine was suffering some of the same qualms as Pletscher—he hated to hold a stock for such a long time, and the potential merger was progressing too slowly for his tastes. He wanted to get the deal moving so he could collect his profit and move his money into another transaction.

One way to insert momentum into a takeover situation is to destabilize the stock of the target company with a buying wave by arbitragers; it makes the target's management nervous and usually forces the executives to view the impending threat more seriously. Levine's attempts to get Jewel stock moving through the arbitrage grapevine had been unsuccessful. So in April 1984, sitting on a stagnant investment of $3.7 million, he decided to try to move the price of Jewel stock by manipulating the news media. And he enlisted as his accomplice Robert Wilkis, who had also bought heavily in Jewel stock.

Late that month, Levine pressured Wilkis to telephone the *Chicago Tribune*'s financial section. Wilkis asked to speak to the reporter covering mergers and acquisitions, and he was connected with Herb Greenberg, a savvy and aggressive reporter.

"Jewel is going to be acquired by a company called American Stores," the caller told Greenberg.

"Who are you?" asked Greenberg.

"I can't tell you that. But my information is good. That should be enough."

"How can you prove what you're saying? How do I know that you know what you're talking about?"

The caller gave Greenberg the expected price of the offer for Jewel and then promised to call back with additional information. Greenberg jokingly suggested the caller use the code name "Deep Freeze." In the meantime, Greenberg telephoned an executive at Jewel, Lawrence Howe, and asked whether the rumor he had heard was true. Howe scoffed at the idea that the chain was talking to anyone about a possible merger. But Jewel, the major supermarket chain in Chicago, had been the subject of takeover rumors earlier in the month, and Greenberg was eager to pursue the story.

When Wilkis called back a few days later, he gave the reporter a vital piece of information: Weston Christopherson, the chairman of Jewel, and L. S. Skaggs, chairman of American Stores, had met the previous week in a Denver hotel. The caller didn't know the name of the hotel, but he gave Greenberg the specific night of the meeting.

Greenberg took the information to *Tribune* financial editor Terry Brown, who suggested that he follow it up by telephoning every hotel in Denver to find out whether Christopherson or Skaggs had a reservation there on the night in question. Greenberg found a reservation for Skaggs on the right night and telephoned Jewel's Howe with his discovery. Howe confirmed that the meeting had taken place. On Tuesday, May 1, 1984, a story appeared in the *Tribune* disclosing the talks between the companies. It contained this paragraph: "Sources indicate that American Stores, a major food and drug retailer, wants to acquire Jewel and is prepared to make an unfriendly offer at a price as high as $75 a share, or about $875 million. Jewel, in which institutions and other large share-holders control more than 50 percent of the common stock, closed in trading on the New York Stock Exchange Monday at $44, down fifty cents."

The story had the desired effect. Not only did it alarm the management at Jewel, it touched off stories in other publications and ignited a buying spree that ran up the price of Jewel stock. On June 1, American Stores announced its offer for Jewel and the companies eventually merged. Dennis Levine sold his stock for a profit of $1.2 million, his biggest score to date. Wilkis, Pletscher, and Meier also sold their shares for substantial profits.

Despite his success with Jewel and other stocks suggested by Meier, Pletscher remained a reluctant investor. Late in 1984, Meier offered to bring him into some options trading that Meier thought would be profitable.

"Is it risky?" asked Pletscher.

"There's always a risk, but it's a good risk," said Meier.

"Well, if you do it for yourself, go ahead for me."

The first few deals were small, and Pletscher earned less than $1,000 a transaction. The money was important, however, as he tried to maintain his standard of living in the Bahamas and support his family in Switzerland. But Pletscher was cautious and proceeded slowly for many months.

In February 1985, one of the options Meier had purchased for Pletscher plummeted and Pletscher lost $3,700. Meier, aware of the effect of the loss on Pletscher, offered to make it up out of his own pocket.

"No, Bernie," said Pletscher. "I lost it, period. You asked me before investing and I said go ahead."

"Okay, I accept that," said Meier. "But don't worry. I'll make up for this loss."

In that moment of guilt and genuine concern over the finances of his colleague, Meier explained what was going on in the Diamond account.

"You must be aware of the fact that Diamond has an excellent track record and that Diamond has made a lot of profits," he said. "Why should you not also benefit from such trades? Diamond is investing in securities, and it happens that most of these trades are related to a takeover situation. This guy must know more than other people."

The explanation sounded reasonable to Pletscher. He recalled his earlier involvement with Levine's trades, particularly the handsome profit he made on Jewel stock. He had also handled several profitable transactions for Levine in recent months when Meier was out of the country on business or holiday.

"Bernie, you know I don't have much money and what I have, I don't want to lose," said Pletscher. "But let me know when you have the next deal coming up."

A few days later, Meier stopped by Pletscher's office. "I have an order from Diamond and you should participate in this one. This seems to be a good deal."

Pletscher agreed and Meier bought 500 shares of stock in American Natural Resources for Pletscher's Yellow Bird account. For his own Ascona account, Meier purchased 1,000 shares. The amounts were minimal compared with Levine's mammoth purchase.

The Diamond account had grown dramatically in recent months, but Meier was unprepared for the investment Levine ordered in American Natural Resources. On the basis of Levine's telephone orders, Meier spent several days in February buying 145,500 shares of stock at a total cost of $7.2 million.

The magnitude of Levine's purchase was so startling that Meier returned to Pletscher a few days after his original approach.

"Bruno, you should increase your ANR," Meier said. "Why don't you buy another thousand? I've been told this is a one hundred percent winner."

"Another thousand? That's too much for me," said Pletscher, who was already so nervous about his $2,500 investment that he was monitoring the price fluctuations almost hourly. Even the gradual upward trend had not eased his worries. "I've already invested a lot of money."

Meier replied, "You can utilize the margin facility and borrow money against the holdings you have."

Even after Meier had described the magnitude of Levine's investment in the stock, Pletscher consented to the purchase of only an additional 500 shares. Meier bought another 1,000 for himself and brought his total to 2,000 shares.

March 1, 1985, was a Friday. After the markets closed for the weekend, Coastal Corporation, a Texas-based energy company, announced an all-cash offer to acquire American Natural Resources at $60 a share. Dennis Levine had been a key player in assembling the deal.

When he arrived at work on Monday morning and found that ANR stock had already gone up to almost $59 a share after trading resumed, Pletscher told Meier to sell his shares. Meier said, "Don't lose your nerve. There's no rush now."

Pletscher agreed to leave the sale in Meier's hands. Later that day, after a call from Levine, Meier sold the stock in ANR that had been purchased by all three men. Meier made $24,518. Pletscher collected almost $12,500 in profit, an amount that left the bank vice president almost giddy with happiness.

Levine had bought his ANR stock for an average price of $49.93 per share and his profit was nearly $1.4 million.

The Bank Leu officers were not the only people copying the successful trading of Dennis Levine.

In September 1983, a broker in Merrill Lynch & Company's Eurobonds division went to Nassau on a business trip. The broker, Martha Malave, met Bernie Meier at Bank Leu and he told her how active the bank had become in the American securities market.

The U.S. securities market was not her territory, so when Malave returned to New York she passed the information on to Brian Campbell, a young broker in Merrill Lynch's international division.

Campbell, a tall, attractive blond, was twenty-six years old. He had come to Merrill Lynch a little over a year earlier after becoming bored as a management trainee at Manufacturers Hanover. Campbell was fluent in Spanish and had a master's degree in international management, so Merrill Lynch placed him in the international division. His job was to develop foreign clients and handle their trading on the American markets.

Campbell telephoned Meier at Bank Leu several times in September and October in an attempt to obtain a share of the bank's trading business. The two men hit it off over the telephone and Meier suggested that Campbell pay him a visit.

At the end of October, Campbell went to Nassau, met with Meier, and returned to New York with a new account, Bank Leu International.

Over the next few weeks, Meier and Campbell established what would become a familiar pattern between them. In almost daily telephone conversations, Campbell would provide Meier with the latest Merrill Lynch research on stocks and Meier would give Campbell a substantial share of the bank's trading business, including chunks of Levine's transactions.

The size of Levine's purchases had sometimes left Meier frantic to distribute the transactions among enough brokers to avoid creating a ripple in the market. So he welcomed the opportunity to place sizable orders in what he viewed to be the competent hands of Brian Campbell.

Whenever he was about to take a trip out of the country, Meier would give a list of brokers and their telephone numbers to Pletscher, who substituted for him as the bank's trader. If Diamond called in a massive order, Pletscher was instructed to split the purchases among the brokers on the list. When Meier handed the list to Pletscher in early 1984, he singled out Brian Campbell at Merrill Lynch as a broker who was especially helpful.

"You can easily give large orders to Brian Campbell since he's giving us the best execution," said Meier. "He's fast and he also has the sense to go slow in situations where it's advisable to go slow. He also gives us a discount on commissions that's one of the best we can get."

When Pletscher asked what Meier meant by going slow, the investment expert explained that Campbell examined the market to see whether the bank's order would be excessive in relation to the amount of trading in that particular stock. Trades larger than the daily average, Meier continued, could "draw attention to our activities."

Meier told Pletscher that Campbell would not abuse what he learned in handling a big order for the bank, unlike two other brokers whom Meier instructed Pletscher not to use because they had been piggybacking on Bank Leu's trades.

"These people talk too much. They pass on the message to their clients and want to show off good information," said Meier. "We're not a supplier of information to brokers."

In fact, Campbell had recognized the remarkable success of Bank Leu in trading takeover stocks and had copied many of the trades for his own account and for some of the commercial accounts he handled at Merrill Lynch.

Later, Campbell would tell the SEC he had no idea that inside information was involved in Bank Leu's successful trading. He said

Meier never told him why he was buying a particular stock; he merely assumed that the bank had a smart customer. He said he made some of the same purchases after checking the trades with Merrill Lynch's research department.

Campbell also passed the bank's trades on to his girlfriend, to a former college roommate, to a partner in a real estate venture, and to Carlos Zubillaga, a broker in Merrill Lynch's Caracas office.

Zubillaga, who was then in his mid-thirties, was a member of one of Venezuela's most prominent social and political families. At one time, he had worked for the Venezuelan government and been in charge of the country's public debt. He had met Campbell in 1982 during a training class at Merrill Lynch and they had become friends, keeping in touch after Zubillaga returned to Caracas.

Zubillaga expanded the piggybacking, not only trading on the information himself but passing it along to another broker in Merrill Lynch's Caracas office, Max Hofer.

Through this series of complex relationships, a single stock purchase by Dennis Levine could be magnified many times across the stock market, from Nassau to New York to Caracas. Levine was buying and so was Wilkis. But Meier and Pletscher and, to a lesser extent, Fraysse were copying. And so were Campbell and his circle and Zubillaga and Hofer.

The trading at EuroPartners Securities Corp. had posed the risk of discovery because of too much concentration. But the solution, to spread the trading among many brokers, had become a problem. If Levine had known about the extensive copying of his carefully orchestrated trades, he might have realized it was only a matter of time before one of the purchases caught the eye of the Securities and Exchange Commission. Perhaps he would have taken steps to stop the copying.

Levine's next brush with the regulators was not the result of piggybacking, however. It grew out of an attempt by Levine to use inside information to enhance his position at Lehman Brothers at the same time that he traded on it illegally.

Chicago Pacific Corporation was created in June 1984 as the successor to the bankrupt Chicago, Rock Island & Pacific Railroad. The liquidation of some rail lines left the company cash-rich in the fall of 1984 and hunting for a major acquisition.

In September, Chicago Pacific hired Lazard Frères to act as its financial adviser for a confidential, unsolicited, all-cash offer for Textron Inc., one of the nation's original conglomerates and a major producer of helicopters and machine tools.

That month, Robert Wilkis learned from a friend at Lazard that Chicago Pacific was preparing an attempt to purchase Textron. Wilkis passed the information on to Levine.

Two years before, Wilkis had switched his secret account from Credit Suisse to the Bank of Nova Scotia in the Cayman Islands, another secrecy haven. He used that account to purchase 29,000 shares of Textron stock in early October.

Levine used his Bank Leu account to buy 51,500 shares of Textron between October 1 and 19. Bernie Meier, Brian Campbell, and Carlos Zubillaga also bought Textron stock, although in far smaller numbers.

Six months before, in April 1984, Lehman Brothers Kuhn Loeb had been acquired by Shearson/American Express and the name had been changed to Shearson Lehman Brothers Inc. More important than the name change, the transaction had ended the longest continuing partnership on Wall Street and left the investment bank in turmoil. Some partners quit and others who would have preferred to leave remained only because of contracts.

Levine remained and lobbied hard for promotion to one of the managing director positions in the mergers and acquisitions department. His primary attribute was his uncanny ability to generate new business for the firm, and he sought to enhance his reputation by signing up Textron.

After learning from Wilkis that Textron was a target, Levine took the information to Stephen Waters, one of the managing directors in M&A at Shearson Lehman Brothers. Levine suggested that Waters call Textron and offer the services of Shearson Lehman Brothers for defense in the takeover.

Waters knew Beverly Dolan, the president of Textron, from previous business dealings and he telephoned Dolan on October 9, 1984.

"My colleague, Dennis Levine, has picked up a rumor that Textron may be the subject of an unsolicited offer and we thought it would be wise to bring this to your attention," Waters told Dolan as Levine sat across the desk.

Dolan said, "That's the first I've heard of it. Thank you very much. Keep calling if you get more information."

On October 24, Chicago Pacific unveiled its $1.5 billion offer for Textron and the price of Textron stock shot up $7.25 a share. Wilkis sold out for a profit of approximately $100,000. Levine sold out for a profit of more than $200,000.

Despite the early warning, Textron did not hire Shearson Lehman Brothers for their defense. Instead, Dolan turned to Morgan Stanley, which orchestrated a successful defense against Chicago Pacific's bid. Unfortunately for Levine, that was not the limit of his bad luck in the Textron deal.

In the days before the announcement of Chicago Pacific's order, the price of Textron stock had risen steadily on purchases that were far larger than those placed by Levine or any of his imitators. The surge was picked up by the New York Stock Exchange's computerized stock-monitoring program, and in November the SEC opened a formal investigation into the possibility of insider trading in Textron.

Dolan told the SEC investigators that the first word he had received of the takeover attempt had come from Steve Waters at Shearson Lehman. Waters was questioned by the SEC and he explained that the rumor had been uncovered by one of his associates, Dennis Levine.

Levine was subpoenaed and, at 10:30 A.M. on November 14, he

sat down in the offices of Shearson Lehman's lawyers on Wall Street and faced two young SEC attorneys, Leonard Wang and Judith Oligny. Levine's testimony was given under oath.

In the first ten minutes, Levine was asked whether he maintained any brokerage accounts and he said no; he was asked whether he had maintained a brokerage account at any time in the last year and he said no; he was asked whether he had trading authority over any brokerage accounts and he said no.

When Wang, who did most of the questioning, moved to the subject of Textron, Levine acknowledged what Waters had already disclosed. Yes, he had heard a rumor about a possible takeover involving Textron. Yes, he had passed it on to Waters and they had contacted Textron.

Wang asked where Levine had heard the rumor. Levine said he had been sitting in the reception area at Drexel Burnham Lambert, a rival investment bank, in early October when he overheard two gentlemen discussing a transaction in rather obscure terms.

The men mentioned Lester Crown, a wealthy Chicago businessman and director of Chicago Pacific, said Levine. The men also mentioned Skadden Arps Slate Meagher & Flom, the takeover law firm, and the First Boston Corporation, a leading investment banking firm. And, said Levine, they mentioned "fireworks in Rhode Island, which is a direct quote."

As he continued his testimony, Levine embellished the story. The men were in their late thirties or early forties. "Dressed in pinstripes, gray suits, just like all of us. They both had briefcases."

From the clues in the conversation, particularly "fireworks in Rhode Island," Levine said, he deduced that the men were discussing a takeover attempt involving Textron, which is headquartered in Providence.

Leo Wang was thirty-one years old. He had joined the SEC enforcement division in May 1982 after four years of private practice in Milwaukee following graduation from the University of Wisconsin Law School.

He was taciturn and rigidly proper in questioning Levine. He showed no emotion during the interrogation and offered no opinion to Levine or his lawyer at its conclusion.

In two and a half years at the SEC, Wang had earned a reputation among his colleagues as a highly skeptical and tenacious investigative lawyer. After listening to Levine for more than two hours, Wang knew the investment banker was lying. It was less a matter of experience than instinct. The question was how much Levine was concealing, and whether Wang and the SEC could get at the truth.

In the previous three years, the SEC had improved its reputation for policing insider trading. About fifty insider cases had been brought since 1981, equal to the total from the previous four and a half decades.

In part, the increase was the result of more aggressive and effective enforcement. When John S. R. Shad, a former Wall Street investment banker, took over as chairman of the SEC in 1981, he vowed that the crime would take on top priority in the agency's enforcement division.

Another factor in the rising number of prosecutions was the rapid growth of mergers and acquisitions activity. More deals created more opportunities to obtain and abuse inside information. The stakes also had gone up dramatically in an era of billion-dollar takeovers. The banks and law firms and retail brokerage houses involved in the new dealmaking had, with a few exceptions, failed to create new internal controls to keep pace with the increasing opportunities for abuses.

The SEC also got a boost through a lurid case involving a former high-ranking Reagan administration official and his mistress. In January 1984, the SEC had accused Paul Thayer, a former assistant secretary of defense, of passing inside information to eight people, including his mistress, while he was a director of two major corporations involved in mergers. Although the woman was not charged, Thayer's prominence and her involvement had created a wave of sensational publicity that bolstered the idea that the regulators and prosecutors were aggressively pursuing cases involving insider trading.

The atmosphere on Wall Street was well short of paranoia, but the old sense that insider trading could not be prevented had been replaced by an awareness that it was no longer a free ride. And rumors about SEC investigations into various stocks were hot gossip on the Street.

So when Ira Sokolow heard through the grapevine at Shearson Lehman Brothers in November that Levine had been questioned about possible insider trading in Textron stock, the young investment banker was concerned. Sokolow had not been involved in the Textron transaction and did not yet know that Levine had traded in the stock. But he was frightened by the possibility Levine had been involved and by the new aggressiveness of the SEC.

"This is all fantasy, Dennis," said Sokolow. "You're going to get caught. It's time to leave it alone. Get off the merry-go-round."

Levine dismissed Sokolow's fears: "That's not me. I never traded in Textron. Stop worrying."

Levine was confident that the SEC had no way to connect him with the Textron trading. He was confident that he had lied with impunity to the two young SEC attorneys.

In boasting to Wilkis about his successful lying, Levine later said: "I can out-con any con in any game. I grew up selling aluminum siding to niggers on welfare."

He was right again. The SEC was unable to uncover evidence linking Levine or anyone else to insider trading in Textron stock. The case was another frustrating dead end for the agency's enforcement division.

But Leo Wang remained convinced that the arrogant investment banker had lied during his sworn testimony. "Dennis Levine" was a name the hard-nosed attorney tucked away in his mind for future reference.

8.

The Rainmaker

There was one element of truth in Levine's explanation of the Textron "rumor" and it was this: he had been at Drexel Burnham Lambert in early October 1984. He had gone there for a job interview.

In November 1981, when he arrived at Lehman Brothers, Levine was confident he was on the road to stardom. He had the title he coveted, division vice president in mergers and acquisitions. He had increased his salary substantially. He was working for a high-profile, old-line firm. And he had found a new mentor, Eric Gleacher, the respected head of M&A.

Levine's duties at Lehman Brothers centered on gathering information. The stock monitor in his office provided a steady stream of trading patterns, but Levine spent most of his time on the telephone. The most prominent feature of the office was the extra-long telephone extension cord that allowed Levine to talk on the phone while he paced the room or stood at the door watching the associates in the bullpen.

On that phone, Levine played the network of investment bankers, lawyers, and arbitragers he had cultivated over the years. He developed a reputation at Lehman Brothers as a "rainmaker," some-one with a talent for bringing in new business. In a profession where a single deal could generate fees of $2 million and up, it was a valuable talent.

Levine's ability to gather accurate information about pending transactions sometimes struck colleagues at Lehman Brothers as brilliant. One former partner recalled that less than a year after his arrival, Levine touted Criton Corporation as a takeover target. When Eric Gleacher called Criton and asked about the possibility, he was told, "You're crazy." But Gleacher and Levine visited Criton executives and convinced them the threat was real. Lehman Brothers was hired to defend against the rumored takeover bid. Two weeks after Gleacher's first call to Criton, Dyson-Kissner-Moran Corporation announced an offer for Criton, and Levine looked like a brilliant analyst who had generated a substantial fee for his employer.

His associates had no idea that Levine had received a tip about the Criton deal from one of his insider sources. Levine made $212,628 from Criton stock.

Levine's reputation as a relentless pursuer of information was so great that several co-workers, including Gleacher, once played a joke on him. They told him they had heard a rumor about a pending takeover and asked Levine to tap into his famous network and check it out. Throughout the day, Levine became increasingly frustrated by his inability to dig out the slightest bit of information about the company or the transaction. He went to Gleacher for help, but his boss waved him away. "I'm busy now, Dennis. Come back when you have the answer." Late that evening, his colleagues laughingly informed Levine that the company did not exist.

Levine was generally well liked at Lehman Brothers. He was affable and good-humored. The atmosphere there was not as stuffy as at Smith Barney and his aggressiveness did not stand out as much. He dressed in expensive suits and projected the image of a well-established investment banker.

As had happened at Smith Barney, however, some of his associates resented what they perceived as Levine's inability to perform the technical evaluations required in mergers and acquisitions. One of them was J. Tomilson Hill.

In July 1982, nine months after Levine's arrival at Lehman Brothers, his old boss from Smith Barney was hired by the firm. He was brought in as a partner, a rank Levine never achieved at Lehman, and, while their relations were cordial, Levine feared that Hill would expose his weaknesses and kill his career at his new firm by assigning him to difficult, technical tasks.

Despite the reservations of some, Levine had impressed Gleacher and had gradually assumed added responsibilities in big transactions. He remained just below the first tier in the M&A department, but he would later note in a résumé that he generated $10 million in fees for the firm in 1982, $15 million in 1983, and reached $20 million in 1984. Not on the résumé was the fact that on almost every big deal, Levine had bought stock for his trading account at Bank Leu.

When Gleacher left in the fall of 1983 to become a partner and eventually head of M&A at Morgan Stanley, Levine worked hard to cultivate his replacement, Peter Solomon. Levine had demonstrated his abilities as a strategist, and he was confident that his talents as a "rainmaker" marked him for promotion to a managing director's position at Lehman Brothers in the near future.

Levine seemed poised for professional success to match the hidden success of his insider trading. Yet the belief that he was about to achieve his dream could not shake Levine's involvement with insider trading. He was too caught up in the thrill of it and kept escalating his deals, placing bigger and bigger stock orders, almost daring the SEC to try to catch him. The excitement of seeing how much stock he could corner, how many millions of dollars he could amass, had become an almost palpable craving that could not be satisfied.

His big frustration was his failure to establish contacts at other investment houses and law firms. He told Wilkis repeatedly how much he hated missing opportunities to trade on deals that he did not know about in advance. He prodded his friend to seek new sources of information within Lazard Frères and he was engaged in his own constant and delicate search for new recruits for his expanding ring.

Despite his frustration, in the spring of 1984, Levine sat at the hub of precisely the type of insider trading network he had envisioned four years before in his lunchtime conversations with Ilan Reich.

Reich himself had steered clear of the ring for more than a year, having stopped providing information in late 1982. In November 1983, he and Levine had been part of a group at a "21" dinner celebrating the closing of a merger in which both of their firms had played roles. Levine, stopping by the table where Reich was sitting with his law firm colleagues, praised his talents, saying that the merger could not have been pulled off without Reich's involvement. Later that evening, in a private moment, Levine whispered to Reich, "We ought to get together again. I'm doing really well."

Reich was doing well, too; he was involved in most of the big, complex transactions at Wachtell, Lipton. A few weeks after the dinner at "21," he and Levine started meeting for lunch again.

At the time, Reich thought his marriage was in trouble and that he might need extra money to pay alimony and support for his infant son. Others would later speculate that Reich was worried that he might not make partner at Wachtell, Lipton, and he wanted the insider money as a hedge against losing his job.

It was true that in late 1983 Reich received a partially negative rating in his annual review at the law firm. The partners recognized his outstanding abilities to devise creative solutions to the most complex problems in a takeover situation, but they were annoyed by his reluctance to pitch in and do the mundane work associated with every deal.

Whatever the reason, on May 3, 1984, Reich got back in. He disclosed to Levine that Wachtell, Lipton had been hired by Warburg, Pincus & Company to begin legal research for the acquisition of SFN Companies. It turned out to be a complicated transaction requiring intricate legal work. Levine used the time to purchase 20,000 shares of SFN, which he sold for a profit of $129,316 the day after the deal was announced on August 23.

Wilkis had also made attempts to get out of the ring, although he never actually stopped supplying information or trading on tips. He remained hooked by the excitement, by Levine's relentless friendship, and by Levine's skillful use of guilt.

Back in June 1982, Wilkis had gone to Levine's office at Lehman Brothers and told him that he was quitting. He said Credit Suisse no longer wanted to handle his account because of unspecified problems, he was not making the kind of money Levine had promised, and he was frightened about being arrested on insider trading charges.

"It's too risky, Dennis," said Wilkis. "I'm scared. It's over for me."

Levine looked at his cohort and said calmly, "The game has been good to me. Don't come crying poor to me later if you get out. I just won't be able to help you."

"Dennis, I can't do this anymore. I can't live with myself. I hate this secrecy."

"Don't be a schmuck," Levine said as he tossed a small booklet at Wilkis. "Turn to the Cayman Islands."

When he picked up the booklet, Wilkis found that it was an airline flight guide. A few days later, he flew to the Cayman Islands and walked down the streets searching for a new bank to handle his account. He picked the Bank of Nova Scotia and transferred his money over from Nassau.

Wilkis remained in the "company," swapping the most sensitive corporate secrets with Levine and trading through his new account in the Cayman Islands. But Wilkis continued having trouble coming up with profitable deals because he did not work in mergers and acquisitions, and Levine constantly berated him for his failures to produce good tips. Eventually, however, Wilkis began to develop better information and his account started showing healthy profits.

Part of the reason for his new success was the addition of another source of information to feed Levine's insatiable appetite.

Randall Cecola had been hired at Lazard Frères as a twenty-two-year-old junior analyst in the mergers and acquisitions office in September 1983. He was a May graduate of Purdue University in West Lafayette, Indiana, who planned to save enough money to go to Harvard Business School. Cecola was bright, ambitious, and the sole support of his mother and two young brothers in Barrington, Illinois, a suburb of Chicago.

Cecola's father had abandoned the family many years before, and Cecola sent a portion of his salary back to Illinois to augment his mother's welfare checks. He also provided money for his brothers, who were both in college on student loans. Cecola still managed to live well in New York, purchasing expensive stereo equipment and taking luxury vacations.

In an attempt to deal with the financial burden, Cecola wanted to trade on the stock market. He did not have the money to buy enough stock to earn what he considered a significant profit, so he decided to enter the risky arena of options. He was confident his talents as an analyst would allow him to transform his meager savings into sizable profits.

Like most securities firms, Lazard required its employees to maintain their trading accounts in-house, where they could be monitored by the firm's compliance department. When Cecola told officials at Lazard he wanted to open an options account with the firm, they refused and cautioned Cecola that options posed too great a danger for a novice trader.

Cecola, still confident he could pick winners and desperate for the money, ignored his superiors and Lazard's requirement that employees trade through the firm. In November 1983, two months after joining Lazard, he had a friend in Indianapolis open a trading account for Cecola's benefit at a local brokerage house. He later had another friend open a second account in Barrington. The accounts were opened in the names of the friends to conceal Cecola's role in case the houses had any contact with Lazard Frères. But the information on what to buy came from Cecola, and he started trading late in 1983.

In May 1984, Cecola became friendly with Robert Wilkis, who had been with the firm for nearly five years by that time. Wilkis saw that Cecola spent an enormous amount of time watching the stock-price monitors and discussing various stock issues. So, one night as they were leaving work, Wilkis brought up the subject of insider trading. He said that he was involved in trading with someone else and he offered to stake Cecola with an overseas account in exchange for information on pending deals from the mergers and acquisitions department.

Wilkis, who had previously relied on second-hand information, suddenly had a source of information inside Lazard's mergers and acquisitions department, and he picked up valuable information from his conversations with the young analyst. For instance, it was Cecola who told him in September 1984 that Chicago Pacific Corporation had hired Lazard to orchestrate financing for an attempt to purchase Textron.

Ira Sokolow also helped expand the pipeline of valuable information by enlisting his best friend from college, David S. Brown.

After Brown and Sokolow graduated from the University of Pennsylvania in 1976, Brown had gone to law school at the University of Michigan and joined the Los Angeles law firm of McKenna, Connor & Cuneo in 1979.

In October 1982, about a year after he began selling information to Levine, Sokolow started passing confidential information on pending deals to Brown. In turn, Brown used the information to buy and sell small amounts of stock and options through two personal brokerage accounts.

In June 1983, Brown took a job as an investment banker at Goldman, Sachs & Co. in New York and began to develop his own inside information. Under the new scheme, Brown provided the tips to Sokolow, who then fenced the information to Levine. Sokolow refused to identify Brown to Levine, telling him only that he had his own source at Goldman, Sachs. Preferring not to trade himself, Sokolow allowed Levine to maintain an "account" for him within Levine's larger account and he accepted periodic cash payments as "withdrawals" from his balance. In turn, Sokolow paid cash to Brown for his tips.

In the course of more than three years, the total paid by Levine to Sokolow was less than $130,000. But Levine complained vociferously to Wilkis about the demands for cash from "Lehman" and "Goldie," and Wilkis had the impression Levine was paying them hundreds of thousands of dollars. At the same time he exaggerated the financial demands of his ring members, Levine guarded their identities from Wilkis, referring to Sokolow as "Lehman" and Brown as "Goldie." Levine also used the existence of the other sources, and the value of their tips, to instill a deep sense of guilt in Wilkis.

Once, around the middle of 1984, when Wilkis was expressing concern about the laws he and Levine were breaking and the trusts they were violating, Levine lashed out: "That's your problem, Bobby. You always believed in the gray area. I'm focused. I took you along. But I keep score. This guy at Goldman, he's just great. And Lehman is a company-oriented guy, working hard for me and giving good tips. You've been in the red every year on your tips. Friendship is great, but I'm running a business here and you've failed."

From the day he opened his first trading account at Pictet & Cie, Levine had conserved his profits and plowed them back into his pool of capital. In a world where success is measured by how much you earn and how much you own, Levine resisted the temptation to withdraw huge sums to finance the lavish life-style that would signal his brilliance but also risk his exposure.

He was far from miserly. He bought his wife expensive jewelry and owned a top-of-the-line BMW sports coupe. They took vacations in Europe and Hawaii and the Caribbean. Occasionally, he flashed wads of cash. But his possessions and expenses were not out of line with his income, which was around the $100,000-a-year level in 1983 and reached nearly $700,000 in 1984.

The restraint vanished toward the end of 1983, when Levine abandoned his cardinal rule of not spending money in ways that could attract attention.

He began by withdrawing $100,000 from his Bank Leu account in February 1983. The real binge did not start until November 3, when he returned to the Bahamas and took out $30,000. Eight days later, he was back at Bank Leu for $160,000. On December 2, he withdrew $200,000. There were a total of $490,000 in cash withdrawals in 1983.

The following year, Levine withdrew precisely the same amount of cash: $200,000 in March, $200,000 in July, $90,000 in December.

The grandeur of his life-style increased. The vacations became more lavish. Levine and his wife loved to dine in New York's most expensive restaurants and they ate out several times a week. The jewelry he bought for Laurie grew increasingly expensive. Once he boasted to Wilkis about a string of diamonds he had bought for his wife. And there was the new apartment.

The heavy withdrawals in 1983 and 1984 coincided with Levine's purchase of a six-room apartment in a vintage building on Park Avenue between Ninety-third and Ninety-fourth streets.

He paid $550,000 for the apartment, putting down 10 percent, $55,000, as a binder. At closing, he put down an additional $225,000 and covered the rest with a mortgage of $270,000. Another substantial expense was the extensive ten-month renovation. Levine, his wife, and their young son, Adam, continued to live in the rented apartment at 225 East Fifty-seventh Street while the work was done on the Park Avenue apartment.

An architect was hired to create a more elegant floor plan. Walls were demolished and new ones were built. A bleached-oak floor was laid in the foyer. An expensive curved wall was constructed at the end of the foyer, with an arch that opened to show a second curved wall.

The walls of the dining room, kitchen, and maid's quarters were removed and an entirely new wing was created. A glass-block wall separated the new dining room from a new bedroom. A bath was added next to a small den for Levine. The kitchen was redesigned and, when the Levines decided halfway through that they didn't like it, the work was torn out and redesigned.

At the other end of the eighth-floor apartment, the master bedroom got a wall of cabinetry complete with a concealed twenty-five-inch television that popped up at the press of a button. A Jacuzzi and an electric towel warmer were installed in the new marble master bath.

When the construction was finished, an interior decorator was brought in to choose an entirely new decor of expensive, contemporary furniture and artwork. Levine, whose idea of a proper painting was one that contained enough orange to match the couch, soon owned a Rodin sculpture, a Picasso etching, and a large painting by Miró.

Ilan Reich was an experienced handyman who had renovated a loft apartment on his own, so Levine often discussed the work on the Park Avenue apartment with him.

Levine had boasted to Reich about his "million-dollar" apartment, but when Reich was invited to inspect the finished apartment in early 1985, he was flabbergasted by the extent and expense of the work. He estimated the cost of the renovation and decoration at $150,000 to $250,000.

Reich's estimate was far short of the mark. The final cost of the renovation and decoration of the apartment was close to $500,000.

But even his own estimate caused Reich to wonder just how much money Levine was making from his insider trading. After that first lunch in which he told how he planned to set up the scheme, Levine had refused to tell Reich very much more. He had played the role of spymaster, divulging information only on a "need to know" basis, claiming he was shielding his confederates from the risk that the discovery of one could compromise the others.

Reich's suspicion that others were involved had evolved into a firm belief, but Levine was adamant in his refusal to identify any of the other participants. Meanwhile, Reich's old worries about whether Levine himself could keep the scheme a secret were rekindled by the evidence of heavy spending on the apartment, and in August he began considering pulling out again.

Before doing so, Reich provided one last bit of inside information.

On August 17, 1984, the family and trusts that controlled half of the stock in G. D. Searle & Company, the pharmaceutical firm and creator of NutraSweet, hired Wachtell, Lipton to serve as legal counsel for the planned sale of 34 percent of its holdings. Reich was not involved in the deal, but he heard about it and passed the information to Levine.

Searle had been mentioned as a possible takeover candidate by chemical companies interested in broadening their holdings in pharmaceutical firms. The roadblock to a takeover attempt had been the high concentration of stock held by the family and trusts. A decision by family members and the trusts to sell their stock was expected to open the way for a takeover bid. It would also open the way for a jump in the price of Searle stock.

Based on Reich's tip, Levine bought 60,000 shares of Searle and took the additional gamble of buying options. But it was a deal that was slow to come together. The Searle family could not make up its mind quickly enough for Levine, so, near the end of September, he once again told Wilkis to telephone the *Chicago Tribune* and push things along with a leak. This time Levine got on the phone, too, without identifying himself. The resulting story applied pressure on the family to speed up the process. At the end of September, when the family announced its plan to seek a buyer for the company or at least sell the major portion of its stock, Levine sold both stock and options for a combined profit of $834,743.

By the time Levine collected his Searle profits, Reich had again quit the ring, at least in his own mind. In the course of the summer, he had experienced the sour taste of self-disgust over his dealings with Levine. It had become something he could no longer endure. In addition, his marriage had improved and he and his wife were expecting a second child. It was time to make a clean break.

Still, Reich lacked the resolve to confront Levine with his decision and he resumed his old ploys, not answering Levine's telephone calls or showing up so late for a meeting that Levine was gone.

Throughout September and into early October, he delayed the confrontation. He knew he was only postponing the inevitable, that he had to end the charade and tell Levine he was out for good. In the middle of the month he arranged lunch with Levine.

They met at a restaurant on First Avenue in midtown Manhattan and, as was their custom, traded talk about their families and jobs. Reich said he felt his performance on some recent deals made him a candidate for partner. He talked with animation about a legal stroke that had forced a holdout to surrender his stock in SFN Companies and paved the way for a successful takeover. Although he had only been at the firm for five years, he said, he had a feeling he would make it when the new partners were chosen in early November.

Levine described his continuing frustration at Shearson Lehman and he brought Reich up to date on his search for a new job. He had gotten positive reactions at three top firms, including Drexel Burnham Lambert, the hottest house on Wall Street. He said he thought things looked good at Drexel, that he might even get the managing director's job he deserved as part of the hiring package.

As they walked along the East Side after lunch, Reich got to the point of the meeting. He told Levine he was getting out of the insider scheme once and for all. He talked about his fears of being caught and the sickness he felt every time he handed over confidential information.

"Dennis, I'm not going to get involved anymore. It was all a big mistake," said Reich.

To Reich's relief, the decision was taken calmly, almost as if it were expected. Then Reich realized it probably was. After all, he had been ducking his friend for weeks and Levine was clever enough to figure out why.

Levine said little. "Your account is up to $300,000. Don't you want your money?" he asked.

"Absolutely not. I feel better because I never took any money in this deal," said Reich.

Reich was relieved. He felt that he might finally rid himself of the sickness of the spirit that he had endured for over four years.

As he walked beside Reich that day, Levine had a different perception of why Reich was quitting. He figured Reich was getting out because he was going to make partner and he didn't need the scheme anymore.

Levine had always been puzzled and somewhat amused that Reich had never taken any money. He had told himself that the lawyer would find something he really wanted someday and change his mind. But if Reich were going to become a partner, his financial worries would be over. Levine knew even a new partner at Wachtell, Lipton would bring home about $500,000 a year.

He didn't press Reich to reconsider. The lawyer might change his mind again down the road, the way he had before. Levine was more concerned about landing his new job at Drexel Burnham.

Despite his success in bringing in new business at Shearson Lehman Brothers and despite what he considered his close relationship with Peter Solomon, the head of M&A, Levine had been passed over for promotion to managing director that summer. Solomon told others at the firm that he just didn't feel Levine was mature enough for the job and that Levine was still weak technically.

As he had been at Smith Barney, Levine was crushed by the setback and had contacted an executive recruiting firm, Hadley Lockwood Inc., to begin the search for a new job.

Wall Street, in the middle of the biggest merger wave in its history, was an environment in which someone with Levine's credentials and contacts proved to be a hot property. Positive responses came from three investment firms. The best offer seemed to be from Drexel, a house where Levine thought he would fit in well.

Drexel Burnham Lambert was the home of the pirates in pinstripes.

In the fall of 1984, Drexel was the most celebrated investment firm on Wall Street and one of the most profitable. It had become the symbol of the tremendous forces that had reshaped Wall Street over the past decade.

In an arena of multimillion-dollar fees for investment banks, Drexel was the toughest competitor on the Street. Its aggressive tactics evoked anger, fear, and envy among other firms. They complained that when Drexel headed an underwriting group, it kept an unfair share of the bonds to sell to its own customers. They complained that Drexel had no reverence for tradition and violated the unwritten rules of Wall Street.

Drexel's partners were among the best paid in the profession. The firm was the very essence of a meritocracy, where the ability to make a deal was far more valued, and richly rewarded, than an Ivy League diploma. The firm seduced many bright young professionals from rival firms with stunning bonuses and the promise of a shot at stardom.

But nothing stirred more anger and envy among its competitors than Drexel's dominance of the controversial junk-bond market, and nothing better illustrated the success of its star system than the man who engineered that dominance, Michael Milken.

Milken began trading in junk bonds in the late 1960s when he first came to Drexel out of the Wharton School. In those days, the only junk bonds around were so-called fallen angels—former investment-grade securities that had been downgraded when the companies that issued them fell into difficulty.

Milken saw a new potential in junk bonds. By selecting the up-and-coming companies from the losers with which the rating agencies lumped them, he developed high-yield junk bonds with surprisingly low default rates.

He was able to convince a broad clientele that carefully selected junk bonds represented a greater value than their ratings showed. Lured by the promise of fat yields from the higher interest rates paid by the bonds, investors loaded up.

It was only a short step for Drexel to begin using Milken's network of institutional and individual investors to sell junk bonds issued by shell companies to raise money to bankroll takeovers, friendly and unfriendly. In doing so, the firm changed the face of finance. Drexel's junk bonds began to displace banks and insurance companies as the prime sources for acquisition funding. Drexel's biggest clients were the corporate raiders and speculative entrepreneurs who were transforming corporate America by using junk bonds to make runs at some of the nation's biggest companies.

Along with fueling Drexel's ascent, Milken became enormously rich, both from his Drexel salary and bonuses—estimated at $15 million to $25 million a year, among the largest in Wall Street history—and from the unconventional practice of investing in many of the deals that he helped finance.

So it was natural that when Drexel wanted to beef up its small mergers and acquisitions department, the firm would turn to the star system.

In 1984, Drexel's executives were trying to expand the firm into a full-service investment bank. With record profits generated largely by the junk-bond business, the firm was hiring people they considered the best at other firms to beef up its bond trading department, its commodities business, and other areas.

That summer, the firm's senior management held a brainstorming session about ways to grab a bigger slice of the lucrative M&A activity on Wall Street. Among those at the meeting were Frederick Joseph, the president and chief executive officer of the firm; Herbert Bachelor, executive vice president and head of corporate finance; and David Kay, the head of mergers and acquisitions.

The executives concluded that there were two ways to jump into the M&A big leagues fast: hire a star from another firm or create their own star.

Kay, who had come to Drexel in 1978 to form its first mergers and acquisitions unit, pushed hardest for bringing in a "star" to upgrade the unit's profile quickly. He was supported by Joseph, the son of a Boston cabdriver who had risen from head of investment banking to CEO in a decade at Drexel.

They compiled a list of the M&A stars on Wall Street that contained such names as Eric Gleacher at Morgan Stanley, Bruce Wasserstein at First Boston Corporation, and Martin Siegel at Kidder, Peabody & Co.

As they went down the list, Kay and Joseph realized that there was little that Drexel could offer the men on the list. They all earned in excess of $1 million a year and they all worked for firms with more prestige than Drexel in M&A.

So they turned to plan two and decided to hire a promising young M&A specialist and turn him into a star.

Toward the end of the summer, Drexel's search for someone with star quality crossed paths with Levine's quest for a vehicle to stardom, and Kay and Joseph began several weeks of discussions and negotiations with Levine.

The résumé the headhunters put together for Drexel at the end of October offers a rare glimpse of Levine's perception of himself and his career, since it was prepared directly from information that he provided to Hadley Lockwood, the search firm. It said, in part:

> Dennis describes himself as a person who truly loves to do two things: do deals and make money. The outstanding success with which he has accomplished the former has not been truly reflected in the latter during his days with Lehman Brothers. His 1984 base salary of $75,000 and a profit participation of approximately $100,000 was finally acknowledged as under-compensation when he received his 1984 bonus from the combined Shearson Lehman/American Express organization. On October 10, 1984, Dennis received his bonus check, which

was slightly in excess of $500,000. He was also promoted to senior vice president and was promised a managing director-ship at the end of 1984/beginning 1985.

The résumé outlined Levine's increased responsibilities at Shear-son Lehman Brothers and discussed what it described as "inter-esting complexities" involved in recruiting him.

Having graduated from schools that do not generally produce investment bankers, Dennis has had great difficulty fighting his way into the major bracket. In the process, he has become something of a workaholic who rarely touches down for an interview except on the shortest of notice, and even then often has to cancel. Once cornered for an interview, Dennis needs to be convinced that the opportunity represented by Drexel Burnham is significantly superior to the one represented by his current employer; he does not like to change jobs and he is an extremely loyal individual.

The résumé, which was redesigned specifically for Drexel, said the environment at Drexel appeared to be "tailor-made for Dennis's aggressive deal-doing skills and new business-generation capa-bility."

Levine proved to be a tough negotiator in his interviews with Kay and Joseph. He said that he had been "enchanted" by the tradition-laden atmosphere at Lehman Brothers when he first joined the firm, but he viewed the merger with Shearson/American Ex-press as a "sellout that betrayed his future." While his future was bright with his present employer, he said he felt obligated to move to another firm because he was unsure about the survival of Shear-son Lehman Brothers.

Drexel conducted a discreet and informal check of Levine's back-ground on Wall Street and found nothing amiss. Joseph Flom and Marty Lipton, two of the most widely respected takeover lawyers in the country, both gave Levine excellent marks, as did other investment bankers.

David Kay, who had become Levine's most ardent booster, saw what he liked to call "star quality" in Levine. He thought Levine possessed a self-assurance and presence that were beyond his years. He sensed in Levine's ambition the ability to transfer his drive and enthusiasm to reluctant clients and kindle a deal from smoldering embers.

"He demonstrated a great understanding of how to get a transaction done and how to create a transaction from nominal beginnings," Kay recalled later. "He had a good feel for the deal, a sense of the potential. Our sense was that he had the kind of attitude that would cause him to do well in the Drexel environment."

On paper, Levine had the professional credentials to warrant Kay's confidence. He had been given increasing responsibility in each job he had taken and appeared to have performed well. In the last year at Shearson Lehman Brothers, he had played a principal role in major transactions, the types of high-profile deals that Kay was eager to land at Drexel Burnham.

Indeed, Levine had traveled a long way in the investment banking profession since his first frustrating attempts to break the barrier from Baruch College. The reminders of his origins were carefully concealed beneath a polite demeanor and a proper formality in his dress, which suggested that he was not going to reinforce any of the inadequacies of his background through slovenliness in manner or appearance.

When Drexel checked Levine's background there were no whispers about his technical weakness and no misgivings were expressed about his amazing ability to generate valuable information. Indeed, the special greed that fueled Levine's illegal enterprise also garnered rewards for him in his career. Colleagues marveled at his ability to get information, at how much he knew, at how often his tips led to new clients.

In late December, Levine reached an agreement to go to work at Drexel. On January 9, 1985, David Kay wrote a letter to Levine outlining the terms of his employment, which was to start on February 4.

Levine would be one of five managing directors. His base salary was set at $140,000, with a minimum guaranteed bonus of $750,000 in 1985. He could draw up to $200,000 of the bonus the day he started work. He would receive 1,000 shares of stock in Drexel Burnham worth about $100,000.

Kay concluded with a note of welcome: "Dennis, all of us are very excited about your decision to join our firm and we all look forward to seeing you at an early date."

As a final cost of hiring Levine, Drexel Burnham paid $267,000 to the executive search firm of Hadley Lockwood Inc. No one at Drexel Burnham had any concept of how much its new star ultimately would cost the investment firm.

After resigning from Shearson Lehman and before starting at Drexel Burnham, Levine slipped down to Nassau on January 28 and withdrew $150,000 from his account at Bank Leu.

9.

Easy Money

The Coastal Corporation's suite on the thirty-eighth floor of the United Nations Plaza Towers provided panoramic north and west views of Manhattan's skyline through floor-to-ceiling windows. But the half-dozen men gathered in the suite on a Sunday night in February 1985 were not interested in the view. They were deciding strategy for a secret, $2-billion plan, code-named "Gull."

The men bent over a table in the room on February 17 were not conspirators in a cloak-and-dagger espionage plot. They were executives from Coastal Corporation, a major gas-and-oil-exploration company headquartered in Houston, and their investment bankers from Drexel Burnham Lambert.

But secrecy was as important to them as to any spy.

Gull was the code for Coastal's confidential plan to take over American Natural Resources, a smaller natural gas company. If word leaked out that a takeover attempt was being planned, ANR stock would rise and so would the ultimate price Coastal would have to pay for the company. Wall Street professionals and corporate executives had seen it happen all too often in recent months.

The executives and bankers had no way of knowing that the plan had already been compromised by one of the men in the room.

Dennis Levine had started work at Drexel Burnham Lambert on February 4, a Monday. He had taken over a medium-sized, glass-enclosed office in the mergers and acquisitions unit on the eighth floor of Drexel's headquarters at 55 Broad Street, two blocks from the New York Stock Exchange.

David Kay and Fred Joseph had decided that the best way to launch their new star was to involve him in the most prestigious acquisition under way at Drexel Burnham at the time, the $2-billion attempt by Coastal to acquire American Natural Resources. When completed, it would be a highly visible transaction, a perfect debut for Levine.

David Arledge, Coastal's senior vice president for finance, had first contacted Drexel Burnham about acquiring ANR in early January. He had come to New York and met with Joseph and John Sorte, a managing director in Drexel Burnham's mergers and acquisitions division. Both men had indicated Drexel Burnham was eager to arrange the financing for the transaction.

Later that month, the men had met for preliminary talks, first at Drexel Burnham's offices and later at Coastal's suite at the UN Plaza Towers, a luxury residential building attached to the UN Plaza Hotel and diagonally across from the United Nations complex. One reason for moving the talks to the apartment was to avoid repeated visits to Drexel by Coastal executives, which could fuel rumors that the company was planning a takeover.

On February 11, Arledge telephoned Sorte and said the Coastal management wanted to lay the groundwork for an all-cash offer of $60 a share. Arledge stressed the need to raise the money in a short period and keep ANR out of the marketplace to avoid a price increase that could make the deal too expensive.

Sorte responded that $60 a share was well above the market

price for ANR stock and told Arledge he was confident the money could be raised quickly and quietly. As added encouragement, Sorte said he would be assisted in the deal by the M&A unit's newest managing director, Dennis Levine.

When he hung up the telephone, Sorte turned to Levine, who had been sitting across from him during the conversation, and outlined the transaction. Levine was enthusiastic about the prospects for success, particularly in view of the plan for an all-cash offer at $60 a share.

Three days later, Levine placed a collect call to Bernhard Meier at Bank Leu and told him to begin buying as much stock in American Natural Resources as possible. He cautioned Meier to proceed carefully in distributing the trades among brokers. The following day Levine called back and asked Meier to check the balance in his account. After being told that it was nearly $7.3 million, Levine said to invest the entire amount in ANR.

"It's a sure winner," Levine told Meier.

The same day that Levine gave Meier his final instructions, Arledge and two other Coastal executives, James Whalen and Austin O'Toole, arrived in New York for a weekend strategy session with the Drexel Burnham team. Levine did not attend the Saturday meeting, but he showed up at Coastal's suite on Sunday during discussions on arranging the financing through a consortium of Arab, Swiss, and Canadian banks.

Levine said little at the first meeting, but as the plan progressed, he played an increasingly prominent role in discussions. He offered advice on the timing of the announcement and on what strategies ANR might take in defense of the takeover.

He told Arledge that he had quietly tapped into his own information network to discover who held substantial blocks of ANR stock and to determine the prospects of those investors selling when Coastal started its takeover. Levine said arbitragers had started buying ANR stock as early as January and held a considerable portion of the company's shares. That was, he explained, a good sign for Coastal. Most individuals buy stocks as a long-term investment and are usually less likely to sell quickly when an outside company launches a takeover bid. But when large blocks of stock are held by arbitragers, a hostile takeover is normally easier because arbitragers can usually be counted on to sell to the highest bidder.

Levine told Arledge he had discovered that one of the arbitragers who had bought heavily in ANR stock in recent days was Ivan F. Boesky, the richest stock speculator in America.

On March 1, as Coastal was preparing the final details of its public announcement of the takeover bid, Levine told Arledge he was confident the deal would be successful because the $60-per-share offer was a fair price.

American Natural Resources initially fought the takeover attempt, buying back two million of its shares and selling off assets to finance the battle. It was not until early May that the two corporations reached an agreement and Coastal completed its acquisition of ANR.

In the end, Coastal had to pay $65 a share and the cost had risen from slightly over $2 billion to $2.45 billion. The arbitragers who had bought into ANR stock in the early going had helped drive up the price; when they sold out they made substantial profits. None made more than Ivan Boesky, who owned 9.9 percent of ANR's stock by the time the deal was consummated and collected $3 million to $4 million in profits.

The heavy buying in ANR stock in the days before the announcement was picked up by the New York Stock Exchange's stock-monitoring unit and reported to the SEC. On March 13, the SEC opened an informal inquiry into the possibility of insider trading in ANR stock, but uncovered insufficient evidence to escalate the inquiry to a formal investigation.

For Levine, who had sold his 145,000 shares of ANR on March 4 for a profit of nearly $1.4 million, the transaction marked the completion of the first act in Drexel's strategy to make him a star. The curtain was set to go up on the second act in the land of stars itself, Los Angeles.

The annual conference on high-yield junk bonds conducted by Drexel each spring attracted leading takeover artists, arbitragers, money managers, and corporate executives from across America. The four-day conference had its share of panel discussions on current events and studious presentations on corporate finances. And the entertainment included such stars as Frank Sinatra and Dolly Parton.

But the real reason nearly 2,000 people showed up every spring was to listen to Michael Milken, whose rousing speeches on the power of junk bonds occasionally lent the conference the aura of a religious revival meeting.

The 1985 conference, held from March 26 to March 30 at the Beverly Hills Hotel, was Levine's first as a Drexel managing director. He basked in the glory of his new position and the recent Coastal-ANR deal.

One of the speakers at the conference was Sir James Goldsmith, the Anglo-French financier who was then perhaps the most complicated and visionary corporate raider in the world.

Born to an old and wealthy family, Sir James is a self-made millionaire many times over. He holds English and French passports; his father was a member of the British Parliament, his mother from the Auvergne. He was born in Paris in 1933 and attended Eton after the family fled France at the outbreak of World War II. He also leads an openly double personal life, maintaining a wife and family in Paris and openly living with a mistress and their two children elsewhere.

In the spring of 1985, he owned townhouses in New York and Paris, a country estate in England, and a farmhouse in Spain. He was the center of a vast network of holdings in Britain, France, and the United States, ranging from diet foods, chocolate, snuff, and chains of grocery stores to L'Express, France's biggest-circulation news weekly, and a Belgian weekly newspaper.

Much of his empire was acquired by hostile takeovers. His principal takeover vehicle was Générale Occidentale, which he used to acquire Diamond International, primarily for its timber holdings, and to make unsuccessful runs at two other timber companies, St. Regis and Continental Group.

In Los Angeles, in addition to speaking about his vision of corporate America—bloated and bureaucratic—he was at the junk-bond session for meetings with advisers from Drexel about his attempted takeover of another timber-rich company, Crown Zellerbach Corporation, begun the previous December.

On the second night of the conference, March 27, Sir James met to discuss the hostile takeover attempt with three M&A specialists from Drexel, G. Chris Anderson, Douglas McClure, and Dennis Levine.

Since December, Sir James had accumulated 8.6 percent of the stock in Crown Zellerbach at a cost of $78 million. The week before the Drexel conference, he had met with William Creson, the chairman of Crown, to announce that he wanted to buy control of the company. Creson had responded that the company was vehemently opposed to a takeover by Sir James, who had made millions by selling off assets from Diamond International and accepting "greenmail" to drop the St. Regis and Continental deals.

Rebuffed by Creson, Sir James had decided to launch a hostile bid for Crown and, when he met with Levine, Anderson, and McClure, it was to discuss strategy and pricing for the cash offer he planned.

The morning after the discussion, Levine sat in Room 289 at the Beverly Hills Hotel and placed a collect telephone call to Bank Leu. Meier was on vacation in Switzerland, so Levine spoke with Bruno Pletscher. Although rumors of Goldsmith's interest had pushed the price of Crown to $40 a share by March 28, Levine was aware that Sir James was willing to go higher. He told Pletscher to buy $4 million worth of stock in Crown Zellerbach.

"There's a deal going through," he told the banker.

Levine was put in charge of the takeover transaction at Drexel, and he provided advice to Sir James and his executives throughout April as Crown launched its defense against the unwanted suitor. The exchanges between Goldsmith and the company were bitter, and both sides filed lawsuits over the opposition's tactics.

In early April, Crown had triggered a so-called poison-pill defense of the takeover bid by distributing stock rights intended to dilute the value of the surviving company in the event Goldsmith succeeded in gaining control. The point was to make Crown a less attractive target and hope Goldsmith relented.

On April 24, Levine learned that Crown had taken the ultimate defensive maneuver and arranged to be acquired by Mead Corporation, another paper products company, in a friendly "white-knight" offer. The $50-a-share, $1.4 billion offer was set to be approved the following day by the boards of Crown and Mead.

Levine telephoned Bank Leu and again got Pletscher.

"It's a short deal," he told Pletscher. "You've got to buy as quickly as possible."

Pletscher bought an additional $200,000 worth of Crown stock for Levine that afternoon and the following morning. He bought $12,000 worth for his own account and telephoned Meier, who was still on vacation in Switzerland, to see if he wanted any stock. Meier declined, telling Pletscher he did not want to buy if he was not going to be present to monitor the stock prices.

Late that night, George Lowy, a partner in the New York law firm of Cravath Swaine & Moore, telephoned Goldsmith at his New York home and informed him that Lowy's client, Mead Corporation, was planning a white-knight offer for Crown. Lowy said he wanted to discuss the offer with Sir James, and the financier invited him to come to his townhouse on East Eightieth Street the following morning.

Goldsmith's townhouse reflects the luxury befitting one of the world's richest men. The courtyard is paved with marble, the furniture is French and antique, the wallpaper is silk damask.

Lowy arrived shortly before 10:00 A.M. to meet with Sir James and his coterie, which included Roland Franklin, one of his closest advisers; several attorneys; and a handful of bankers from Drexel. Levine was one of them.

The board of Mead Corporation was holding a simultaneous meeting at a community college in Dayton, Ohio, where the company has its headquarters. The agenda for the meeting included final approval of the acquisition of Crown Zellerbach.

Arbitrager Ivan Boesky had accumulated 7.4 percent of the stock in Crown, and Mead's lawyers were certain he would be happy to sell his stake for $50 a share. Their concern was reaching an agreement with Goldsmith to buy his 19 percent of the stock without a court fight or a costly bidding war. From Mead's point of view, the deal was dead unless Goldsmith cooperated.

Levine and the others remained downstairs when Lowy accompanied Sir James, Franklin, and Blaine Fogg, one of Goldsmith's lawyers, to an upstairs living room. Lowy explained that Mead and Crown had agreed on a friendly acquisition at $50 a share, and the company wanted to reach an accord with Sir James to purchase his Crown stock. Goldsmith responded that, although he wanted control of Crown, he did not want to pay $50 a share. That, he said, was too rich for him.

He agreed to sell his stake to Mead, and the four men spent the next two hours negotiating details of the transaction before heading back downstairs for lunch.

Goldsmith proved a charming and voluble luncheon host as he held forth on American business and French culture and politics. He is considered generally more conservative than even the right-wing parties of Europe, and he spent a considerable portion of the lunch complaining about the state of the socialist government in France.

Near the end of the lunch, Lowy was called away from the table to take a telephone call. It was one of his partners who was attending the Mead board meeting in Dayton.

The senior management at Mead had kept its negotiations with Crown secret inside the company, but they fully expected the board to approve the deal. Instead, Lowy was told the board had rejected the proposal. Mead was in the process of recovering from the slump that had plagued the entire paper products industry in 1982, and the board did not want to take on the added corporate debt involved in the acquisition of Crown.

As Lowy hung up the telephone, his first thought was how to get out of the townhouse without returning to the luncheon table. When he walked back into the room, he announced to Goldsmith and the others:

"You're not going to give me dessert. The board didn't approve the deal."

Sir James expressed disappointment and said he would simply proceed with his plan to acquire Crown. But he and Franklin noticed that Levine reacted strongly to the news that Mead had dropped its offer. He turned gray.

After the lunch broke up, Goldsmith and Franklin speculated on Levine's obvious concern over the collapse of the deal. They assumed he had bought a large number of shares in Crown.

"He was anxious to get to his broker as quickly as possible," Goldsmith joked to Franklin.

The matter was no joke to Levine. Immediately after leaving the townhouse, he went to a pay phone and telephoned Pletscher.

"The deal didn't go through," he told the banker. "Sell as quickly as possible."

Pletscher sold all of Levine's stock that day and managed to salvage a small profit of $82,000 for his client. He also sold his own 300 shares and broke even on the deal. Goldsmith ultimately won control of Crown Zellerbach on July 25, and the stock closed at $38.25 a share that day.

The takeover was the first victory over a poison-pill defense, and a Drexel assessment of the transaction declared it a "convincing success." A sizable portion of the credit was given to Levine for his tactical advice.

In the first months after Levine's move to Drexel, Wilkis found his friend to be completely intoxicated with his new station in life, bragging endlessly about his successes and his high-stakes pals, Jimmy Goldsmith and Ivan Boesky.

"They love me, they love me," Levine exuberantly told Wilkis at

dinner one night after Levine's return from the junk-bond conference. Waving his arms across the table at his friend, he said: "I'm
not a banker. I'm a thespian."

Yet a few nights later, an upset Levine telephoned his friend at
home around midnight and asked Wilkis to meet him near the
Museum of Natural History on Central Park West, not far from
Wilkis's apartment. When Wilkis arrived he found Levine crying
over a slight he had suffered from his wife.

"She pissed on my parade," Levine complained. "I'm getting rid
of the bitch. It'll probably cost me a million dollars. But I'm going
to find someone worthy of my station in life. Or else I've got to get
down and find a proper mistress."

At Drexel Burnham, David Kay, Fred Joseph, and the other executives were pleased with Levine's performance on the Coastal
and Crown Zellerbach deals. Both were highly visible transactions
on Wall Street and had showcased the firm's rising star.

As Levine's profile rose, they expected him to generate more of
the megabuck deals that would help Drexel's M&A division achieve
the type of dominance it enjoyed in the junk-bond market. After
all, the two operations went hand in hand: an aggressive corporate
raider who relied on Drexel to finance his deal also would be able
to turn to the firm's mergers and acquisitions staff to carry it out.
The result would be more fees for Drexel.

Alongside his role as a principal dealmaker, Levine began to
cultivate an image as a mentor to the young associates in the M&A
division. The young MBAs from Harvard and Stanford and Wharton
gathered in his glass-enclosed office to learn the game.

By 1985, investment banking was attracting so many top graduates that the nation's leading business schools were concerned
that the concentration of talent on Wall Street might leave too few
bright managers for industrial America.

For instance, 14 to 15 percent of the graduating class at Harvard
Business School traditionally took jobs in investment banking. By

1984, the percentage had increased to 19 percent and, in 1985, a full 28 percent of the graduates took jobs with investment firms. A third of Yale University's 1985 graduating class interviewed with First Boston Corporation that spring.

One reason Wall Street was gobbling up so many bright young business school graduates was the geometric growth of trading, mergers and acquisitions, leveraged buy-outs, and other deals consummated by the investment banks. In 1980, the revenues of the twenty firms that dominated investment banking totaled $10.9 billion; by the end of 1985, they would almost triple to $28.8 billion.

The demand for young bankers to do the rising number of deals created a competition among the leading firms that was reflected directly in the enormous money offered to the new graduates. A freshly minted MBA from Harvard could reasonably expect a starting salary and guaranteed bonus of $75,000 to $100,000. He or she could be earning half a million dollars a year by the age of thirty.

The money bought a lot of Porsches and BMWs, a lot of upper-bracket East Side apartments and summer houses in the Hamptons. However, there was often little time to enjoy the material wealth. Investment banking in the eighties was not a job for young idlers.

Long working hours were routine and in the heat of a takeover, one-hundred-hour weeks were normal. The pace was exhilarating, with its late-night strategy sessions, respectful receptions from the captains of industry, and a role in decisions that were restructuring American industry. And the gratifications were almost instant. There was no waiting for a year-end financial report to determine success, no months spent anguishing over whether a new toothpaste would catch on. Deals were done in a few weeks or even days, and then it was on to the next transaction.

As Felix Rohatyn, one of the most influential figures in the profession, put it, the young investment bankers were the "rock stars" of the 1980s.

Small wonder that the young associates at Drexel Burnham were eager to learn from Levine how to make the deals happen, how to jump into activities that would generate fees and boost their year-end bonus.

During his first months at Drexel, Levine made occasional trips to Nassau to review his account. To disguise his absences, he often traveled on a weekend or over a long holiday. Once in a while, he flew to Nassau at the end of a business trip, before returning to New York. On the few occasions he could not avoid leaving work without another excuse, he explained to Kay and others that he was visiting his ill father-in-law in Miami.

Once he said he and his brother Robert had taken a trip to the Bahamas to do some scuba diving. Kay thought the trip was unusual because Levine was suffering from a severe cold that would have made diving dangerous to his hearing. But neither Kay nor anyone else at Drexel had reason to dig for any further explanations.

As he had at Smith Barney and Shearson Lehman, Levine spent hours on the telephone, talking to arbitragers and lawyers and investment bankers, talking to the financial press, even helping a reporter who was writing a book on Drexel's rise to prominence.

At the same time, Levine's profits were building at Bank Leu. He invested more money with more certainty in the outcome because his information was better. By the spring of 1985, Levine had perfected his system and was on the verge of his biggest jackpot ever.

Although Reich was out for good, Levine's information was more accurate partly because he had reached a level in the profession that put him at the center of the big deals at Drexel. He no longer had to rely on office gossip or his vantage point as a second-tier player.

Similarly, Wilkis had been floating in various sections of corporate finance at Lazard Frères, including mergers, which had improved the quality of his tips. And in May 1985, there was the added potential bonus when Wilkis switched jobs and moved up to become a first vice president in mergers and acquisitions at E. F. Hutton & Company. For the first time in his career, Wilkis was happy in his work, feeling that Hutton provided him with a freer atmosphere, one in which his talents would surface. So Wilkis began holding out on information, refusing to discuss any Hutton deals with Levine. In late 1985, Wilkis was to close his trading account and transfer his money to certificates of deposit.

Ira Sokolow, whom Levine had begun cultivating when Sokolow was an intern in 1980, had been promoted to vice president in Shearson Lehman's M&A department, which left Levine an excellent source of information at his former employer's. Sokolow was also passing on the tips he received from David Brown.

In the midst of his demanding involvement in the Coastal and Crown Zellerbach transactions and his illegal purchases of related stocks, Levine found time for a number of other insider deals in the spring of 1985.

On March 14, McGraw-Edison Co. hired Goldman, Sachs as its financial adviser in connection with a proposed leverage buy-out by Forstman Little & Company. Brown heard about the proposal and immediately telephoned Sokolow with the tip. Sokolow in turn passed the information to Levine, who telephoned Bank Leu on his lunch hour and bought 79,500 shares of McGraw-Edison at a cost of $3.4 million.

Later that week, Wilkis bought 15,000 shares and Meier bought 1,000 shares. On March 22, the buy-out was announced and Levine sold his stock for a profit of $906,836. Levine paid cash to Sokolow, and Sokolow split the money with Brown.

On March 28, at the same time he telephoned Pletscher with his first purchase order for Crown Zellerbach, Levine also bought 21,800 shares in Multimedia, which he had learned was involved in a leveraged buy-out. He sold the stock a week later for a profit of $129,000.

In mid-April, Wilkis learned from Cecola that Houston Natural Gas Corporation had hired Lazard Frères as an adviser in connection with a proposal by InterNorth Inc., another energy company, to acquire HNG. On April 30, Cecola met Wilkis at Saks Fifth Avenue and told him that the transaction would probably be completed early the next month.

Wilkis passed the information to Levine, who telephoned Meier in Nassau and told him, "This is a firm deal, a sure deal, and I'm going to make an easy 20 to 30 percent." Levine purchased 74,800 shares of HNG for $4 million.

Meier told Pletscher of Levine's newest order and suggested that Pletscher buy some HNG stock. When Pletscher protested that he was leaving on a business trip and did not want his money tied up in a stock he could not watch, Meier said, "Don't worry. This is going to be a good deal; you shouldn't miss this one."

Pletscher relented and Meier bought 500 shares for Pletscher's account at the same time he purchased 1,500 shares for his own. Wilkis, through his Cayman Island account, bought 35,000 shares, and Cecola, using the Indianapolis account opened for him by a friend, bought options.

On May 2, InterNorth's offer for Houston Natural Gas was announced and the price of HNG rose. Levine sold his stock for $4.9 million, precisely within the 20 to 30 percent return he had predicted to Meier. Meier earned $28,749 in selling his 1,500 shares, and Pletscher collected more than $9,000 for his 500 shares. Wilkis made $540,000. Cecola, who had invested about $1,000 in options, sold out for a profit of $46,687. Two months later, Cecola left Lazard to enroll at Harvard Business School.

. Levine usually received his information from Sokolow over lunch, as he had done with Reich and continued to do with Wilkis. After he started work at Drexel, Levine began to put the lunches on his expense account and list them as "recruiting" sessions with the young banker from Shearson Lehman.

On May 6, a Monday, Sokolow and Levine met for lunch at Palm Too, an expensive restaurant where Levine invariably ordered a thirty-ounce steak. Sokolow described his newest project at Shearson Lehman Brothers—the possible merger of Nabisco Brands Inc., the big food company, with R. J. Reynolds Inc., the tobacco giant—explaining that Nabisco had hired Shearson Lehman as its financial adviser and that the deal appeared to be promising.

Before he returned to work, Levine telephoned Meier and told him to begin buying Nabisco. He advised Meier to go slow because the deal was not yet certain.

Over the next two weeks, Sokolow provided Levine with updates on the secret negotiations between Nabisco and Reynolds. On May 21, based on Sokolow's reports, Levine telephoned Meier and ordered the balance of his account invested in Nabisco.

Two days later, Levine and his wife flew to Barbados for a five-day stay at a luxury resort, the Sandy Lane Hotel. Levine kept in touch with Drexel about various deals that were pending, and he kept in touch with Sokolow on the status of the Nabisco-Reynolds talks. He billed $333 worth of long-distance calls to Drexel.

Levine returned to work on May 28, the day after Memorial Day, two days before Nabisco announced its exploratory merger talks with Reynolds. Levine had invested $9.2 million in 150,000 shares of Nabisco. His average cost per share was $61.30. The announcement of the talks sent Nabisco stock up almost 33 percent, and Levine sold his entire holdings at an average price of almost $80 a share.

His profit from the Nabisco tip was $2,694,421.26—the biggest jackpot of Dennis Levine's career as an insider.

10.

The Russian

It was a mark of Levine's elevation to the big leagues that he met Ivan Boesky during his first weeks on the job at Drexel Burnham Lambert.

Levine had a reputation for possessing first-class sources among New York's arbitragers. Yet he had never crossed paths with the man regarded as the richest and most influential risk-taker of them all.

For his part, Boesky had never heard of Dennis Levine before the young investment banker became a managing director at Drexel, where Boesky maintained close relations with Michael Milken and his colleagues in the junk-bond end of Drexel's business.

Boesky and Levine were brought together by Levine's first deal at Drexel, the Coastal Corporation bid for American Natural Resources.

Ivan Boesky had everything Dennis Levine wanted.

In a decade, the gaunt forty-eight-year-old with the spectral grin had become a Wall Street legend by turning $700,000 from his late mother-in-law's estate into a personal fortune estimated at $200 million.

Boesky's principal arbitrage vehicle was the Ivan F. Boesky Corporation, a private investment holding company that specialized in merger arbitrage and venture capital and, through a trading subsidiary, owned a seat on the New York Stock Exchange.

Wall Street experts estimated that he had nearly $1 billion at his disposal for arbitrage through the limited partnerships he established with investors.

He controlled many other investment entities, including a major investment trust in Britain, Cambrian & General Securities PLC, in which he had holdings of roughly $50 million. He and his wife owned 53 percent of the Beverly Hills Hotel, a plush California landmark worth more than $100 million.

He lived on a 163-acre wooded estate in upper Westchester County, with formal gardens, tennis courts, pools, indoor racquetball and handball courts, and spas. His splendid, antique-filled Georgian mansion had ten bedrooms and was valued at $10 million. He was driven back and forth to New York in a limousine, and he was known for working prodigious hours, starting his day at 6:00 A.M. and arriving home at 1:00 A.M.

Boesky ran his empire from a sleek suite of offices on Fifth Avenue that was once occupied by Marc Rich, the financier who fled the United States for Switzerland in 1983 to avoid tax-evasion charges.

In his office, Boesky surrounded himself with elaborate high-tech equipment. Banks of video monitors tracked the activities of his traders in other rooms and Quotron monitors flickered green with the current stock market prices. A telephone with 160 direct lines and 300 buttons kept him in touch with a vast network of corporate raiders, corporation executives, and investment bankers. Even the phone in his limo had three lines.

From that office, Boesky dominated the risk arbitrage business. He was a principal player in virtually every major takeover in America. His trademark was the enormous amount of stock he bought in major takeovers, usually four or five times more than any other arbitrager. Along the way, he had taken risk arbitrage from a little-noticed specialty profession to the pinnacle of Wall Street, and every major investment bank followed his lead by creating its own aggressive risk arbitrage department.

His spectacular success paralleled the transformation of Wall Street and the wave of mergers and acquisitions that had changed the face of corporate America. He was aggressive, highly competitive, driven by a compulsion to bet more and win bigger than anyone else, relentless in his pursuit of money.

Not long after he met Levine, Boesky was commencement speaker at the business school at the University of California, Berkeley, and he shared the essence of his philosophy with the new graduates:

"Greed is all right, by the way. I want you to know that. I think greed is healthy. You can be greedy and still feel good about yourself."

If it is shocking that Boesky could say that at a business school graduation, it is a measure of the cynicism and rampant materialism of the decade that he was greeted with applause and laughter.

Boesky's doggedness in amassing the wealth that made him the king of arbitrage was nearly equaled by his determined cultivation of an image as the statesman of arbitrage.

Although his own alma mater was a small school in Detroit, he donated hundreds of thousands of dollars to Harvard University, which helped him secure an appointment to an advisory panel at the school. The appointment qualified Boesky for membership in the Harvard Club of New York and he often held court there. He taught a graduate-level business class at New York University and was on its board of trustees. He contributed heavily to many philanthropic and cultural institutions. He contributed $2 million and a valuable manuscript collection to the Jewish Theological Seminary of America and, in 1983, the seminary named its modern library after Boesky and his wife, Seema. His generous financial backing of Republican political campaigns eventually earned him an appointment as an adviser on Jewish affairs to the chairman of the Republican National Committee.

Like Levine, Boesky came from modest roots in a family of Jewish entrepreneurs. His father, one of five brothers who arrived here from Russia in 1912, owned and operated three successful restaurants in Detroit.

Boesky often purposely left the false impression that he had grown up poor. And he loved to tell the story of how, as a thirteen-year-old, he bought an old truck and drove it, without a license, through Detroit's parks selling ice cream. He said he earned $150 in nickels and dimes and "it taught me to appreciate the green kind," referring to paper money. His educational career was lackluster. He attended three colleges without getting a degree before entering Detroit College of Law in 1959. The law school did not require a college degree and, after withdrawing twice, Boesky received his law degree in 1964.

While in law school in 1962, he married Seema Silberstein, a daughter of Detroit real estate tycoon Ben Silberstein. When he was unable to get a job with any of Detroit's prestigious law firms, he spent a year as a clerk for a federal judge who was a friend of the Silberstein family. After his year as a clerk, Boesky reapplied to the big-name law firms. He was rejected again. He finally was hired as an accountant, but he soon quit because the work did not interest him. A year out of law school, twenty-seven years old, with a wife and a baby, Boesky got his first nickname when his father-in-law called him "Ivan the Bum."

Boesky took his wife and child and headed to New York in 1966. A former high school wrestling teammate from Detroit was working as an arbitrager with an investment bank and the job intrigued Boesky. His first job was with L. F. Rothschild, but he left after being given little opportunity to do arbitrage. He moved to First Manhattan, where he found little money available for arbitrage. Then he went to a firm called Kalb Voorhis. He was fired the first day after losing $20,000 on a deal.

It was several months before Boesky could find another job. Meanwhile, he and his family lived in a posh apartment on Park Avenue that had been provided for them by his father-in-law.

In 1972, Boesky was hired to run the arbitrage department at Edwards & Hanly, a small brokerage house. He began to exhibit the traits that would later become part of his legend. At one point, the New York Stock Exchange censured Boesky and fined him $10,000 for selling securities in excess of the firm's ability to deliver. He also flouted the rules of cooperation observed by most arbitragers and frequently bought all the available stock in a company, without regard to whether he drove up the price or shut out his peers. He picked up another nickname, "Ivan the Terrible," and this was one that would stick.

Edwards & Hanly was undercapitalized from the start of Boesky's tenure there, and when the firm went bankrupt in 1975, Boesky decided to go out on his own. His mother-in-law had died recently, and Boesky's wife received her $700,000 bequest early so that her husband could open Ivan F. Boesky & Company on April 1, 1975.

From two small trading rooms in the former offices of Edwards & Hanly, Boesky placed advertisements in the *Wall Street Journal* soliciting investors for a limited partnership devoted exclusively to risk arbitrage. He offered the same split he was selling ten years later: 55 percent of the profits to him, 95 percent of the losses to them. Only the minimum investment had changed by 1985: $75,000 then, $5 million to $10 million in 1985. In 1975, the standard arbitrager's cut was 20 percent, and the business standard for losses was 80 percent.

Boesky assembled a staff of a dozen people in the cramped quarters and drove them daily until the early hours of the morning under intense pressure and for cheap wages. He was just as tight with clients as he was with his staff, charging almost triple the fee normally asked by arbitragers. So Boesky had to take more risks than most arbitragers to make his partnerships attractive investments. He had purchased a seat on the New York Stock Exchange soon after starting his own business and, as a member, he could leverage up to four times his fund's capital, compared with two times for the average investor. The leveraging greatly increased profits on the deals that went well but exposed the investors to enormous risks.

But Boesky proved adept at playing a hot market and racked up impressive returns in his first years: 97 percent in 1976; 95 percent in 1977; 18 percent in 1978, a year the average stock market return was only 6 percent; and 51 percent in 1979. As a result, investors showered him with money and by 1980, the $700,000 stake had turned into $90 million in capital.

But then came the day in March 1980 when the Hunt brothers failed to meet a margin call in their silver trading and it appeared that their broker, Bache & Company, would have to liquidate its huge arbitrage portfolio. The fears of a glut sent the market plunging, and the takeover stocks in which arbitragers had invested their millions plummeted. Some say Boesky lost $10 million in a single day. Boesky finished the year 6 percent ahead.

For the five years between 1975 and 1980, Boesky's investors had trounced the stock market average. Someone who invested $1 with Boesky in April 1975 would have had $7.54 at the end of 1980 compared with $2.19 if the money had been invested in the stock market.

But in 1980, Boesky decided he was going to get out of the arbitrage business. He declared that the takeover wave had ended and there was a scarcity of investment opportunities. Protracted negotiations to sell the firm to his employees failed; it was taken over eventually by another arbitrager and renamed Bedford Partners.

Boesky officially closed down Ivan F. Boesky & Company in January 1981, declaring he was done with the arbitrage industry. Some former employees speculate that Boesky may actually have shut down his first company for tax reasons. In any case, within three months he was raising funds for Ivan F. Boesky Corporation, which started operation in May 1981 with a list of investors that ranged from wealthy individuals to giant insurance companies.

Boesky's financial record with the new firm illustrates why he earned a reputation as an enormous risk-taker. In 1982, his rate of return was a healthy 57 percent compared with a drop of almost 11 percent in the stock market, based on Standard & Poor's 500.

In 1983, Boesky had his first unprofitable year, with a 33 percent loss on investments. The losses were largely the result of Gulf Oil Company's decision to withdraw its offer to buy Cities Service in August 1982, which was part of Boesky's 1983 fiscal year. Many arbitragers had large blocks of stock in Cities Service and were hurt badly when the deal collapsed. Boesky, because of his penchant for gargantuan positions, owned an estimated two million shares and lost between $11 million and $13 million when the price plummeted.

Boesky rebounded spectacularly. Merger activity increased dramatically near the end of 1983 and set new records for size in 1984. So did Boesky's profits, stemming largely from two megadeals involving oil companies.

The acquisition of Getty Oil by Texaco and the acquisition of Gulf Oil by Standard Oil Company of California were the types of deals that can make arbitragers rich.

In small or medium-sized deals, the price of stock in the target company can rise quickly because the finite amount of stock available cannot meet the demand from the arbitragers. But the two oil deals were multibillion-dollar transactions, which meant stock was plentiful and the price remained low enough for arbitragers to take big positions.

As usual, no one took a bigger stake than Boesky, and no one made more money when the deals were completed. For his investors and himself, Boesky made an estimated $50 million on Getty stock and $65 million on Gulf Oil stock. The Gulf profit was particularly satisfying because Boesky had lost significantly the previous year when Gulf quit the Cities Service deal.

By the end of Boesky's fiscal year on March 31, 1984, his rate of return was a staggering 142 percent. His reputation as the king of the arbitragers and his prestige among the money men jumped by a similar increment.

Through his influential role in the major takeovers, Boesky developed relationships with the financiers, brokers, and corporate raiders who were at the center of the megadeals. Like many traders, Boesky spent his days in the free and frantic exchange of rumors, gossip, and tips. He devoted hours on the telephone to pumping his sources for information, and he frequently talked with the nation's leading corporate raiders, such as T. Boone Pickens, Jr., chairman of Mesa Petroleum Company, and Carl Icahn, who would eventually control TWA.

Boesky also had close ties to Drexel, which had raised millions of dollars in junk-bond financing for his arbitrage activities in recent years in return for millions in fees from Boesky. In addition, Boesky was a big investor in junk bonds issued by other Drexel clients. And Drexel invested its own money in some of Boesky's ventures, including buying 7 percent of a California motel chain controlled by Boesky.

Investors in Drexel junk bonds were often investors in Boesky's partnerships, too. For instance, Rapid-American Corporation's chief, Meshulam Riklis, was a Boesky investor and a backer of junk bonds issued by Drexel to finance takeovers by raiders.

While there is nothing illegal or inherently wrong in these convoluted clusterings of traders, raiders, and financiers, their existence has irritated regulators and other investors because of the potential for conflicts of interest in the volatile world of takeovers. The irritations became particularly acute on those occasions when it was discovered that Boesky had bought big stakes in a deal prior to its announcement.

In a typical takeover, the raider will line up financing for his takeover attempt through an investment bank. Often the financing for raiders comes from junk bonds issued by Drexel Burnham. With the financing under way, the raider might buy a million or so shares of the target company on the open market through a broker. The rules of the Securities and Exchange Commission require the raider to announce the extent of his holdings and his intentions toward the company once 5 percent or more is in his grasp. The announcement will trigger an increase in the price of the target stock as arbitragers jump in to buy as much as they can. This is perfectly legal.

The illegality comes in when the raiders and the arbitragers get together and arrange to buy blocks of stock in tandem just below the 5 percent line to avoid the SEC's disclosure requirement and delay the public announcement of the raider's plan. The raider benefits because he can be sure that a substantial portion of the target's stock is in friendly hands, and the arbitrager benefits by getting in before stock prices increase.

The investment banker can also play a role in the scheme by feeding information about a pending deal to various arbitragers. This tactic puts more shares of the target in the hands of the arbitragers, who can be expected to sell out to the raider's high bid. Once the deal is announced, it also applies pressure to the target's management because they know the raider can purchase a sizable interest in the company from the arbitragers.

While there have been no charges of wrongdoing, the potential for large-scale speculators to add momentum to a takeover was illustrated by the campaign for control of Phillips Petroleum Company in early 1985, which involved Boesky and Carl Icahn.

Depositions in private lawsuits show that Boesky bought enormous blocks of Phillips stock about the time of Icahn's hostile takeover attempt in early February. The documents also show that Icahn had frequent telephone conversations and several meetings with Boesky just before Icahn announced the bid.

"He calls me every day," Icahn said in one deposition when asked about his relationship with Boesky during the Phillips deal.

On January 28, Icahn bought 2.7 million shares of Phillips stock from Boesky in a private deal totaling about $47 a share. On Monday night, February 4, Icahn delivered his offer of $55 a share to Phillips and the takeover bid was announced publicly.

Five days later, Boesky went to dinner at Icahn's New York

residence and discussed the possibility of joining with Icahn in his takeover bid. Icahn could not remember whether it was during dinner or a few days earlier that Boesky told him he had bought another four million to five million shares of Phillips.

During the next month, Icahn and Phillips reached an agreement under which Icahn dropped his bid in exchange for $25 million in cash to cover his expenses. Phillips offered all shareholders a package of securities with a face value of $62 a share. By March 31, the end of his 1985 fiscal year, Boesky had sold all of his shares.

Boesky was desperate for a big winner in the Phillips deal. The performance of his investment fund in fiscal 1985 had been lackluster. At a time when the stock market was doing well and takeovers were plentiful, Boesky's partnership fund was about to return a yield of only 7.7 percent for its investors.

What fueled his desperation was far more than a desire to recoup his personal losses and rejuvenate the fund's performance in time to report acceptable earnings or repeat his incredible performance of 1984. What drove Ivan Boesky was the fear of losing his reputation.

Many wealthy businessmen are content to amass their fortunes in relative obscurity, sometimes even going to great lengths to ensure their privacy. For them, the money and its accumulation provide enough gratification.

But Boesky cultivated personal fame with the same compulsion that he sought great wealth. He was never content with anonymity or even a modest measure of prestige on Wall Street. He hired publicists and invested thousands of dollars of his own money in promoting his book on the mysteries of arbitrage. He reveled in his self-created image as a financial wizard who worked longer and harder than anybody else, the guy who took the biggest risks and reaped the biggest rewards.

So in early 1985, with his performance slumping and his outsized ego in jeopardy, Boesky was a perfect candidate for recruitment into Dennis Levine's network of insiders. The tips generated by Levine and his organization could shore up the arb king's sagging fortunes, make him appear to be the wizard of Wall Street once again.

From Levine's point of view, Boesky was an equally important catch. Boesky represented an opportunity to escalate his insider dealings to a level that would make him even richer without increasing his risk of exposure.

In the simplest terms, Boesky was a kind of insurance for Levine. Tipping Boesky on a pending takeover would mean that Boesky's own purchases of a target company's stock would be large enough to create a surge in the price of the stock. In addition, Boesky's reputation for getting in early on takeover stocks meant his trades were carefully monitored by other arbitragers. Once they saw Boesky buying a stock, they would jump on the stock, too, and contribute to the price increase.

All Levine had to do was make sure that he bought into the stock a day or even a few hours ahead of Boesky and could thereby ride the surge created by Boesky's buying and the next surge of the copycat buyers. Levine and his informants would be in a sensitive enough position to learn early if a deal showed signs of falling through; he could then sell out quickly and still retain his investment, if not a small profit. The Crown Zellerbach–Mead deal had convinced Levine of that.

Boesky also represented a potential asset on the professional side of Levine's ledger: getting large blocks of stock into Boesky's hands improved the chances of success for a hostile takeover.

There have been disputes over whether Levine first telephoned Boesky or Boesky first contacted Levine.

What is clear, however, is that Levine provided Boesky with inside information in connection with the Coastal Corporation's hostile takeover bid for American Natural Resources, and Boesky began buying ANR stock before the deal was announced publicly.

By the time the deal was consummated, Boesky owned 9.9 percent of the stock in ANR and he sold out at a premium price.

Over the next weeks, Levine continued to share the confidential fruits of his job and his insider network with Boesky. Levine did not ask for anything in return. While the tips involved deals taking place outside Drexel, Levine was careful to make sure that Boesky never learned the identity of his other sources of information. And Levine was the only ring member who ever dealt with Boesky, although he boasted to Wilkis that he was working with the legendary arbitrager.

Levine's insider trades had grown substantially by the spring of 1985, but his purchases were dwarfed by the positions that Boesky took on the basis of Levine's tips.

Boesky had several advantages that allowed him to buy huge chunks of stock on the open market without attracting the type of scrutiny that Levine feared. He did not have to hide his purchases through a foreign bank and split the purchases up among many brokers. His history of taking big positions on risky stocks provided the perfect cover for his illegal buying. Regulators and competitors alike would simply assume Boesky was taking another big risk, and they were accustomed to his risks paying off with frequency.

Further, where Levine had been forced to guard his limited capital, particularly in the early days of his trading, Boesky could invest $20 million or more in a single deal and risk little financial exposure in the event of a collapse.

The best camouflage of all, however, was Boesky's profession itself. Arbitragers could pursue information about a pending takeover legitimately and buy stocks on the basis of rumors and research and good guesses. How were the regulators going to separate the good guesses from the illegal tips?

On May 1, the day after he had made his own purchases in Houston Natural Gas on the basis of information from Wilkis, Levine told Boesky that InterNorth was planning a tender offer for HNG.

Using his vast resources and a network of nearly one hundred employees, Boesky invested more than $16 million in 301,800 shares of common stock in HNG, more than four times the amount bought by Levine. When InterNorth and HNG announced their merger agreement the following day, Boesky sold his stock for a total profit of $4.1 million.

Later that same month, Levine let Boesky in on what would turn out to be Levine's most successful deal, the merger talks between Nabisco Brands and R. J. Reynolds Inc. Having completed his own purchase of 150,000 shares of Nabisco on May 21, Levine passed the information on to Boesky the next day. Boesky began a week-long buying binge and, by May 29, he had spent more than $25 million on 377,000 shares of Nabisco. When the exploratory merger talks were revealed the following day, he sold his entire stake for a profit of $4 million.

"I tipped the Russian on Nabisco," Levine told Wilkis one night in early June of 1985 as they headed for dinner at Palm Too.

"The Russian" was Levine's code name for Boesky. Wilkis knew that Levine was infatuated with Boesky and with the arbitrager's vast wealth and high profile. And Levine had told Wilkis that he had tipped Boesky on a handful of earlier deals. That night in June Levine repeated his explanation for sharing their valuable commodity with Boesky: "I'm trying to win him over. He can be important for our future. If we go into business for ourselves, the Russian can put money behind us."

But Levine really had other plans for the Russian, and he kept them to himself.

Boesky's growing mystique on Wall Street, along with the size of his positions, gave him unrivaled access to corporate executives, raiders, and investment bankers. Many of those contacts involved the exchange of information, and Boesky was famous for the pressure he applied in an attempt to obtain the slightest edge. The line was blurred between the legal information obtained through this type of contact and the illegal inside information. If his relationship with Levine had never gone further than exchanging information, Boesky might never have crossed that shadowy line. But not long after the Nabisco tip, Levine said to Boesky: "I'm helpful to you. What's in it for me?"

Boesky, who was impressed with the quality of Levine's information and searching for a way to repeat his astounding successes of 1984, agreed to sit down with Levine over dinner and discuss an alteration of their arrangement.

As David Kay had learned when trying to hire him, Levine could be a demanding negotiator. He was well aware of his value to Boesky and he was astute enough to sense the other man's vulnerabilities. At the same time, Boesky had built his empire on arrangements with investors that were far more generous for him than the standard deals, and he was reluctant to give up more than necessary to keep the information flowing.

In the end, several negotiating sessions were required, and the agreement was changed and refined over several weeks. The final arrangement set forth two formulas to determine Boesky's payments to Levine.

If Boesky had no shares of a company's stock before Levine provided him with information on a pending deal, Levine would be entitled to 5 percent of Boesky's profit from the sale of stocks bought on the basis of the tip. For instance, if Boesky had held no shares of Nabisco prior to Levine's tip, Levine would have been entitled to 5 percent of the $4 million profit earned on the shares bought after the tip, or $200,000.

Under the second formula, Levine would receive a lesser percentage of the profits if he provided information to Boesky about a company in which Boesky already held an interest. This information would still be of value because Boesky could sell or buy based on Levine's updates, but the value would be less. The precise percentage of Levine's share was subject to various negotiations, and the two men finally settled on 1 percent of the profits. Under the second formula, if Boesky had already held Nabisco when Levine provided his information, Levine would have been entitled to 1 percent of the $4 million profit, or $40,000.

Boesky also added a "penalty clause" to the agreement with Levine: any losses that Boesky suffered as a result of Levine's tips would be subtracted from Levine's payments.

The agreement leaves no doubt that Boesky was aware he was receiving confidential inside information from Levine. But Boesky had always been a gambler and he was willing to take the risk. Indeed, the arrangement was very similar to one that Boesky had with another major figure on Wall Street.

Martin Siegel had a middle-class upbringing in Natick, Massachusetts, a suburb of Boston. His father owned a successful women's shoe store that had been in the family for years. Siegel was an exceptionally bright youngster who dreamed of becoming an astronaut. He worked his way through Rensselaer Polytechnic Institute, graduating with a chemical engineering degree at the age of nineteen, and then worked briefly for Eastman Kodak and the Raytheon Company. When Siegel was twenty years old, his father's shoe store failed and the father was forced to file for bankruptcy. The event left an indelible impression on Marty Siegel, who abandoned his dream of a career in space and entered Harvard Business School.

After graduating from Harvard in 1971 at the age of twenty-three, Siegel headed for Wall Street, where his good looks, personality, and Harvard degree netted him a job as an investment banker at Kidder, Peabody & Co. Siegel soon distinguished himself as a bright, hard-driving banker, and, when the new era of mergers and acquisitions dawned in 1980, he was poised to take advantage of the changes.

"I wasn't going to have some senior partner telling me, 'This is how it was done in 1942,'" Siegel said in an interview with *Institutional Investor* magazine. "It was a way to make a quick identity.

The easiest investment bank product to sell is a good M&A idea. Everyone will listen. It cuts through traditional banking relationships like a hot knife through butter."

The same article contained this illuminating quote from Siegel: "There's the one Marty Siegel, and he's the guy who does all the deals, and he's all geared up and on the go and, geez, what a ball of fire," he said. "Then there's the other Marty Siegel, and he's the guy who just wants to go home and spend time with his kids. When that second Marty Siegel reads about the first one, it gets a little surreal. It's almost bifurcated in his mind."

Haunted by his father's bankruptcy, Siegel lived modestly for many years and saved money compulsively. But in 1981, he married his second wife, also an investment banker at Kidder, Peabody and the following year they had their first child. The couple built a large cedar-and-glass house, complete with a tennis court and gym, on the coast of Long Island Sound in an exclusive Connecticut enclave. They also kept an apartment on the Upper East Side of Manhattan, hired a nanny for the baby, and began commuting to Wall Street by helicopter from Connecticut. The new life-style outstripped Siegel's salary and bonuses, and he began to dip into his savings. In 1982, he thought he had discovered the answer to his problems.

In August of that year, Siegel met with Ivan Boesky in the grill room at New York's Harvard Club. Siegel had known Boesky for several years, and they regularly exchanged information over the telephone about stock positions and company valuations as part of the routine gossip of Wall Street. They had also formed a personal relationship and, like Levine later, Siegel was awed by Boesky's wealth; when he was invited to dinner at Boesky's sprawling estate, he found that it dwarfed the house Siegel had built on Long Island Sound; when Boesky came to Siegel's house for tennis, he drove up in his pink Rolls-Royce.

Over lunch that day in August, Siegel revealed some of his personal financial difficulties and Boesky responded by volunteering to make some investments on Siegel's behalf. By the end of the conversation, the two men had worked out a formula under which Boesky would pay a small percentage of his own profits to Siegel in exchange for information. In return, Siegel was to provide information early enough for Boesky to buy into a stock well in advance of any public announcement, which would ensure avoidance of detection by the SEC.

Soon after his conversation with Boesky, Siegel was hired by Martin Marietta Corporation as the company's chief strategist to defend against a hostile takeover offer that was being planned by Bendix Corporation. It was a role that would thrust Siegel into Wall Street's limelight and seal his deal with Boesky.

Under Siegel's guidance, Martin Marietta developed a response that would depend on the boldest of tactics: it planned to launch a "Pac-Man defense." Named after the video game, the plan called for the target company to devour its unwanted suitor with a counteroffer. The Pac-Man defense had been tried in other instances, but never before had it been used on such a mammoth scale. Essential to its success would be persuading Bendix that the market was taking the Martin Marietta counteroffer seriously, which would force Bendix to begin talks with Martin Marietta. What Martin Marietta needed to do was get Bendix into play, pushing up the price of its stock. The Bendix bid for Martin Marietta was announced on August 25, 1982, and the next day, Siegel telephoned Boesky and told him that Martin Marietta was planning a $1.5 billion counteroffer for Bendix. Using Siegel's information, Boesky bought 52,500 shares of Bendix stock and eventually realized a profit of $120,000.

The Pac-Man defense succeeded in putting Bendix in play, and the company was eventually purchased by Allied Corporation. Martin Marietta survived, and Marty Siegel's victory propelled him into the center of the nation's takeover boom. Siegel and Kidder, Peabody parlayed his new fame into a prosperous practice that specialized in defending companies against unwanted suitors. But Siegel felt that he was not properly rewarded at Kidder, and he frequently complained to friends about his low pay in comparison to more senior partners who contributed less to the firm.

In December 1982, Siegel asked Boesky for $125,000 in cash and the arbitrager agreed happily, even though the amount exceeded Siegel's profits on the Bendix deal, the only tip Boesky had received from him at that point. Boesky viewed the money as an investment. He placed the cash in a suitcase and arranged for a courier to meet Siegel in the lobby of a New York hotel. When Siegel gave the courier the agreed-upon password, the man handed over the suitcase. Siegel dipped into the cash over the year, using it to pay employees and as spending money.

Siegel and Boesky developed a pattern in which Siegel would call Boesky and arrange a meeting when he had information, or Boesky would telephone Siegel for a meeting if he needed information. They frequently met in an alley in the Wall Street area or at a coffee shop near Boesky's Fifth Avenue office. Between February and May of 1983, Siegel leaked information to Boesky about efforts by one of Siegel's clients at Kidder, Diamond Shamrock Corporation, to acquire Natomas Inc., and Boesky eventually realized profits of $4.8 million on the transaction. Siegel tipped Boesky on several other Kidder deals, the biggest of which seemed to be the perfect insider transaction.

In April 1984, Siegel was retained by Carnation Company as its financial adviser in connection with a possible acquisition or change in corporate control of the company. Siegel used the information to predict that Carnation would eventually be sold, and he passed on his educated guess to Boesky, who began acquiring Carnation stock. In the course of several months, Boesky bought 1.7 million shares of Carnation and, after it was announced on September 4, 1984, that Nestlé Holdings Inc. planned to buy Carnation, he sold his stock for a profit of $28.3 million. The cleverness of the scheme was that Boesky was able to amass his stock well in advance of the Nestlé announcement and minimize the risk of any detection by the SEC.

At the end of both 1983 and 1984, Boesky and Siegel sat down and reviewed the balance sheet for the year's leaks to determine Siegel's fee. The two end-of-year cash payments, which were both delivered by couriers in public places after the exchange of passwords, totaled $575,000.

But Siegel began to worry about the security of the arrangement after reading an August 1984 profile of Boesky in *Fortune* magazine. Entitled "Ivan Boesky, Money Machine," the article was a balanced account of Boesky's rise from nowhere to become "one of Wall Street's most daring—and controversial—arbitragers." It was the controversial part that bothered Siegel because the article contained this sentence: "Boesky's competitors whisper darkly about his omniscient timing, and rumors abound that he looks for deals involving Kidder, Peabody and First Boston."

When Siegel confronted him with his fears, Boesky was not rattled. He merely suggested that Siegel establish a foreign bank account to handle the payments. Siegel blanched at the idea. It seemed too obviously criminal. Although he accepted money from Boesky at the end of 1984, the Carnation tip was the last information he provided to the arbitrager. Throughout 1985, he resisted Boesky's efforts to obtain more information and refused to accept any more money.

Despite a salary and bonus that totaled $1.7 million in 1985, Siegel's impression that he was not compensated in relation to his worth at Kidder persisted. In early 1986, he decided to accept an offer to become co-head of the mergers and acquisitions department at Drexel Burnham. His multiyear contract called for a salary in the millions of dollars. Siegel was afraid of Boesky's reaction to the news of his move and, when he summoned the courage to face the arbitrager, he found that Boesky was indeed furious. Siegel, however, had no way of knowing that Boesky was angry because he already had an excellent source inside Drexel—Dennis Levine.

11.

HO-1743

Sometimes when a single thread is pulled, the entire curtain unravels.

On Wednesday, May 22, 1985, the day before Levine headed for his vacation in Barbados, a strange letter arrived at the headquarters of Merrill Lynch in the heart of New York's financial district. The letter was typed and addressed to the compliance department. It bore no return address or sender's name and the postmark was Caracas, Venezuela.

The letter was riddled with grammatical mistakes and spelling errors, but the point was clear.

The letter read, in full:

> Dear Sir: please be informed that two of your executives from the Caracas office are trading with inside information. A copie with description of ther trades so far has been submitet to the S.E.C. by separate mail. As is mantion on that letter if us customers do not benefit from their knoleg, we wonder who surveils the trades done by account executives. Upon you in-

vestigating to the last consequecies we will provide with the names of the insider on their owne hand writing.

At the bottom of the letter were the names Max Hofer and Carlos Zubillaga.

Merrill Lynch & Company is the biggest retail brokerage firm in America, with 1,100 offices and 45,000 employees around the world. Partly because of its sheer size and partly because a giant retail firm depends on an image of integrity, Merrill Lynch has the largest compliance division on Wall Street, with a staff of seventy-five.

The Caracas letter was routed initially to Merrill Lynch's international division because of the foreign postmark. Two or three days after its arrival, however, it wound up on the desk of Richard Drew, a vice president in the compliance division.

Drew is a lawyer who had spent fourteen years with the New York Stock Exchange before coming to Merrill Lynch in 1981. At Merrill Lynch, he was in charge of twenty-three analysts who monitored trading in the firm's accounts and reviewed suspicious situations.

Drew looked at the letter and said to himself, "Let's see what's going on here." He assigned the task to Steve Snyder, a senior analyst in the unit.

Among the analysts and lawyers who handled Merrill Lynch's compliance cases, Snyder was regarded as a relentless digger. Sometimes his zeal disturbed lawyers who worked with him on sensitive matters, but there was never any question that he was a first-rate sleuth.

The first thing Snyder did was pull the statements containing the trading records of Carlos Zubillaga and Max Hofer for the previous twelve months. The records included trades for the accounts of their clients and for their personal accounts.

In reviewing the hundreds of trades, Snyder found that both

MAY 22 1985

       Dear Sir:please be informed
that two of your executives from the Caracas office are
trading with inside information.A copie with description
of ther trades so far has been submitet to the S.E.C. by
separate mail.As is mantion on that letter if us customers
do not benefit from their knoleg,we wonder who surveils the
trades done by account executives.Upon you investigating
to the last consequecies we will provide with the names of the
insider on their owne hand writing.

            executives max hoffer 14899052
                     carlos zubillaga 14899073

            mr frank granados might like to
            have a copie

                    ZU

                 OfICP

men had bought stock in corporations involved in prominent take-over transactions, such as Textron, G. D. Searle, Sperry Corporation, and Houston Natural Gas.

The discovery deepened Snyder's curiosity. He pulled the records of both men's personal cash management accounts, which are combination checking-savings-trading accounts maintained at Merrill Lynch.

In examining the transactions in Zubillaga's account, Snyder found another curiosity: the Venezuelan had written two checks totaling about $8,000 to Brian Campbell.

Snyder recalled that Campbell was a broker in Merrill Lynch's international division and he took the records into Drew's office.

"It's strange that a guy from Venezuela would be sending Campbell checks," Snyder told his boss.

"Let's pull Campbell's records," suggested Drew.

Snyder found that Campbell had left Merrill Lynch in February to take a job at Smith Barney, Harris Upham & Co. He also found that Campbell and Zubillaga had been in the same training class for brokers at Merrill Lynch in 1982. And, in examining the hundreds of trades in Campbell's personal and commercial accounts, Snyder found the same takeover stocks that had been purchased by Zubillaga and Hofer, only Campbell had bought them a day before the brokers in Caracas.

Snyder and Drew knew they had uncovered evidence that the brokers were at least talking with one another and making lucky buys on takeover stocks. They suspected it might be more serious. Snyder kept digging.

Campbell's biggest commercial customer had been Bank Leu International in Nassau. The bank's location was an immediate flag to Snyder because he knew illegal trades were often conducted through offshore institutions.

He found another flag when he reviewed Bank Leu's trades. The bank had purchased the same takeover stocks as Campbell and the other brokers, only in blocks of 5,000 or 10,000 shares. Not only were the purchases far larger, but the bank had bought stock in many more takeover targets than the brokers.

Drew and Snyder mulled over the possibilities presented by the evidence. The bank traded in its own name, so there was no way for Merrill Lynch to discover who was picking the takeover stocks. Perhaps, they thought, it was only some smart or lucky trader.

But Drew had spent too long investigating insider trading, and Snyder was too suspicious by nature to assume that luck was involved. So they called in Robert Romano, the firm's expert on insider trading.

Romano had been a federal prosecutor in New Jersey in the mid-1970s before joining the SEC as an enforcement attorney in 1977. Over the next six years, he was involved in several critical insider cases for the SEC and had helped the agency learn to employ the tougher investigation techniques he had picked up as a prosecutor, including the tape-recording of conversations to gather evidence. Just before leaving the SEC, Romano had led the investigation into the insider dealings of Paul Thayer, the former Reagan administration official who went to jail for four years on charges of obstruction of justice.

Since coming to Merrill Lynch in late 1983, Romano had handled most of the firm's insider trading problems and worked in cooperation with the SEC on several matters.

After listening to Drew and Snyder describe what they had found, Romano was fairly certain that someone was trading on inside information at Bank Leu.

"Somebody down at that bank is wired," Romano said confidently.

In the middle of June, Zubillaga and Hofer were brought to New York and questioned separately at Merrill Lynch's offices. Hofer said he knew nothing about inside information. He had traded on advice from Zubillaga and he thought Zubillaga had received his information from Campbell.

Under questioning at Merrill Lynch, Zubillaga acknowledged receiving tips from Campbell and trading on them. He denied any involvement in insider trading. He said he simply thought Campbell was copying the trades of a hot client and passing on the tips.

As for the payments to Campbell, Zubillaga said he had given Campbell an interest in his personal trading account as a result of the tips and the $8,000 was Campbell's share of the trading profits.

Drew, Romano, and Snyder were at an impasse. They had traced the trading backward from Zubillaga and Hofer to Campbell and through Campbell to Bank Leu. Merrill Lynch could not question Campbell because he had left the firm, and the brokerage house certainly could not pierce the secrecy of a foreign bank.

Snyder's thorough examination of the bank's trading records had turned up trades in twenty-seven stocks of companies involved in one type of merger or another. The trades amounted to thousands of shares and hundreds of thousands of dollars in profits.

At that point, Romano suspected that what had been uncovered was part of an active SEC investigation of possible insider trading through Ellis AG, a large Swiss brokerage house. Bank Leu was Swiss and several stocks involved in Merrill Lynch's inquiry were under scrutiny in the Ellis AG probe. The rumors on Wall Street were that the Ellis AG inquiry could be the biggest insider case in history, involving dozens of stocks and up to forty brokers and investment bankers in the United States. The rumors also indicated that the SEC was having trouble putting the case together.

On June 28, a Friday, Romano telephoned Gary Lynch, the SEC enforcement director in Washington. He thought he was providing Lynch with a piece of the Ellis AG puzzle.

Lynch had been SEC enforcement chief for just four months. He was thirty-five years old and had spent his entire career as an SEC attorney. Soft-spoken and poker-faced, he had a reputation as a fair but tenacious investigator. He had taken over from John Fedders, who had been forced to resign in February as a result of publicity about his personal problems, including the admission by the six-foot ten-inch lawyer that he occasionally beat his wife. Lynch was well liked by his colleagues and his promotion to enforcement director in March had averted any long-term impact on morale among the division's personnel.

When Romano got Lynch on the telephone he said, "Gary, I think I've got something for you."

"What is it?" asked Lynch.

"I think we've got an offshore bank that's hitting on every recent takeover," Romano said.

"What do you mean?" asked Lynch.

Romano simply listed the stocks: "Textron, Searle, Sperry, Jewel Companies."

"Jesus," said Lynch.

"Gary, there's a lot of it here."

Lynch called in his associate enforcement chief, John Sturc, switched on his speaker phone, and the two men listened carefully as Romano described the evidence uncovered by Merrill Lynch's internal inquiry.

John Sturc was balding, bespectacled, and approaching his thirty-fifth birthday. His father was a career official at the International Monetary Fund and, except for college at Cornell University and law school at Harvard, Sturc had never lived outside Washington, D.C.

After five years as a federal prosecutor there, he had gone to work for a private law firm. He lasted less than six months before deciding private practice wasn't for him. He had come to the SEC in 1982, attracted by the challenge of working on sophisticated investigations and the chance to return to public service.

During the weekend, he mulled over the information provided by Bob Romano. The brokerage firm's inquiry had crystallized concerns that Sturc and the SEC had in several arenas. Bank Leu had come up in earlier SEC inquiries, and most of the stocks on the Merrill Lynch list had been examined by the SEC at one point or another.

Sturc did not think the information was part of the Ellis AG inquiry, and he was too cautious to speculate about where the trail might end. He just knew that he and the young attorneys who worked for him would follow it as far as possible.

On Monday, Sturc had a formal order prepared authorizing an investigation into the evidence from Merrill Lynch. The order would grant the SEC attorneys power to subpoena records and testimony from anyone under its jurisdiction. The following day, July 2, the order was approved by the SEC commissioners and investigation number HO-1743 officially began.

Sturc would have ultimate responsibility for overseeing the investigation, but the actual supervision would come from Paul Fischer, an assistant enforcement director. Fischer assigned day-to-day responsibility for the investigation to one of his best investigative attorneys. The attorney's name was Leo Wang.

Wang was joined in the investigation by Peter Sonnenthal, who had recently joined the SEC after several years in private practice. Together they examined the trading records that had been sent to Washington from Merrill Lynch in New York. They pieced together a chronology of the trading, matching the bank's purchases and sales with the dates of takeover announcements, and then adding the corresponding trading dates for Zubillaga and Hofer.

In the middle of July, the SEC issued subpoenas for Zubillaga and Hofer. The two brokers were questioned under oath in separate sessions by Wang and Sonnenthal. They told the SEC essentially the same story that they had told Merrill Lynch. They also speculated that the letter had been sent by a colleague in Caracas who was jealous of their trading success. Wang sent copies of the transcripts of the sessions to Merrill Lynch to confirm that there were no inconsistencies.

Campbell first learned of the inquiry into his trading activities at the beginning of July from the compliance department at Smith Barney, which had been alerted to the situation by Merrill Lynch. Campbell assured his employers that he had nothing to do with any insider trading. Campbell then telephoned Bernie Meier at Bank Leu, telling him that the Smith Barney compliance officers were examining Campbell's trading and he expected they would also have questions about the bank's trades.

When Campbell was subpoenaed by the SEC later in July, he again telephoned Meier and told him.

"Keep your chin up, Brian," Meier said. "You'll be all right."

Over three days in early August, Campbell was questioned at the SEC headquarters in Washington by Wang, Sonnenthal, and another SEC attorney, Edward Harrington. He testified under oath and was accompanied by his personal attorney, Peter Morrison.

Campbell discussed his first contacts with Bernie Meier and described opening the account for Bank Leu. He said Meier never told him why he was buying a particular stock, but Campbell acknowledged that he soon recognized Meier's success in picking takeover stocks.

He repeatedly said that he did his own research on the stocks purchased by Bank Leu before buying them. He said he had no idea who owned the trading account for which Meier was placing the orders with him. Campbell also acknowledged that Meier had agreed to loan Campbell $10,000 as an investment in a real estate deal. From their questioning, it was evident that the SEC attorneys were still searching for evidence that would lead them to the source of the inside information. The SEC was also intensely interested in discovering the identity of the author of the anonymous letter to Merrill Lynch. The letter had offered to provide the "names of the insider on their owne hand writing," and Wang and Sonnenthal thought the author might be able to identify the person behind the trades. It was a theory that ran counter to the evidence indicating the trading had originated through Bank Leu, but it was one of many theories that had to be pursued. So the SEC pressured Merrill Lynch for permission to question every employee in the Caracas office.

If the trading had indeed originated at Bank Leu International, the SEC would have to overcome a number of formidable legal obstacles in order to discover the identity of the insider.

Nearly 10 percent of the transactions on the New York Stock Exchange originate abroad. Electronic trading has linked stock markets in America with exchanges around the world, especially in London and Tokyo, and twenty-four-hour trading is nearly a reality.

Only a small fraction of the foreign-based trades may involve insider trading or other abuses, but the potential for misusing foreign bank secrecy is a growing problem for regulators in the United States as well as for their counterparts abroad.

The U.S. State Department had negotiated an agreement with Britain and the Cayman Islands, a British colony, that made information related to narcotics cases more accessible to U.S. investigators. Similarly, a treaty with the Dutch government and the Netherlands Antilles made financial information easier for U.S. investigators to acquire. At the SEC, one of John Fedder's successes was progress in reaching similar agreements with foreign governments in cases of insider trading and other securities abuses.

In 1982, the United States and Switzerland agreed to allow the SEC and Justice Department access to information about Swiss bank accounts in certain cases of insider trading in the U.S. securities markets that might also have violated Swiss law. The agreement, however, was subject to several limitations, including the provision that allowed the records to be withheld if a commission established by the Swiss Bankers Association determined the case did not involve a violation of Switzerland's more liberal insider trading laws.

The 1982 agreement, called a Memorandum of Understanding, was the direct result of pressure on Swiss banks by two federal judges in two cases in New York. The first case involved allegations by the SEC that several Arab businessmen had made $7.8 million by trading options on inside information about an upcoming takeover of the Santa Fe International Corporation. The SEC had discovered that the proceeds were being held in a private Swiss bank, in the Swiss accounts of two American banks, Citibank and Chase

Manhattan, and in the account of a New York securities firm owned by Credit Suisse.

In a precedent-setting ruling on October 26, 1981, U.S. District Court judge William Conner ordered the profits frozen in the various accounts until the case could be resolved. The lead SEC lawyer on the case was Bob Romano and, after he left the agency in 1983, it was taken over by John Sturc.

The second case began on March 27, 1981, when the SEC filed a complaint against "certain unknown purchasers" of stock and options in St. Joe Minerals bought just before the announcement of a takeover bid by Joseph E. Seagram & Company. Federal judge Milton Pollack then froze all the suspected insider trading profits in Banca della Svizzera Italiana's New York branch after the SEC expressed fears the money would be transferred out of the country because the unknown defendants were operating through foreign banks and corporations.

In November, Pollack went a step further. He threatened to impose a $50,000-a-day fine on Banca della Svizzera Italiana of Lugano, Switzerland, unless the bank divulged the identity of traders in St. Joe Minerals Corporation stock and options. Faced with the seizure of its assets in the United States to pay the fines, the bank persuaded one of the principal traders in the scheme to waive his secrecy rights. The bank was then able to identify him and three Panamanian companies under his control without breaching Swiss law.

Pollack's order sent shudders through the Swiss banking community and resulted in the temporary agreement of 1982.

While representing crucial victories for the SEC, the St. Joe and Santa Fe cases also illustrated the difficulty of protecting U.S. markets from violators who use accounts in Switzerland or other bank secrecy havens. The names of the insiders in the Santa Fe case were not disclosed to the SEC until May 1985, following four and a half years of court battles in Switzerland. In the fall of 1985, the St. Joe traders were still free. Their illegal profits remained frozen while their lawyers fought the case on every detail.

During the last week of August, Wang and Sonnenthal met with Paul Fischer to review the status of the investigation and determine strategy for the next phase. Clearly they needed some way to pierce the secrecy of Bank Leu.

Not only did they face the legal hurdles imposed by Swiss law on a subsidiary of a Swiss bank. The problem was compounded by the secrecy laws of the Bahamas. The SEC had recently been rebuffed in an attempt to learn the identity of an account holder, and negotiations between the two governments over a mutual assistance treaty regarding bank secrecy and money laundering had been stalled since 1979.

The SEC lawyers decided first to seek the bank's voluntary cooperation by telephoning Bernhard Meier, who appeared to be the bank executive who would know the most about the trading. If that did not work, they could always try the formal route and issue subpoenas.

Shortly after noon on August 28, Bernie Meier stormed into Bruno Pletscher's office at Bank Leu. His face was red with anger.

"Now we're in the shit." Meier was almost shouting.

Pletscher was taken aback by the demeanor of the normally unflappable Meier.

"What are you talking about?"

"I just got off the phone with the SEC. Our friend went too far. They want to know about a lot of things, about his stocks," Meier said.

"What are you talking about?" Pletscher repeated.

Meier calmed down enough to tell Pletscher the SEC had telephoned seeking information about twenty-seven stocks that had been traded through Bank Leu. The caller said the stocks involved takeover situations, and the SEC believed the trades may have been made on the basis of inside information.

When the caller listed the stocks, Meier knew he was talking about the Diamond account and realized that the SEC had tracked the trading through Campbell to Bank Leu. After Campbell first told him of the inquiry in July, Meier had informed Levine that the SEC was questioning a broker about some of the stock transactions that the bank had placed on his behalf. Levine had assured Meier the inquiry was a routine matter that would not go anywhere, and Meier had tried to put it out of his mind. But now that the SEC had placed a direct call to Bank Leu and demanded information about twenty-seven transactions, Meier was suddenly very worried and angry. Clearly the SEC knew more than Meier had imagined, and perhaps Levine was wrong when he said the inquiry would not proceed.

Meier told Pletscher that it was ridiculous for the SEC to attempt to obtain information from a Swiss bank operating in the Bahamas. He said the American agency had no right to the information. It was an argument Pletscher accepted. As a Swiss banker for nearly twenty years, he was deeply imbued with the tradition of privacy for clients. He also did not believe any laws had been broken by Levine's trading.

"I was under the impression that what we do is in the gray zone, not something we cannot do," he told Meier, meaning that he thought copying Levine's trade violated no law, although the practice might have violated bank guidelines.

"We never had confirmation that he is an insider," said Meier. "We never knew it for sure."

Meier, who was still upset and nervous, said the SEC had demanded an immediate response to its request for information. Did Pletscher think the bank would have to respond in any way?

"It doesn't look good," said Pletscher, and then turned the question back on Meier. "What do you think we have to do? Do you think we have to give the SEC the information they requested?"

It was clear that neither man knew how to respond. As is often the case in rigid Swiss society, their initial reaction was to obey the demand from someone in authority, even a foreign government. Pletscher suggested that they contact the home office in Zurich and seek legal advice on how to proceed. In fact, if they had contacted the home office at that time, they probably would have been told to ignore the call and let the bank's lawyers in Zurich handle the matter. But Meier said he could not wait for Zurich's response; he would have to respond sooner than that. He said he had to call the SEC back immediately.

Pletscher asked, "Can you call Diamond?"

"No, but we've had frequent telephone calls lately regarding trading and I'm sure he'll call within the next few days."

"Let's stall until we can talk to Diamond," Pletscher suggested.

Pletscher accompanied Meier to his office while Meier called the SEC. Meier told the SEC that the bank would require notification in writing and that he was seeking legal advice on how to respond.

The first SEC ploy had failed. On August 30, the agency sent a formal telex message to the bank seeking information on twenty-eight stocks, one more than had been mentioned in the telephone call. A similar message was mailed to the bank's home office in Zurich. The SEC also asked the U.S. Customs Service to notify the agency if Bernhard Meier entered the United States.

The same day the telex arrived, Levine telephoned Meier, who told him the SEC inquiry had led to Bank Leu and urged him to come to Nassau immediately. Levine was calm. Assuring Meier that they could deal with the inquiry easily, he agreed to come to Nassau as soon as possible.

Back in July, after Meier had first mentioned the SEC inquiry to him, Levine had told Robert Wilkis that the bank had run into a minor problem. He assured Wilkis that he would be able to handle the problem by working with the bank to cover his tracks. The news about the SEC telephone call annoyed Levine only because it meant he would have to make an extra trip to Nassau and deal with the problem. He didn't want to go again so soon; he had just been to Bank Leu to withdraw $150,000 the day before Meier got the SEC call.

"It's a fucking institutional problem at the bank," Levine told

Wilkis after learning of the SEC call to Meier. "I'm going to tell those yo-yos that they have to clean this up."

Levine told Wilkis that he had met with Boesky: "I told him I have a friend who has a problem with the SEC. The Russian told me, 'Tell your friend to get Harvey Pitt. He's the best and he's taken care of my scrapes with the SEC.' "

"Do you think it's wise to hire a lawyer at this point?" asked Wilkis.

"You fucking moron," Levine responded, "I'm not gonna hire him. I'm gonna have the bank hire him."

"What if it becomes an institutional problem for the bank and their interests don't match yours?" asked Wilkis.

"That won't happen. I'm gonna work with the bank."

September 2 was Labor Day and Wall Street was shut down. Levine used the holiday to go to Nassau, where he met with Meier and Pletscher at the bank. He could see that the two Swiss bankers were still in a state of high anxiety over the SEC snoops.

Levine was irritated that the bankers would even be bothered by the regulators, but he concealed his anger and set about employing his well-honed charms to soothe their nerves and win their cooperation in the plan he had conceived to dispense with the SEC inquiry.

Meier began by outlining the telephone call from the SEC. He showed Levine the telex, which had added a twenty-eighth stock to the original list.

"You don't have a problem. We can deal with this," Levine said reassuringly as he sorted through several slips of paper that he had pulled from his pocket and placed on the top of the oak conference table.

Levine said he had experience in handling SEC inquiries through his responsibilities at work. He knew the agency was filled with bureaucrats and lawyers who couldn't find jobs in the real world. He had himself lied to the SEC and said he knew others who had done the same thing. The SEC lawyers probably suspected they were all lying but could not prove anything.

"They don't understand what they are doing and you don't have to worry about them," Levine said persuasively. "You have to approach them very strongly and just tell them what you have to say. The main thing is to have a good lawyer who represents you and you turn them away. They don't have any right to interfere in a Swiss bank and they don't have any right to interfere in a bank in the Bahamas."

The approach sounded logical and reasonable to Pletscher and Meier, particularly the notion that the SEC had no business interfering with the bank, and they listened intently as Levine outlined his plan for thwarting the agency.

"The only thing you have to do is tell them that you studied the markets and you bought these stocks on your own decision. You are the smart guys. They don't have a single bit of proof otherwise and that turns them away."

Levine said the SEC should be informed that the stocks had been bought through the portfolio of investor accounts that Meier managed for the bank's clients. Meier was certainly not an insider. He was a professional investment adviser, and the SEC should be told that he had chosen the stocks on the basis of his own research and of advice from his brokers. The bank could refuse legally to provide the SEC with any documents and the agency would have to accept his story about the managed portfolio, Levine explained.

An important element of the strategy was hiring a lawyer who could be told the false story and convey it convincingly to the authorities. As part of the cover-up to convince the lawyer to accept the lie, the three men decided to alter bank records, creating an agreement for Levine to sign in which the bank was appointed manager of his investment account.

Meier left the room and returned with the bank's standard portfolio agreement. Levine suggested that language be added to the document specifying that he had instructed the bank to invest in "speculative situations," including takeover stocks.

The finished document was given to Levine, who said he would have his Bahamian lawyer review it and return it later. Meanwhile, he signed a temporary form for the bankers.

As another element of the scheme, Levine promised to look for brokers' reports and newspaper articles to support buying the take-over stocks then under SEC review. Meier could use the material to help explain to the lawyer why he had purchased the stocks.

Levine asked Meier and Pletscher if the bank had a good lawyer who could deal with the SEC. When the bankers said they did not, Levine picked out one of his slips of paper and looked at it.

"I recommend that you hire Harvey Pitt of Fried, Frank," he said, handing Pletscher a piece of paper bearing Pitt's name and telephone number.

"Why him?" asked Pletscher.

"I know Harvey Pitt from other cases," said Levine. "He used to be general counsel at the SEC and he knows the business inside out. You can convince Pitt of the story and he can convince the SEC for you."

As Levine laid out his plan, the tension in the room eased. Pletscher and Meier began to believe that the SEC could be handled smoothly. Until the inquiry was over, however, Meier suggested that Levine might alter his trading pattern.

"We've got to be careful not to trade further in securities that are subject to takeover situations," he said to Levine.

Levine said he would be more careful and select only stocks involved in takeovers that were either public or the subject of wide-spread rumors. But he cautioned against stopping their trading completely, warning that such a halt might indicate to the SEC that the bank had something to hide.

"Did the SEC tell you anything about what triggered all this?" Levine asked.

Meier said the SEC had mentioned nothing about the origins of the inquiry, but he repeated to Levine that Brian Campbell, one of the brokers Meier dealt with in New York, had testified before the SEC in August. Meier explained that Campbell had left Merrill Lynch in early 1985 for a different brokerage firm and had taken most of Bank Leu's business with him. He thought that Campbell's successor at Merrill Lynch might have initiated the inquiry by passing on information to the SEC because he was angry about losing the bank's business. In any case, while at Merrill Lynch, Campbell had copied some of the bank's trades and the SEC questioned him about the purchases.

Levine had never heard of Campbell and he complained about the broker's "stupidity" in piggybacking, then dropped the matter.

After Levine left, Meier and Pletscher went to Jean-Pierre Fraysse's office and informed the bank manager about the meeting and the plan the American had outlined for dealing with the SEC. They told Fraysse the bank's interests would be served best by going along with the scheme. The SEC should not be concerned with trades executed by a bank based in the Bahamas, and Levine's plan appeared to be the best way to dispense with the inquiry quickly and protect both the client and the bank.

"Yes, this seems to be the best way to deal with this problem," Fraysse agreed.

Pletscher said Levine had suggested hiring an American lawyer named Harvey Pitt to represent the bank with the SEC, and he asked whether the bank manager had ever heard of Pitt.

"No, I've never heard of him," said Fraysse. "But I'll certainly call him up and see if we can retain the services of Mr. Pitt."

12.

"Just Lie"

Harvey Pitt had become one of the leading securities lawyers in the United States in the seven years since resigning as general counsel to the Securities and Exchange Commission and joining the Washington office of the large and prestigious law firm of Fried, Frank, Harris, Shriver & Jacobson. He had represented corporations trying to take over other companies and companies defending themselves against unwanted corporate suitors. He had overseen the expansion of the firm's securities division into a major profit center. He also specialized in handling insider trading cases and negotiating on behalf of clients at the SEC.

A forty-year-old native of Brooklyn, Pitt was an imposing figure: self-assured and aggressive, with a full beard and portly build, he liked to hook his thumbs through a favorite pair of suspenders emblazoned with little red devils. As a lawyer, he was tenacious and fanatically thorough. Soon after he started at Fried, Frank in 1978, he was featured in a book about workaholics, and his pace had never slackened. He employed three shifts of secretaries for round-the-clock support.

As is the case with most prominent lawyers, Pitt was not cheap.

He billed his time at $300 an hour and often charged multiples of that figure for intricate corporate work.

Near the end of the first week in September 1985, Fraysse telephoned Pitt's office in the Watergate complex in Washington and left a message asking him to phone back. In the ensuing call, Fraysse said he would like to meet with Pitt to discuss the possibility of hiring him to represent Bank Leu in a pending SEC inquiry. They arranged a breakfast meeting for early the following week at the Westbury Hotel in New York, where Pitt spends a day or two each week.

Before the meeting, Pitt's paralegals did preliminary research on Bank Leu International Ltd. in Nassau. They found that it was a subsidiary of Switzerland's oldest private bank, Bank Leu, and that the parent bank was a respected financial institution.

Pitt circulated a memo in the law firm's New York, London, and Washington offices to determine whether the firm would have a conflict of interest if it were retained by Bank Leu. The only response to the memo was a telephone call from Michael Rauch, a senior litigation partner in the firm's New York office.

Rauch was forty-seven years old, a graduate of Princeton University and Harvard Law School. He lived on the Upper West Side of Manhattan and favored cigars and suits that were a bit more fashionable and flashy than the somber uniforms of his partners.

After law school, Rauch had spent four years as an assistant state attorney general in New York before joining Fried, Frank in 1968, where he came to be regarded as one of the very best trial attorneys, with a reputation for never losing his temper or making a rash judgment or statement. When Leon Silverman, the head of litigation at Fried, Frank, was appointed to investigate Raymond Donovan, Reagan's former secretary of labor, in 1982, his first choice as a special assistant was Rauch.

At Fried, Frank, Rauch had handled many cases involving securities-fraud litigation, most recently representing Credit Suisse in the Santa Fe International Corporation insider trading case. Now, he offered his assistance if Pitt needed a litigator familiar with foreign secrecy cases, an offer Pitt accepted. It was a partnership that would prove vital to their success.

Pitt's breakfast meeting with Fraysse the following week was brief and routine. Fraysse said Pitt had been recommended by several sources in the securities business who knew of his experience at the SEC and of his private practice. The Frenchman then explained that the bank had received a request for information from the SEC concerning possible insider trading in twenty-eight stocks. He said the trades had all been conducted by Bernhard Meier, the bank's portfolio manager, for accounts managed by the bank.

Pitt outlined the SEC process to Fraysse, explaining U.S. insider trading regulations in broad terms. Fraysse left Pitt a copy of the SEC inquiry and a letter about the bank.

A few days later, Pitt and Rauch arranged a conference call with Meier and Richard Coulson, an expatriate American lawyer who was a special adviser to the bank. Pitt and Rauch agreed to meet with Meier as soon as possible to review the various trades under SEC scrutiny. Meanwhile, the bank would have to weigh a variety of options, including whether it wanted to respond to the SEC at all, since it was outside American jurisdiction and the Bahamian bank secrecy law might prohibit disclosure of any information to the SEC. Whatever the decision, Pitt and Rauch offered to meet with Meier in Nassau. Meier rejected the offer, saying he had to come to New York the following week on bank business and would meet with Pitt and Rauch then.

Meier's initial jitters over the SEC inquiry had been replaced by a determination to defy the regulators. He would adhere to Levine's fabrication that he had made all the trades on behalf of the bank's managed accounts. But if the SEC inquiry were to be dispensed with promptly, the American lawyers had to be convinced of this story. Arriving at Fried, Frank's Wall Street office on September 18, a Wednesday, he spent the entire day regaling Pitt and Rauch with his investment prowess and, in particular, with his ability to pick takeover stocks by analyzing "the fundamentals" of the companies. Meier was bitter about the SEC's audacity in trying to interfere in the operations of a Swiss bank in the Bahamas and he was ready to take a tough stand. He would refuse to cooperate with the inquiry in any way.

Shortly after Meier returned to Room 2341 at the Waldorf-Astoria, there was a knock on his hotel room door. When he opened it, a smiling man handed him an envelope containing two subpoenas from the SEC. One subpoena was a broad demand for the bank's business records from October 1, 1983, until the present. The other demanded Meier's personal and business records.

The SEC had abandoned any hope of voluntary cooperation from Meier or Bank Leu, and the border watch placed on Meier by the Customs Service had paid off. In filling out his U.S. immigration papers in Nassau, Meier had said he would be staying at the Waldorf-Astoria in New York. The Customs agents had alerted the SEC.

Faced with the subpoenas—and especially with the demand for his personal records—Meier's confidence vanished. He frantically dialed the Fried, Frank law offices and got Pitt on the telephone. Pitt tried to calm his distraught client, arranging a meeting with Meier in Nassau for the following Sunday and sending a messenger to the hotel to pick up the two documents.

When Meier hung up the telephone, he slipped into a mild state of paranoia. He was sure he had been followed from Nassau. Looking back, he thought he had detected some surveillance at the airport in Nassau and again when he landed in New York.

Pletscher was scheduled to join Meier in New York the next day for a business meeting with a prospective client. Now Meier telephoned him in Nassau, telling him about the subpoena and his new fears.

"The U.S. Customs people behaved strangely at the airport when I left," Meier said. "I think I'm being watched. You must be very careful when you leave."

Pletscher, who had also reserved a room at the Waldorf-Astoria, told Meier he would switch to the Helmsley Palace in case the SEC was also watching him. He was scheduled to arrive late in the day on Thursday for their client meeting on Friday. He said he would telephone Meier immediately upon his arrival.

Meier ordered a drink and sandwich from room service and tried to relax. Soon, however, the telephone rang. It was Levine calling from a pay phone in a restaurant at Ninety-fifth Street and Third Avenue, about two blocks from his Park Avenue apartment.

Meier had told Levine several days earlier that he would be meeting with the lawyers. Now the investment banker was calling to get a rundown on how the session had gone. Levine also wanted to send over some background material on several of the stocks under investigation. But instead of giving Levine a review of his meeting with the lawyers, Meier launched into a description of how he had received the subpoenas, telling the banker he thought he was being followed. He was frightened, he said, that he would be ordered to testify before the SEC. While he thought his story had held up well in front of the lawyers, Meier was not sure he could carry out the lie under questioning from government lawyers.

As he had when the inquiry first arose, Levine remained calm. "You just lie to the SEC and you'll get out of it," Levine advised. "They'll know you're not telling the truth, but they won't have a single bit of evidence to prove the opposite."

Bruno Pletscher had been uncertain about the chances of lying successfully to the SEC from the start. The subpoenas unnerved him. They were dramatic evidence of the seriousness and reach of the American government. En route to Nassau International Airport late on the afternoon of September 19 for his flight to New York, he feared the customs agents had his name and Swiss passport number in their computer. When he arrived at the airport, Pletscher found that a power failure had cut off all electricity. A good omen, he thought. The immigration clerks were using candles to check passengers for the last flight out and, better still, the computers were all down. There was no way the authorities would be able to check the list of suspect travelers.

Although Pletscher had no way of knowing it, the SEC did not even know his name in September 1985 and would not learn of his involvement for many weeks.

After arriving in New York and checking into his room at the Helmsley Palace, Pletscher walked to the Waldorf. There, he used the house phone to call Meier, who met him in the lobby within minutes. Meier was still frightened and suggested that they leave the hotel immediately to avoid any possible surveillance.

They went to the Helmsley Palace and, once inside Pletscher's room, Meier handed his colleague copies of the SEC subpoenas.

"How can the United States ask for these things from a person who does not live in the United States and is not a U.S. citizen?" asked Pletscher.

"I don't know," said Meier. "I don't know if they can or not, but it worries me very much."

The men decided to cancel the next day's meeting and return to the Bahamas on a Friday morning flight. Meier cautioned Pletscher not to leave his room and, as he got up to go, he said, "For heaven's sake, don't open the door."

About ten minutes after Meier's departure, there was a knock on Pletscher's door. He was terrified. The SEC must have tracked him down, after all. He considered Meier's parting advice. The knock came again, more firmly. Pletscher walked to the door and opened it slowly.

The night service maid smiled and handed Pletscher his complimentary Swiss chocolates.

Harvey Pitt travels extensively on his job. He flies first class, sometimes charters jets to make it to crucial meetings, and always stays at luxury hotels.

When he saw the room Meier had booked at the Nassau Beach

Hotel, he wondered if the banker were trying to tell him something. He telephoned Rauch and found that his partner's quarters were equally small and offered the added advantage of being situated directly over the lounge, where a loud calypso band was playing. Later that night, Pitt found there was no hot water and took his first cold shower since high school.

On Sunday afternoon, Meier stopped by Pitt's small room for a lengthy meeting that ran into the evening. Meier did not want the American lawyers visiting him at Lyford Cay Club, the resort complex where Meier made his home and whose excellent hotel would have provided much more convenient accommodations. Worse, Meier was hesitant about having the lawyers come to Bank Leu. It seemed as if Meier was embarrassed to be involved with them, perhaps also wanting to avoid arousing the curiosity of bank employees. But the next day's meeting would be held at the bank.

Before the lawyers arrived at the bank, Meier met with Pletscher in his office to go over their story. Pletscher still had reservations, and Meier sought to eliminate them.

"We should go along with this plan for Diamond, saying we chose the stocks," Meier said. "If the lawyers are convinced, such good lawyers, we should finish with the SEC in no time."

"As a matter of fact," Meier continued, "I'll do the talking. You don't have to bother. I'll say that you only filled in while I was away and even when I was away, you checked with me on trades. I called on a daily basis."

There are lawyers who prefer not to know the truth about a client's involvement in a crime. Guilt or innocence does not matter to them and does not affect their defense strategy. They may believe that a client is entitled to the best defense available, regardless of guilt, or they may not wish to burden their own consciences with the knowledge that they are defending a guilty person.

There also are lawyers who insist on full disclosure before proceeding. They may do so out of regard for the truth or because they cannot mount an effective defense without knowing precisely what it is they are defending. They may be motivated by a combination of both reasons.

In complex corporate crimes, guilt or innocence can be a matter of degree. There is nothing as black and white as a corpse on the boardroom floor. In these instances, lawyers are more likely to demand a full disclosure from their clients. Insider trading certainly fits in the category of complex crimes, particularly when the people involved are foreigners not subject to United States law.

Pitt and Rauch had to come to grips with two conflicting accounts about the twenty-eight takeover stocks on the subpoena. The SEC thought the purchases reflected insider trading; the bank contended they had been bought "on the fundamentals." It was important for the two lawyers to ensure that they were being told the truth by their clients; otherwise, defending the bank could be an impossible task.

When Pitt and Rauch arrived at the bank on Monday, they were taken to the large conference room where they were greeted by Pletscher, Meier, and Richard Coulson. Michael Barnett, a Nassau lawyer, also attended the meeting to offer advice on Bahamian bank secrecy laws. The bank officials heard Pitt explain that lying to their lawyer was the worst mistake clients could make. They were told he and Rauch would be unable to defend them effectively without knowing the truth.

"Here are the obvious facts on both sides of the ledger," Pitt said. "You've got the SEC subpoenas, which were delivered after an electronic border watch picked up Meier's entry into the U.S. That means they are very serious about this investigation and it's a very hostile situation. You also have a list of twenty-eight stocks under scrutiny, and many of them appear to me to have been purchased just before takeover deals were announced. And you have fourteen SEC enforcement people on the formal investigation order, an extraordinarily high number.

"On your side, you have your statements that these were managed trades for your portfolio. Either the commission is way, way off base or you guys may be reluctant to tell us the truth. We're very good lawyers and if you tell us the truth, we can probably help you."

"No, no, don't worry," said Coulson. "Bernie did the buying on fundamentals. That's all that's involved."

Coulson was in charge of responding to the lawyers on behalf of the bank. He was fifty-four years old, an American who had moved to Nassau many years before. A graduate of Yale University Law School, he had been a lawyer at Cravath, Swaine & Moore in New York and an investment banker, so he was familiar with the laws involved. Coulson assured Pitt and Rauch that they all understood the importance of telling them the truth. Coulson insisted that the trades had all been made by Meier for managed accounts on the basis of his own analysis of the stock situations.

The bank officials were questioned carefully, partly to see if there were any obvious flaws in the story and partly to allow the lawyers to begin assembling evidence for their defense. Meier was asked how he picked specific stocks, and he reviewed his investment strategies and described the help he got from his network of American brokers.

Pitt then asked how Pletscher bought stocks when Meier was away on vacation or business. Pletscher had said little during the meeting, and Pitt and Rauch had assumed he was a lower-level functionary at the bank, despite his title.

Pletscher represents the essence of the Swiss persona. He is polite, reserved, and cautious. But that day he was quieter than usual because he was very uncomfortable with what was occurring. He did not trust the American lawyers. He was unfamiliar with the American legal system, and he viewed Pitt and Rauch as intruders. He had wanted and would have preferred legal advice from the head office in Zurich. In addition to those factors, Pletscher had doubts about whether the cover-up would succeed.

It took time but finally he answered Pitt: "I stayed in contact with Bernie all the time."

"If Bernie is on vacation, how can he keep up with the brokers and how did he always catch the right time, since Switzerland is six hours ahead of Nassau and New York?"

Meier tried to answer, but Pitt interrupted and instructed Pletscher to respond.

"I kept in contact with the brokers and passed the information on to Bernie," he said. "I made some small trades on what the brokers said, but Bernie always made the decisions on the big trades."

As the meeting ended, Pitt promised that he and Rauch would return to the Bahamas soon, saying they would want to see the details of the trades involving the twenty-eight stocks, including the bank statements from the managed accounts to which Meier had allocated the trades.

Pletscher's discomfort had increased in the face of Pitt's probing questions and detailed demands. After the lawyers left, he told Meier, "It's clear to me I was talking bullshit. Surely they can see that, too. We should contact Zurich."

"Ah, they don't know anything about this SEC business in Zurich," said Meier. "They don't have that much business in the U.S. stock market and they don't understand it."

"I want to get them involved anyway," insisted Pletscher.

Early Tuesday, Pletscher telephoned the bank's home office in Zurich and spoke with Hans Peter Schaad, the bank's general counsel. He told Schaad that the SEC inquiry was more serious than they had thought initially, and he asked him to come to Nassau as soon as possible to "get the whole picture." Schaad said he would consider the request and take it up with Hans Knopfli, the home office executive who served as chairman of the board of the subsidiary, Bank Leu International.

Pletscher's reservations remained, but he felt some relief in sharing the situation with Schaad and passing responsibility to the

highest levels of the bank, where, for the past three weeks, he had
felt it belonged.

Pitt and Rauch were scheduled to leave at mid-morning on Tuesday. At 7:00 A.M., the telephone woke Pitt. It was Coulson. He
wanted to meet for breakfast in half an hour in the hotel restaurant.
He needed to talk with the two lawyers before they left the country.

Pitt telephoned Rauch, waking him up. He told his partner they
were having breakfast with Coulson in less than thirty minutes.

"Either he's going to confess or we're going to be fired," Pitt
predicted.

Neither event occurred. Coulson was cordial over breakfast as
he reviewed the situation and emphasized the requirements of Bahamian secrecy laws. The three lawyers agreed to talk further the
following week, after Pitt and Rauch met with the SEC.

Later that same week, an auditing team from Bank Leu in Zurich
arrived in Nassau for a routine inspection of the bank's records.
The chief inspector and his deputy had already set up shop in a
small office when Meier and Pletscher asked to speak with them
about a special matter.

It would turn out to be a confusing meeting for Pletscher, one
of a series of events in which he may have misinterpreted signals
from his superiors and been left with more responsibility than he
intended to accept.

Meier had been speaking with the American lawyers because he
was more comfortable with them, and the plan would be in his
hands anyway. It was Pletscher, whose background was as an accountant and Bank Leu International's chief financial officer, who
explained the situation to the auditors. Pletscher described the SEC
inquiry into the trading of certain stocks through the bank and
indicated the investigation might involve insider trading. He told
them Fraysse had authorized hiring the two American lawyers to

represent the bank in the inquiry, but, he added, he, Pletscher, had also contacted the legal department in Zurich for help. Now, Pletscher had learned that Knopfli, not Schaad, was coming to Nassau the following week. The seriousness of the situation necessitated legal advice from the home office, however, and Pletscher asked the chief auditor to contact Zurich and reinforce the need for Schaad to come.

To demonstrate the seriousness of the inquiry, Pletscher explained that the bank had one major account through which the trades under SEC scrutiny had been booked on direct orders from the client. He acknowledged that the bank's position had been compromised because he and Meier had added to the client's trades by purchasing stocks for their personal accounts as well as for accounts managed by the bank for investors.

As the auditors listened without comment, Pletscher described the plan the client had come up with to get rid of the SEC: telling the agency that the trades were placed through the bank's managed accounts on the basis of Meier's judgment.

Meier then said the bank might have to create some documents that concealed the true nature of the trades and the single account and supported the story about managed accounts. The document he had in mind was the management agreement giving the bank discretion over Levine's trading account. He also said he was assembling public material to support the idea that he had based the trades on his own judgment based on information from brokers and other sources.

This, concluded Pletscher, seemed to be the best way to protect the client and the bank. If the problem were not solved, he warned, the bank could face a fine of up to $40 million.

The figure shocked the auditors. Pletscher explained that he and Meier had calculated the customer's profits at $10 million. He said their American lawyers had told them that U.S. securities law allowed a court to demand reimbursement of the profits and impose a fine of up to triple the profits.

Faced with this prospect, the auditors proceeded to review some of the records of Levine's trades. There are times, they concluded, when, in order to protect the bank's interest, certain documents have to be brought up to date. They used the French phrase "*à jour*" for up to date.

Pletscher asked what the auditors meant, and they responded that the documents he and Meier had produced should reflect the story they were telling.

It was enough. Pletscher and Meier felt the auditors had approved creating the fake agreement giving the bank discretion over Levine's account. Later, the auditors would tell Pletscher that the two had misunderstood them: they had meant only that Meier should assemble the public material necessary to support his position that he had chosen the stocks.

The chief auditor, recognizing the potential seriousness of the problem, agreed to telephone Zurich the next morning and repeat Pletscher's request that Schaad come to Nassau. As a result of the call, the auditors were instructed to change their itinerary and return to Zurich through London, rather than New York as planned, to avoid the possibility of any further U.S. subpoenas.

But the auditors were also told that it would still be Knopfli, not Schaad, who would arrive in Nassau at the beginning of the next week to deal with the difficulties. Before the current week was out, however, Meier and Pletscher would receive a call from another visitor and take an irreversible step down the path laid out by Levine.

13.

"Under No Circumstances"

Behind his neutral Swiss exterior and polite demeanor, Bruno Pletscher was struggling. As September came to a close, he had been dealing with the tensions and deceit of the cover-up for nearly a month, and he fought a constant battle to keep the strains from surfacing.

The demands of the SEC inquiry had distracted him from his other responsibilities at the bank. Work had piled up. Since summer, Jean-Pierre Fraysse had been traveling more and more, leaving the everyday operation of the bank to Pletscher. That would have been burden enough, without the sessions with the lawyers and the auditors and the constant whisperings with Meier.

Throughout the month, Pletscher remained firm in his belief that the American authorities had no right to interfere with bank affairs. But his reservations about the chances for lying successfully to them persisted.

On Friday, September 27, Pletscher wanted to straighten out some accounting and personnel matters that had to get done before he started a one-month vacation at the end of the following week. He was angry when, about mid-morning, Meier interrupted with a reminder that "Diamond" was expected to arrive soon. (Although both bankers knew the client's real name, they always referred to him as "Diamond.") Levine had telephoned collect the previous day to say he would stop by the bank for a few hours. Pletscher told Meier he was too busy to spend much time with the American. That was true. It was also true that Pletscher wanted to avoid involving himself any further than necessary in the scheme. He promised to stop by the conference room later so that Diamond could review his account files with both men.

When Pletscher eventually walked into the conference room he found the two men seated at the table, Meier writing furiously in a notebook as Levine described the financial history of one of the companies on the SEC list. Pletscher realized Levine was dictating the explanations, stock by stock, that Meier would need to convince the lawyers and, if necessary, the SEC that he bought the takeover stocks on his own knowledge.

They interrupted their work and Pletscher, glancing at the Diamond Holdings files on the table, asked, "Is there anything in particular you wish to review?"

Levine wanted to check the files to determine whether they contained documents that could identify him. But first he wanted a report on how the meeting had gone with the lawyers earlier in the week.

"What have you told your lawyers?" he asked.

"We reported that every security trade mentioned in the subpoena was made on our decision and the trades were allocated to managed portfolios," said Meier.

"That's the right thing to do. You'll see. With Fried, Frank as your counsel, you'll get the SEC off your back in no time," said Levine.

Levine then asked to see his account files, and Pletscher retrieved the master file for Diamond Holdings Inc. from the stack. It contained the account opening forms, pledge agreements, and other legal documents that are maintained from the start of an account until it is closed.

The first document to grab Levine's attention was the photocopy of his passport, including his photograph, which was stapled to the master file. Alongside it was the signature card he had completed for the original individual account in the code name "Diamond." On the card were his real name and signature.

"What are these documents doing here?" Levine asked, waving the file in front of the two bankers. "This passport doesn't belong in this file. This signature card doesn't belong here either. This is the account of Diamond Holdings, and my name and identity shouldn't appear anywhere in this file. These are from the old file, Diamond only, and they should not be here."

Meier was silent. Pletscher thought for several seconds and said: "You are right. This was an oversight. The Diamond account is closed. There was no need to maintain these documents. However, we don't have complete corporate documents for Diamond Holdings. We have no real beneficiary for the account if these documents are not here."

Since creating the Panamanian front company in October 1981, Levine's lawyers had neglected to provide the bank with all of the necessary documentation, Pletscher went on to explain.

"Never mind," Levine said curtly. "I'm establishing a new company. The new company will produce all the proper account documents. Then we'll close the existing company. We don't need these documents anymore."

He pointed to the passport photocopy and the signature card and ordered: "Make sure you take them out of the file and destroy them. They don't have anything to do with the company."

Levine continued through the files until he discovered the receipts he had signed on the various occasions when he had withdrawn cash from his account. The receipts were the only record the bank maintained of a customer's withdrawals and, for the protection of the client and the bank, they had to be signed in the customer's real name.

"These show my real signature," said Levine. "They must be destroyed, too."

Pletscher balked at the new order. He said he could not destroy the withdrawal forms.

Pletscher was an accountant, with an accountant's belief in maintaining proper records. He was also vice president of Bank Leu International and ultimately responsible for the sanctity of the bank's accounting system. He was the bank officer who had to report directly to the home office auditors, and their recent visit was fresh in his mind.

He also knew that destroying the withdrawal slips in Levine's account would be insufficient. The bank maintained two other copies, one in the master accounting files and another for cash accounting. But the papers in these files were the originals and they were the slips that Pletscher insisted on retaining.

The slips were scattered throughout the account file, and Pletscher resisted as well Levine's attempt to group them into a single file. He was concerned that Levine might grab them and destroy them in a single moment, or that Meier might later open the files and remove them if they were easily accessible.

Pletscher did see the logic in destroying the passport photocopy and signature card from the Diamond account. The documents were, as Levine said, obsolete. But the withdrawal slips were essential to the integrity of the bank's accounting system.

For the moment, Levine accepted Pletscher's decision. He finished reviewing the file and moved to the next item on his agenda. He wanted to create a new Panamanian company to add another layer of secrecy to his trading, in case the SEC obtained any documents from the bank. He had therefore instructed his attorneys to begin preparing documents to close Diamond Holdings Inc. and create a new company, called International Gold Inc. It also would be registered in Panama and ownership would be through anonymous bearer shares. Levine wanted to transfer the assets of Diamond Holdings to the new company without creating any link between the two entities. He asked the bankers if they had any ideas for concealing the transaction.

Create a temporary intermediate company, suggested Pletscher.

The money could be transferred out of Diamond Holdings into the intermediate company and deposited in a money-market fund at another bank in Europe in the name of the intermediate company. The money could then be transferred into the new account, International Gold. Pletscher said the amounts of withdrawals from Diamond Holdings should be varied, to be redeposited later in International Gold in different amounts. The transfers could take place over several days to add another cloaking layer. Pletscher was sure the process would work, and he and Meier agreed to begin the transfers as soon as they received the papers for Levine's new corporation from his lawyers.

Levine was pleased with the transfer arrangement, but he was not satisfied with stopping there. He wanted to create a new, safer system for withdrawing cash from his account. He had considered it before the meeting and the discovery of the withdrawal slips increased his resolve.

"I don't want to sign any official bank documents for cash withdrawals from now on," he said. "This is a weak point in the way we've been doing things, and I don't want to have a weak point in case the SEC inquiry goes on too long."

Instead of signing bank receipts for cash, he wanted to authorize Meier and Pletscher, as two senior officials of Bank Leu International, to withdraw up to $250,000 in cash from his account upon his request. The cash would be handed over to Levine and he would sign a plain piece of paper as a receipt. He said his new company would pass a resolution to establish the procedure.

The bankers agreed to implement the new system, with proper authorization from International Gold.

At Levine's request, Meier showed him the copies of the subpoenas he had received from the SEC. Levine read them over and dismissed their significance with an indifferent shrug. He said they were standard documents that should cause little concern.

"As a Swiss bank operating out of the Bahamas, you're not obliged to comply with all these requests," he said. "You would have to give the SEC nothing more than the bank's omnibus accounts

showing the total of trades. You don't have to show them any allocation of trades to individual accounts. If you did that, it would
be going too far and it would be breaking the Bahamian secrecy
law.

"If you show them an allocation of the trades, the SEC will easily
figure out that the majority of the trades were passed through one
account and they'd focus on that particular account. Just show
them the omnibus account. They don't have any right to get any
single account."

But Meier realized that Pitt and Rauch were insisting on seeing
individual accounts, even if the documents could be withheld from
the SEC.

"If you had ten accounts with us, it would look better," he told
Levine. "We could divide your account in subaccounts and allocate
the trading to each of those accounts. All we would need is the
names of ten people as the beneficial owners of those accounts.
The company documents would say that the shareholders are 'so
and so' and 'so and so.' Then we can produce the account showing
actually ten accounts."

Pletscher agreed with the idea. "You need to get friends or lawyers to front for you. You have to have real people, real corporations."

But Levine rejected the plan: "I can't do that. I don't want anybody to do that. I don't want anyone else to know about this. That
would be too risky and too expensive. Nobody knows my account
exists and if I appointed beneficiaries, more people would know
about it. Even my wife doesn't know. Anyway, I'd have to pay these
people and that would be too expensive. I want you to go on with
the scheme the way we've decided."

"Well," said Pletscher, "if we don't have ten beneficiaries then
we can't do it."

"You don't have to worry about splitting up the account," said
Levine. "The lawyers don't have to see the detailed information."

As Meier had moments before, Pletscher recognized that Levine's assertion flew in the face of Pitt's demand for the account
statements.

Pletscher left the room a few minutes later and returned to his office down the hall. He tried to busy himself with paperwork, but his mind kept returning to the SEC inquiry. He feared the inquiry was getting more dangerous, that it would not be so easy to turn away the American investigators.

How had he gotten into such a mess? Where did the best interests of the bank lie? Where did client loyalty end? Could they fool the lawyers into believing Meier had made the trades? Did the American agency have any right to demand bank records? Was "Diamond" as smart as he claimed to be? Should they destroy the passport photocopy and the signature card?

The last question was the most troubling because it was the most immediate. He agreed with Levine that the documents did not belong in the file for Diamond Holdings. He understood the idea that they were obsolete. But Pletscher was a cautious man and he had been an accountant too many years to find it easy to destroy any type of records.

His troubling thoughts were interrupted by a knock and Meier's entry. It had been a long and demanding week for both men and the strain showed on Meier. His complexion was pale and his shoulders were hunched as he dropped the Diamond files on Pletscher's desk and sank into a chair. On top of the stack was the master file, with the passport photocopy and the signature card stapled to the folder.

"Shall we destroy them or not?" asked Pletscher.

"Yes, as Diamond said, these documents do not belong in that file and they are obsolete," said Meier.

Then, trying to relieve the tension, Meier joked, "Are you going to destroy them or am I going to do it?"

"You do one and I'll do one," Pletscher said with a feeble smile.

Like most businesses that generate reams of paper, Bank Leu has an ample supply of paper shredders. Pletscher had one in his room and he opened a panel to pull it out. Switching on the machine, he detached the passport photocopy from the master file.

With a slight shrug, he dropped it into the shredder. Meier stood up, pulled the signature card from the file, and dropped it down the shredder.

Neither Pletscher nor Meier was fully aware of the significance of what they had just done. They were bankers, not lawyers, and not even Americans. Neither was familiar enough with U.S. law to recognize that the destruction of any relevant documents after receiving subpoenas could constitute obstruction of justice, a serious violation of the law.

Pletscher and Meier had no way of knowing that dropping two documents they believed to be obsolete into the shredder was an irrevocable step that would jeopardize their futures in a far more serious way than executing five and a half years' worth of insider trades for Levine had done.

Hans Knopfli was one of the highest ranking executives in the Bank Leu organization. He was chairman of the management board for the parent bank and chairman of the board of directors of the subsidiary, Bank Leu International.

On Monday morning, September 30, he arrived at the bank offices in Nassau for a visit that had been planned several weeks before. The unpleasantness of the American regulators and their inquiry was a small matter to him. He had to deal with the resignation of Jean-Pierre Fraysse, who had informed bank officials in June that he intended to leave Bank Leu.

Knopfli spent most of Monday in meetings with Fraysse and some of the bank's directors. At the end of the day, he called Pletscher into the manager's office, which he was using.

Since arriving in Nassau in late 1979, Pletscher had risen in stature with the home office. His technical work had never been in doubt and he had been a pleasant surprise as he grew more adept at dealing with customers. Pletscher would never possess the easy charm and polish of Fraysse or Meier, but he was a solid, hardworking executive.

Pletscher was also comfortable in the Bahamas. His first marriage was over and he had met a young Bahamian woman, Sherrill Caso, who worked at a local trust company. His intention was to return to Switzerland someday, but he was content to remain in Nassau for a few more years, particularly if he received Fraysse's position.

Fraysse had first mentioned to Pletscher in June or July of 1985 that he wanted to leave the bank. When Pletscher sat down across the desk from Knopfli late that Monday afternoon, he received his first good news in a month: Fraysse would depart on December 31, and he was to be promoted to general manager of the bank, effective January 1, 1986.

Knopfli asked Pletscher to keep the news quiet, since it would be several weeks before Fraysse's departure would be announced, but he congratulated Pletscher and promised that his future with Bank Leu was bright.

Pletscher and Caso celebrated later with dinner and a bottle of wine. More than ever, Pletscher wished that the SEC inquiry would go away.

On Tuesday, Knopfli set aside time to meet with Pletscher and Meier to discuss the SEC inquiry. Pletscher had been surprised that Schaad had not come and feared the home office did not recognize the growing seriousness of the situation. It was a critical miscalculation on the part of Bank Leu in Zurich not to send Schaad or another lawyer. Pletscher was determined to explain the facts to Knopfli and obtain the advice of a superior on how to proceed.

"How much is involved?" Knopfli asked when he learned of the subpoena.

"We have clients, we have one big client, and we have the bank and staff involved in the purchases," said Pletscher.

"Put that together on a piece of paper for me so I can see it," Knopfli asked.

Meier had spent the previous weekend compiling data about the stock purchases. He now consulted his notes and wrote out a quick summary of the transactions that went beyond the twenty-eight stocks and covered most of Levine's dealings with the bank since 1980. It listed purchases through Levine's account, those made on behalf of bank investors, and those made by the various staff members.

By Meier's rough calculations, Levine's profits exceeded $12 million, Meier had made more than $150,000 in profits, and Pletscher about $46,000.

Meier explained that the subpoena might require him to testify to the SEC and that, while he was not comfortable with the decision, he was prepared to lie.

At the mention of lying to the SEC, Knopfli almost jumped out of his chair. "Mr. Meier, under no circumstances can you go to an authority and lie," he said firmly.

"This is the only way that we can get the SEC turned away from the bank and solve this matter in the best interests of the bank," Meier said.

Knopfli agreed that the matter should be resolved as quickly as possible, but he repeated that Meier could not lie.

"We have to find another way to deal with this matter," he said.

"This is in the bank's interest, and if we don't do it, we run the risk of getting a fine of forty million dollars," said Meier.

Knopfli asked Pletscher what he thought of the situation. Pletscher said he agreed that the best interests of the bank would be served by claiming the stocks had been purchased on Meier's judgment for managed accounts.

The banker from Zurich appeared to Pletscher and Meier to be uncomfortable with the entire subject, and he sought a fast finish to the unpleasantness by saying: "This is a critical situation. I want you to do what is best for the bank. However, do not go and lie."

Rauch and Pitt had still not determined that the bank was required to provide any information or testimony to the SEC, although Meier and Pletscher clearly assumed that Meier would have to testify. The conclusion of the meeting with Knopfli, however, did not leave the two men with a clear sense of what Knopfli wanted them to do. He had told them not to lie, but he had also told them to act in the best interests of the bank. Just as the auditors had the previous week, Knopfli avoided giving any explicit direction to his subordinates for dealing with the growing problem. They were left to their own interpretation of what he meant them to do.

"I think Mr. Knopfli doesn't understand the consequences," said Meier.

"I understand Mr. Knopfli's remark and I understand that Mr. Knopfli cannot admit to you to go and lie," said Pletscher. "However, if he tells us to do what we think is best for the bank, and this includes a lie, then we should do it. I feel in that respect you have Mr. Knopfli's blessing."

Knopfli would later deny that he had authorized the bankers to proceed with the cover-up. He would point to his explicit orders not to lie to the authorities and demand that Pletscher provide him with a written statement that it was only Pletscher's interpretation that he had intended them to lie. But on October 1, 1985, Meier and Pletscher decided that they had authority from the bank's chief executive to carry on with the cover-up.

Pletscher was scheduled to begin a month's holiday at the end of the week, and he could go off to Switzerland buoyed by his impending promotion and a clearer conscience about the cover-up scheme. But Meier immediately began to pressure Pletscher to move the cover-up a critical step forward and help him create the ten fraudulent subaccounts for Levine's trades, despite the American's objections.

"It's essential now to produce the documents to affirm what we're saying vis-à-vis the SEC, including producing subaccounts for Diamond," Meier insisted after they returned to Pletscher's office.

"Bernie, we don't have legal documents to justify subaccounts, therefore I cannot do that," said Pletscher.

"Why don't you just go into the computer and change things and produce ten subaccounts?" said Meier.

"Bernie, I will not go into the computer and change anything."

Meier switched tactics, bringing up the subject of his personal trading account. The SEC had also demanded the records of that account, he reminded Pletscher, and it contained purchases of more of Levine's takeover stocks than the twenty-eight on the SEC subpoena.

"There are other shares in my account that could lead the SEC to further investigation," said Meier. "I'd like to have my account split up into two accounts. One would be with only the stocks under investigation and the others would be excluded, like a subaccount. Can't you change that in the computer?"

"Bernie, under no circumstances will anything be changed in the bank's computer," Pletscher said firmly.

Pletscher's stubborn resolve was again rooted in his training as an accountant. While he believed he could have produced subaccounts with Levine's authority, he would not do so without it. He certainly would not alter the bank's computer.

But Pletscher recognized the pressure on Meier. He realized it was Meier who was faced with the possibility of testifying before the SEC and so he offered an alternative.

"Okay, Bernie, if you want to do that with your own account, we can do that," said Pletscher. "We'll leave the main statement unchanged in the accounting department and in the bank's mainframe computer. We will have that original statement. But what you produce for the SEC is actually your own business.

"If we split up your account into two accounts, and you give them only one, that is again your own business. And to produce such a statement, I can write you a program for the personal computer, like a word processing program, and you can type on the statement what you want to have on it and we can print it out."

Meier's real account listed trades involving far more than takeover stocks, for he was an active investor. But the danger involved the Levine-inspired takeover stocks that were not on the SEC's list of twenty-eight suspicious purchases. Pletscher agreed to show Meier how to create a second account statement for Meier to give the lawyers that would list only the twenty-eight stocks in the subpoena, along with his many purchases of nontakeover stocks unrelated to Levine. The statement would not contain the other takeover stocks.

Since opening his Bank Leu account in 1980, Levine had bought and sold stock in more than one hundred companies. There were several reasons why the SEC subpoena listed only twenty-eight of the stocks. First, the subpoena was based solely on records supplied from Merrill Lynch, and Bank Leu had not opened its account there until October 31, 1983. So the inquiry asked only for bank records dating from October 1, 1983, forward. Second, Campbell had not copied every trade by the bank and the SEC was still piecing together information about other stocks in the Merrill Lynch records. Third, even after the account was opened at Merrill Lynch, not every trade was moved through that brokerage house. Occasionally, if Meier were away from the bank and Pletscher handled a trade, he would skip Campbell despite Meier's instructions.

As a result, the SEC had not yet uncovered the full scope of Levine's insider trading, and Meier did not want to tip the investigators to any more suspicious trades by providing accurate records of his own activity.

Meier urged Pletscher to create the program immediately and also pressed him to change his mind and create Diamond's new subaccounts without authorization.

"You should not go on vacation now," Meier told Pletscher. "You should stay so we can change Diamond's statements."

Pletscher remained adamant. He would use the personal computer in his office only to help Meier create a second version of his "Ascona" account. But setting up the computer program for Meier's fake account would take many hours; it would have to wait until he returned from vacation.

Late Thursday, over Meier's protests, Pletscher left for Zurich aboard the same plane as Knopfli. During his month's holiday, Pletscher spoke many times on the telephone with Meier, who cursed him for leaving Nassau without creating the subaccounts for the Diamond account or setting up Meier's personal account.

Had Pletscher created fake documents for Levine's account, the scheme might have worked. Spreading Levine's trades among ten or more subaccounts would have been more complicated and time-consuming than setting up one new account for Meier. But the same basic process could have been applied to an unlimited number of accounts. It still wasn't foolproof, but the chances of success would have been much greater.

Meier's managed-accounts story depended for its plausibility on suppressing the truth about Levine's account. Pitt and Rauch had to be convinced that Meier picked the stocks himself and allocated them to accounts that he managed for individual investors or corporations. If the lawyers were shown apparently authentic bank records dispersing the trades among ten or twenty or more accounts, they might be convinced the story was true.

Even Levine's fears of letting people in on his trading could have been overcome. Levine could have paid a fee to his law firm to set up ten new front corporations using lawyers or their secretaries as beneficial owners. He had done essentially the same thing in creating his Panamanian companies. The cost for each Panamanian company had been less than $2,000 a year for director's fees and registration stamps.

If Levine had authorized it and provided the names of ten corporations as beneficial owners, Pletscher would have been willing to create ten new subaccounts. Pletscher would have left the bank's records untouched, but the new documents would have appeared to be authentic. Meier could have presented them to Pitt and Rauch and used them to convince the lawyers he was telling the truth. Unknowingly, Pitt and Rauch would have gone to the SEC with the documents and argued that the inquiry was off base. They could have said that, to the surprise of everyone, Meier had bought the stocks for the bank's managed accounts and there was no evidence of insider trading.

If the SEC were unconvinced, they would have been forced to go to court in an attempt to obtain the records of a Swiss bank operating in the Bahamas. Despite the progress of recent years, the legal battle would have been waged in U.S. courts, Bahamian courts, and probably Swiss courts. Even if the SEC had prevailed, it could have taken years to discover who was really behind the trading at Bank Leu.

In the meantime, Levine could have withdrawn his money from Bank Leu and set up his scheme elsewhere. He could even have taken his millions of dollars and gone straight. He could have run off to any one of a number of foreign countries that do not extradite people to the United States for crimes such as insider trading.

It might have worked, except that Dennis Levine thought it was too risky to involve others and didn't want to spend the extra $20,000 or so. And Bruno Pletscher refused to alter the official records of Bank Leu International without Levine's authorization.

14.

Risk-Balancers

Harvey Pitt and Dennis Levine had dinner together in the middle of October. It was a "relationship dinner," a genre of event common to any professional subculture in which business dealings depend, at least in part, on personal relationships.

Fried, Frank and Drexel Burnham had done a modest amount of business together over the years and the dinner was arranged to explore the possibility for further dealings. Arthur Fleischer, the law firm's leading mergers partner in New York, had invited David Kay, head of mergers and acquisitions at Drexel, suggesting he bring along some of his key people. Since Fleischer made the reservations, the dinner was at his favorite spot, Lutèce.

In addition to Fleischer and Pitt, the Fried, Frank contingent included Stephen Fraidin, a mergers specialist and Ivan Boesky's longtime lawyer, and Thomas Vartanian, an expert on savings and loans from the firm's Washington office. Kay brought along Stanley Stein, a former Fried, Frank lawyer who had joined Drexel as an investment banker, and the newest star in his department, Dennis Levine.

Pitt knew Kay from several transactions and, of course, he knew Stein from his law firm days. He had only a vague recollection of meeting Levine previously, and the lawyer's impression of Levine was not strengthened that night.

Later, Pitt would be reminded that Levine had been there. He would recall that Levine sat against the wall and said little during the dinner conversation. And Pitt had a vague recollection that Levine was dressed a little more flashily than the average investment banker.

Levine was normally good company at the combination social-business occasions that are so much a part of an investment banker's routine. He could be witty and friendly. He was subdued that night by the surprise of finding himself at dinner with the man who, on his own recommendation, held his future in his hands, even if Pitt did not know it. Levine later told Wilkis that, during the dinner, he had been praying for Pitt's success with the SEC.

If Levine hoped to hear Pitt's unguarded assessment of the Bank Leu case, he was disappointed. Secrecy surrounding a case is second nature to Pitt, primarily because so much of his work involves sensitive takeover matters. When he is out of town, his secretaries are instructed never to disclose his whereabouts to a caller lest they tip someone to a pending deal by merely mentioning a particular city.

By the middle of October, he and Rauch had had their first exploratory meeting with the SEC and were still trying to determine how to respond to the agency's subpoenas. If the lawyers decided Bahamian law allowed a response, and the bank officials authorized a response, Pitt and Rauch then had to decide how much information and documentation to provide. But the conferences were closely guarded even within the law firm, and there was no way Levine would hear a word at a business dinner.

Not long after hiring Levine, Drexel president Fred Joseph was attending a dinner party with several other Wall Street heavyweights. While discussing Drexel's recent rapid growth, Joseph boasted that he had recently hired Dennis Levine.

"Dennis who?" asked one investment banker.

David Kay had a similar conversation about Levine during the complicated and widely publicized attempt by Pantry Pride and its chief executive, Ronald Perelman, to take over Revlon Inc. He was in Miami with Peter Solomon, Levine's former boss at Shearson Lehman Brothers, working on part of the deal. Solomon, who was outspoken and occasionally sharp-tongued, was telling Kay about the troubles at his firm since the merger. Only the M&A department seemed to be immune from the exodus of real stars, Solomon said.

"We're so strong that Dennis—he was good, of course, but he was never able to make the first string with us," said Solomon.

Joseph and Kay had known from the start that making a star would be harder than buying one, but they had persisted. Levine had been handed prominent deals and thrust to stage center. He was being showcased in every possible arena, including business dinners like the one at Lutèce. And it was about to pay off.

Levine's performance in the highly visible Coastal and Crown Zellerbach transactions had established him as a power within Drexel Burnham while polishing his image outside the firm. His easygoing, helpful manner made him popular with corporate clients. And, as he sat against the wall at the corner table at Lutèce, Levine was on the verge of the victory that would put him over the top.

Since raising $2 million to purchase 40 percent of a jewelry retailer in 1978, Ronald Perelman had become one of Wall Street's shrewdest takeover artists with business interests ranging from cigars and licorice to home videocassettes and film processing. His early acquisitions had been savvy but friendly. At the beginning of 1985, however, after a bitter proxy fight, he acquired a controlling stake in Pantry Pride Inc., a chain of supermarkets and drugstores.

Perelman had a reputation as a raider who actually liked to manage the companies he bought, rather than stripping them of their assets to pay off his financing and earn a fast profit. But when he gained control of Pantry Pride, he immediately began selling off

$200 million worth of its assets to raise cash to go after his next target, Revlon Inc., the cosmetics and health-care giant whose lethargic earnings made it a prime takeover opportunity and offered Perelman the chance to revive an ailing company. His investment banking firm was, of course, Drexel Burnham.

In August 1985, Levine had taken on the role of Perelman's chief adviser in the $2.4 billion attempt to take over Revlon. Levine showed that, in addition to being charming and good on the telephone, he could be intense, serious, and hard-driving through weeks of complex maneuverings, which included defeating Revlon's poison-pill defense.

The transaction required an extraordinary amount of time from Levine, and much of it was spent on the phone with his sources in the arbitrage community trying to determine who held the big chunks of Revlon and how high the price would have to be to win the company. After the bid became public, Levine spent a considerable amount of time on the phone with reporters, explaining strategy and trying to tailor their stories in a way that would keep momentum going for the deal.

Distributing credit for a takeover's success is, in large measure, subjective and, therefore, subject to manipulation. This is particularly true in the case of a complex, high-profile transaction involving dozens of lawyers and investment bankers. How much credit goes to the investment banker who plotted strategy? How much to the banker who came up with a move to beat the poison pill? Or the lawyer who saved the deal with a last-minute technical change? Because reputation is a large factor in an investment bank's ability to attract clients, and since the evaluation of contributions is imprecise, bankers often compete for this credit.

Some participants later said that the real credit for Pantry Pride's successful takeover of Revlon should have gone to Eric Gleacher, who had moved from Lehman Brothers to Morgan Stanley, even though Morgan Stanley played a subsidiary role in the deal. But the lion's share of the acclaim wound up going to Levine. His dealings with the press, his long hours, and his unerring information from the arbitragers had drawn new attention to him and certified him as a star on Wall Street.

In a sense, the Pantry Pride victory was a rite of initiation for Levine, a symbol that, at the age of thirty-three, he had been accepted into the loose confederation of investment-banking movers and shakers who were involved in all the big-money deals on one side or another. Levine had spent his entire career trying to gain entry to that group and, with the calculated boost of Drexel Burnham, he had made it. When the Pantry Pride–Revlon transaction was sealed on November 1, he bought a case of champagne for his colleagues. He put it on his Drexel expense account.

Levine's miserliness, whether it was complaining about the $10 charge for his collect calls to Bank Leu or sticking Drexel Burnham with the tabs for his lunches with Wilkis, Reich, and Sokolow, was not reflected in the way he spent his illicit money.

The lavish spending that had begun near the end of 1983 had turned into a pattern: Levine would withdraw a big chunk of cash, $150,000 or $200,000, out of his account following a string of trading successes. A sizable amount of the money went into the down payment and renovation of his apartment. But he also used it to finance the luxury vacations he enjoyed after a rigorous spell at work. The spending seemed to ease the twin pressures of his job and his secret trading operation.

By June 1985, after working long hours on the Coastal and Crown deals and making his biggest insider killing ever on Nabisco, Levine felt he needed another vacation. He decided to make it a special trip for his wife, who would celebrate her thirty-second birthday on June 21.

On June 7, he flew to Nassau and withdrew $200,000. On June 20, Laurie and Dennis Levine sat aboard the Air France Concorde to Paris. They spent three days in Paris, staying at the Royal Monceau Hotel and eating at fine restaurants. On June 23, they flew to Nice and rented a car for the three-hour drive to Antibes, where they spent a week at the Hotel du Cap before returning to the United States in the first-class section on a Pan Am flight.

By the beginning of September, Levine was again juggling the twin pressures of glory and greed. A morning of conferences with Perelman or others involved in the Pantry Pride deal would be followed with a business lunch squeezed in before a round of afternoon meetings. Whenever he was not behind closed doors in a meeting, he was on the telephone pumping his network for information on Revlon stock. Evenings often were devoted to strategy sessions or business dinners.

He also traveled extensively that fall, sometimes on Pantry Pride business and sometimes to meet with prospective clients in their home cities. He was in St. Louis, Detroit, and Washington. He flew to Minneapolis on business on September 26 and managed a one-day trip to Nassau the following day before returning to New York for weekend meetings.

Despite the pressures of work, Levine felt the Nassau trip was important. He wanted to make sure the cover-up was on track and go through his files for incriminating material, just in case the bank decided to provide the SEC with documents, and he wanted to consult with his lawyer, Hartis Pinder, on setting up a new Panamanian company.

In addition to his trips to Nassau on September 2 and again on September 27, he accumulated voluminous reports on the twenty-eight stocks listed by the SEC, combing through his files for brokers', reports and summoning additional public information from Drexel's research department in order to construct his defense. And unlike Pletscher, Levine had neither fear of discovery nor pangs of conscience. He remained confident that the SEC could be thwarted by lies. After all, look what happened with Textron. He just had to find the time to deal with everything.

Despite his confidence in the outcome of the inquiry, Levine had agreed with Meier that he would slow his trading. In fact, he had stopped completely. It was a decision based more on his desire to keep the Swiss bankers in line and not spook them with more big winners than one of caution over the SEC. But it had the side benefit of relieving some of the pressure on him.

While Levine felt none of the sense of siege that plagued Pletscher, he was straddling two demanding obligations and, perhaps to relieve the pressures, he indulged in another luxury.

Ever since the days when a motorcycle was all he could afford, Levine had admired fast cars. The faster and more expensive, the better. He drove a top-of-the-line BMW, but he had always wanted something more exciting. In the fall of 1985, he saw no reason not to have it.

Steven Kessler Motor Cars on East Thirty-fourth Street in Manhattan is an upscale car dealership that handles only Ferraris, Maseratis, and Alfa Romeos. Levine had pondered the choices for a few weeks and shopped for the best price before ordering a new red Ferrari Testarossa, one of the sleekest, fastest, and most expensive production cars available. Only a limited number of Testarossas are produced.

On October 8, he drove into the traffic of midtown in a car that cost $95,000. He had put one-third down and assumed an auto loan for the remainder, similar to what he had done in buying his apartment. There was no point in tying up too much investment capital in a car or apartment.

He rented a garage for the car and only drove it at night or on weekends, when he would speed across one of the bridges out of Manhattan and head for the isolated country roads of Long Island, where he could crank up the car to more than a hundred miles an hour and zoom away from all the pressures represented by the soaring skyline behind him.

There was no hiding this prize. Levine boasted about his car to co-workers and had a professional photographer take a portrait of the Ferrari to hang on his office wall. If third-year associates at the firm drove BMWs and Porsches, surely one of Drexel's managing directors could afford a Ferrari without raising any eyebrows.

Leo Wang rides the subway to work. That fall, he and Peter Sonnenthal were also very busy. Sonnenthal, under Wang's watchful eye, had devoted several weeks to analyzing the trading information provided by Merrill Lynch, slowly assembling the evidence that would be necessary if the case went to court. He isolated the transactions of the bank and the Merrill Lynch brokers on each stock and then compared the purchase and sale dates with announcements of takeovers or other corporate actions.

In response to an SEC request, any brokerage firm registered to do business on the U.S. markets is required to disclose the names of its account holders and a list of every transaction made through any account. While most brokerage firms comply voluntarily, physically retrieving the information can require an extensive commitment of time and labor.

Sonnenthal prepared separate requests for every brokerage firm in New York. He asked whether they had an account for Bank Leu International or Bernhard Meier. If such an account existed, he requested a list of every trade made through the account since its inception.

In addition, he had forms, called "blue sheets," sent to brokerage houses requesting information on trading in all twenty-eight stocks on the list. He also went back through the agency's investigative files and retrieved information generated by earlier inquiries into some of the same stocks, such as Textron and Thiokol. Checking the files on those stocks uncovered the stalled inquiry into Euro-Partners, which added another layer of information. An intriguing element was the fact that one of Bank Leu's officers sat on the EuroPartners board until mid-1985.

As the information began to flow in from the brokerage houses, there was no easy way to sort through it. Bank Leu had accounts at more than a dozen firms and the bank traded thousands of shares through those accounts. Not every purchase involved a takeover stock, but every transaction had to be analyzed.

Sonnenthal began to see that the bank's purchases through Merrill Lynch in the twenty-eight stocks were only part of the story. Simultaneous orders for the same stocks had been placed through brokers at E. F. Hutton, Dean Witter Reynolds, and many other houses. And the number of takeover stocks was growing.

Sonnenthal devoted all of his time to the expanding Bank Leu investigation, working sixty to seventy hours a week assembling and analyzing records. Wang did not have that luxury. In February, he had been promoted to a branch chief in the enforcement division, which meant he supervised the work of seven or eight other lawyers. But he kept in close touch with Sonnenthal, partly because the other lawyer had been at the commission less than a year and still needed some supervision, partly because he was intrigued by the case.

Neither lawyer knew where the investigation might lead. Perhaps it would turn out to be another dead end. But there were tantalizing hints that they were on to something big. An offshore bank was involved and the extent of the trading was growing with each batch of documents. Plus, there was the pattern of scattering purchases among many brokers, rather than simply placing the order through one or two houses. Someone appeared to have gone to a lot of trouble to avoid creating a stir in the market. They just had to find out who.

On a shelf in John Shad's office at the SEC building in Washington is a pair of size-ten hobnail boots. Soon after taking over as chairman of the agency in 1981, Shad had told a reporter the SEC was going to come down on insider trading "with hobnail boots."

The remark created a minor sensation on Wall Street and not long after making it, Shad was scheduled to testify before Congress. His staff presented him with the boots as a gift and wanted him to wear them over to Capitol Hill for his testimony. He didn't have the guts.

Shad, who began as a young stock analyst in New York after graduating from Harvard Business School in the 1940s, invested wisely and earned a personal fortune in the stock market. He was vice chairman and head of corporate finance at E. F. Hutton when President Ronald Reagan appointed him to the SEC post in 1981.

Sharing the Reagan administration's emphasis on deregulation, he presided over fundamental changes in the relationship between the agency and the nation's business community, such as the creation of the SEC's shelf-registration rule, which allows companies to file a single registration statement to cover securities they expect to sell over the next two years. It saved business a small fortune.

Shad also worked hard to replace the adversarial relationship between the SEC and Wall Street with a more workable and co-operative arrangement. But there was no place in that arrangement for tolerance of insider trading.

Some free-market enthusiasts would have preferred Shad to take a more laissez-faire attitude toward insider trading. They contend that chasing insider trading is a waste of government resources. Let stock prices reflect all information, inside or not, they argue. Further, they say, policing insider trading is an impossible task that employs vast amounts of SEC resources at the expense of more efficient and important regulatory activities.

Others compare insider trading to a rigged poker game: if you know some players have aces up their sleeves, you are less likely to play the game.

Shad and his supporters, including the executives of the major stock exchanges, view insider trading as a serious threat to the integrity of the markets. It is an integrity based as much on perception as on reality, and the small investors must maintain the perception that they have the same opportunity for the benefits as the big boys.

Delivering on the promise to clean up the game, however, had turned out to be difficult.

Part of the reason was the explosion of information that had accompanied the takeover wave of the 1980s. No longer was confidential information on a pending corporate matter restricted to a longtime investment banker, an in-house lawyer, and a handful of corporate executives. There were forty-five takeovers of $1 billion or more from 1981 to 1984 compared with twelve in the previous decade. The size of the deals led to a new complexity that ballooned the number of people with insider knowledge. Up to one hundred lawyers, bankers, consultants, corporate executives, public relations experts, secretaries, and proofreaders may legitimately be aware of a major merger or acquisition.

To deal with the blizzard of suspects, the SEC developed a computer program to compare the times of transactions with the times of news announcements, grouping traders by name, address, and broker, and cross-referencing officers and directors of the companies involved. But printouts can be two feet high and analyzing them can take months.

Another part of the reason a crackdown was so hard was something that had been clear to Levine for a long time: the SEC has great difficulty disproving a lie.

Ira Lee Sorkin, who had been a federal prosecutor in New York, was an attorney in private practice before he was named head of the SEC regional office in May 1984. Although he was not involved in the Levine investigation, Sorkin is an aggressive attorney who was frustrated to find that insiders could often lie to the agency with little chance of getting caught.

"I'd look in on a deposition, where a young attorney was taking some guy's testimony, and I'd listen for a while and I'd hear enough to know the guy was lying," says Sorkin, who has since returned to private practice in New York. "The young attorney would come out and shake his head. He knew it, too. These are very tough cases to make. You don't have bloodstains. You don't have eyewitnesses to the bank robbery. You have two guys talking to each other and if they both deny they spoke, how do you make the case?

"A guy could tell you, 'I'm dating a Gypsy and she's got a crystal ball,' and you can have a tough time proving he's lying."

One of the SEC's recurring complaints was that penalties for insider trading were not stiff enough. Until 1984, the standard punishment for someone caught trading on inside information was the "disgorgement" of their illegal profits. Timothy Wirth, then a Democratic congressman from Colorado and later elected senator, responded by sponsoring the 1984 Insider Trading Sanctions Act. It enabled the SEC to sue a violator for up to three times his illegal profits and demand the return of the profits as well. Suddenly, the risks of insider trading were greater.

The SEC still lacked the authority to bring a criminal case against anyone for insider trading or other securities frauds. Criminal jurisdiction remained with the Department of Justice. Relations between the two law enforcement agencies have sometimes been tender. Gradually, however, relations between the SEC and the Justice Department improved in the early 1980s and, as a result of that new cooperation, the U.S. Attorney's Office in Manhattan developed an interest and expertise in insider trading that proved invaluable to the SEC in many investigations.

With the Justice Department involved, anyone who lied to the commission or concealed evidence faced charges of perjury or obstruction of justice, with the possibility of jail terms. In addition, the SEC could impose its civil sanctions and the Justice Department could turn around and file criminal charges of securities fraud or, when the profits were not reported, income tax evasion.

Slowly, the number of insider cases brought by the SEC began to mount: twenty cases in 1982, twenty-four in 1983, thirteen in 1984, and twenty in 1985. Yet the problem not only persisted, it seemed to get worse. There was criticism that the SEC had launched most of its insider trading cases against people far removed from Wall Street's inner circles. The Paul Thayer case had deflected some of that criticism, but the sentiment on Capitol Hill and within the financial community in 1985 was that the SEC was letting too many real insiders get away.

On April 29, 1985, *Business Week* magazine published an influential cover story entitled "The Epidemic of Insider Trading: The SEC Is Fighting a Losing Battle to Halt Stock-Market Abuses." The magazine commissioned an analysis of activity in the stock prices of all the takeovers, mergers, and leveraged buy-outs involving companies listed on the New York and American stock exchanges during 1983 and 1984. In looking at the price one month before and one day before the transaction was announced, the study found that in 72 percent of the cases the price rose. Expressing an assessment widely held on Wall Street, the magazine wrote, "Insider trading is running rampant, despite a major law enforcement crackdown and toughened penalties."

The article angered John Shad, and the heat was turned up on the enforcement division and its new chief, Gary Lynch. The word had to go out: insider trading was no longer worth the risk.

Insiders often are professional risk-takers and are aware that trading on confidential information involves taking a calculated risk. If they determine the chances of getting caught are slim, particularly balanced against the potential rewards, they will take the risk. If they find the chance of getting caught is too great, presumably they won't take the chance. Another element of the equation involves punishment. Before 1984, insiders only had to return their illegal profits; the 1984 act gave the SEC the right to seek the return of the profits plus a penalty equal to three times the profit. In addition, the more active cooperation with the Justice Department increased the chances a person convicted of insider trading would go to jail.

The SEC enforcement division had a staff of about 110, and its responsibilities extended beyond insider trading to a full and time-consuming range of securities-law violations. Even at the height of the crackdown, only about 10 percent of the division's resources were devoted to insider trading.

What the division needed was to create the impression that its ability to detect insider trading was far greater than in reality it was—what one lawyer called "the illusion of three dimensions." The lawyers, investment bankers, and stockbrokers had to believe that insider trading was no longer a safe crime, that the risk of getting caught had reached the point where it was no longer worth the gamble. The concept is called deterrence in some circles, scare tactics in others.

The news media rarely create public reaction; they respond to it. Insider trading is not a cosmic event that demands press attention or public interest. In order to achieve the deterrence sought by the SEC, a case would have to become a major news story and dominate the media. The SEC needed something that would capture the public imagination and drive the message onto the front pages and evening news for weeks. The agency could not create a case to fit its needs. But with the right combination of luck and hard work, anything was possible.

Pitt and Rauch got a chilly reception from the government on October 1 when they had their first meeting with Wang, Sonnenthal, and Paul Fischer, the SEC lawyers handling the investigation. The agency lawyers pressed for information about the bank's position and, while they were willing to give the bank more time to comply, the government attorneys wanted to know what the institution's explanation would be for the trading. Pitt and Rauch said there were legal considerations involving Bahamian law. They refused to disclose how they intended to respond to the subpoenas or how the bank would explain the trades. They refused even to concede that they represented the bank.

This was a critical point because the subpoena for bank records that Meier had received did not clearly cover the bank and could be challenged in court. Meier was not a director of the bank or an officer with control over its records. Serving the bank's subpoena on him may have been convenient, but there were legal questions about whether it was proper and could thus demand any response from the bank.

Meier, on the other hand, had been properly served with the demand for his personal records, so they told the SEC that, for this meeting, they represented only Meier. Meier's subpoena had demanded his records by October 1, and Pitt and Rauch argued that they should have until the end of the month to comply with the request. When the SEC lawyers refused to grant that much additional time, Pitt said they would take it anyway.

After leaving SEC headquarters, Rauch and Pitt wrote a letter to the agency complaining about the failure to grant the extension and repeating that, because of the time involved in obtaining the documents, they were taking until the end of October.

Throughout October, a team of paralegals from the law firm assembled public information about the twenty-eight stocks in an attempt to confirm Meier's story. In an exhaustive task that paralleled Sonnenthal's research, the paralegals built a chronology for each stock, listing the dates any takeovers or other major corporate news was announced and checking the availability of public information about each stock prior to the announcements. If Pitt and Rauch were to defend Meier's claim that he had made the trades based on information in the public domain, the lawyers needed to know how much information had actually been available regarding each stock at the time of the purchases.

There were also frequent telephone conversations with Coulson and Meier in Nassau. When Pitt and Rauch had left the Bahamas in September, they had a rough game plan in mind, though they had not yet received final authorization for it from the bank. They intended to tell the SEC eventually that the agency would not receive the names of any bank clients because of restrictions under Bahamian law. They would explain that the names did not really matter because the clients had passive roles. Meier had made the trades on his own judgment and allocated them to the various accounts managed by the bank.

If the SEC insisted on the names, Pitt and Rauch would warn that the bank was prepared to fight the demand in court, a process that could tie up the case for years. However, if the SEC agreed to its proposal to withhold the names of customers, the bank would provide some of its records without the names of the customers and Meier would testify before the agency about how he had selected the stocks.

By mid-October, Coulson had approved the proposed plan.

The story got its first test flight in November. Anyone who believed in omens might have recognized one that day. Pitt and Rauch were scheduled to return to the SEC and make the proposal to the same three lawyers. The meeting was scheduled for 11:00 A.M. on the fourth, and Rauch was flying in on the 9:00 A.M. shuttle from New York. As soon as Rauch took his seat, however, the pilot announced that air traffic would delay the departure for at least an hour. That meant Rauch would miss the meeting, so he got off the plane and telephoned Pitt to see if he wanted to postpone. In the face of the SEC's recent accusations of stalling, postponing did not seem like a good idea to Pitt, so he asked another partner, James Schropp, to accompany him.

Across a table from Wang, Sonnenthal, and Fischer, Pitt explained his understanding that the trades had been made for accounts managed by the bank. As a result, he said, there appeared to be no customer involvement. He offered to negotiate an agreement with the SEC that would allow the agency to obtain certain bank records and the testimony of the bank's portfolio manager, Bernhard Meier, to back up the story. The documents, he said, would be "redacted," a legal term for removing certain information, to eliminate material identifying clients.

From the government's standpoint, the agreement would avoid litigation and speed its investigation. But the SEC lawyers were suspicious of the managed-accounts story. They demanded to know how soon they could see the supporting documents.

Pitt said he needed more time. He and Rauch had returned from Nassau without inspecting the statements that Meier said would support his story. Pitt was not about to sign an agreement to provide documents that he had not inspected.

The bank had, however, authorized Pitt and Rauch to cooperate with the SEC to a limited extent in an attempt to end the inquiry. The bank could have gone to court and fought the investigation, but the service of the subpoena on Meier had weakened their case somewhat. Furthermore, the public relations impact of a court fight with the SEC might damage the bank's standing in Nassau and the international financial community. If the managed-accounts story and Meier's testimony were accepted by the agency, the bank could dispense with the inquiry without a costly and potentially embarrassing court fight.

15.

Liquidating Positions

On November 4, Bruno Pletscher returned to Nassau from a month's holiday in Switzerland. He found himself right back in the middle of the cover-up scheme.

Meier had spent most of October working on the stories he was preparing for the lawyers explaining why he bought each of the takeover stocks. He had blocked Pitt's repeated requests for documents with a variety of excuses about the press of other business and his inability to locate the material he required.

On Pletscher's first day back in the office, Meier gave him a set of the typewritten stories—fat paragraphs analyzing each company's financial position, trends in particular industries, references to newspaper stories and broker's reports. They were the truths upon which the lie was to be based.

He explained to Pletscher that these were rough drafts of the documents he intended to present to the lawyers and, if necessary, later to the SEC. He said they had been compiled from information provided by Diamond, but that they were incomplete. Diamond was bringing additional information to Nassau later in the week.

He had other news. The documentation had arrived establishing

Diamond's new company, International Gold. Pletscher's return provided the second signature required to withdraw the money from Diamond Holdings and transfer it to the intermediate company, Midu Enterprises. The funds would be invested in the name of Midu for a short time and then transferred to the International Gold account.

Before starting the transfers, however, Meier's first priority was enlisting Pletscher's guidance in creating his bogus personal account for the lawyers. He was aware that negotiations between the SEC and Pitt and Rauch could result in his having to testify soon and require him to provide his personal trading records. He wanted the false record to be ready.

"Bernie, I'll have to get the computer program completed and then you can put in the information as you like," Pletscher told him.

In snatches of time over the next two weeks, Pletscher created a special program on his personal computer at the bank to reproduce an account statement for Meier, who went through his trading statement and marked the items that he wanted excluded from the new account.

Once the program was completed, Meier sat down at the terminal in a small office. Pletscher watched as he typed the information into the new statement. Along with excluding specific stock purchases, Meier withheld several money transfers recorded in the official statement. One involved several thousand dollars to a bank in Delhi, New York, in August 1984. Meier said the money involved a real estate venture that had nothing to do with the SEC inquiry. Meier asked Pletscher to alter the bank's backup documentation for the transaction and Pletscher agreed reluctantly. Meier provided no further explanation of why he wanted the transfer so thoroughly erased, but the date coincided with his $10,000 loan to Brian Campbell, the former Merrill Lynch broker.

Meier stored the altered statement on a disc until the process was completed. Then Pletscher printed it for Meier on bank stationery. Meier's original, unaltered statement was put in a sealed envelope and the envelope was placed in a file apart from the regular bank account statements.

The authentic appearance of the new statement surprised and pleased Meier. It also reminded him of the possibilities for creating an entire array of new accounts for the Levine trades. He had learned from Pitt during October that the bank might have to produce statements for the managed accounts for the SEC. He also had learned that the names on those statements probably would be blacked out so the bank would not violate Bahamian secrecy laws by identifying a customer.

Any number of nameless new accounts could be created and Meier could allocate the trades from Levine's account to them. He could sit down at the terminal and conjure up an unlimited number of anonymous new accounts where he could park transactions covering thousands of shares of stock from Levine's account. Since the names would be blacked out, no one could know there were no actual names for the accounts. It was a way around Levine's refusal to come up with real beneficiaries and create real companies for his subaccounts. And it was a way to do it without altering the bank's computer, which he knew Pletscher would not allow.

"You've got to make up a series of accounts," he insisted to Pletscher. "You can make forty or fifty accounts for Diamond's trades."

But Pletscher refused: "If you want me to say that there was more than one account for Diamond, you have to have Diamond authorize the paperwork."

Meier looked at Pletscher with disbelief. The solution was so simple, so easy. How could he reject it? But Pletscher would not budge. He still believed that only the customer could authorize any changes in his account. Levine had refused to authorize the creation of subaccounts. As far as Pletscher was concerned, Levine's refusal shut the door on any attempt to allocate the Diamond trades to fictitious accounts.

Levine had been working on his own defense tactics during the fall. One of his chief concerns was how he would explain all of his trips to Nassau if the SEC learned of them through the U.S. Customs Service or Bahamian authorities. He told Wilkis that he had devised two explanations. One plan was to claim that he was a gambling addict who had gone to Nassau for the action in the casinos. To buttress that contention, he told Wilkis he was considering joining Gamblers Anonymous. His second cover story would be that he had been shopping for a condominium in Nassau; he considered buying a condo that fall to support the claim.

There was also an escape plan. Levine told Wilkis that he had kept "getaway money" in case he had to flee the country in a hurry. Levine would go to Brazil, which he had learned did not extradite people to the United States for insider trading crimes.

At the end of the first week of November, Levine arrived at Bank Leu carrying a plastic shopping bag bulging with the documents he had assembled to back up Meier. He accompanied Meier to the large conference room and, when Pletscher stopped in later, the men were going over this new batch of material.

"Have you heard anything new about the SEC?" Pletscher asked Levine.

"The SEC is on a fishing trip. You don't have to worry that they could prove anything," Levine said.

He assured Pletscher that he had been careful not to leave any trace of his identity in his trading. He said he traveled to and from the Bahamas through different cities, used cash to buy his tickets and pay other expenses, and avoided staying overnight in the islands.

Levine was confident that he was smarter than the other insiders who had been caught by the SEC in recent years. "It's just a fishing trip," he repeated. "They can't find any pattern to these stocks. Not all of the trades were in stocks where my firm was involved. I was only involved in negotiations on a few of the twenty-eight takeovers they're looking at."

As always, Levine was self-assured, speaking authoritatively to the Swiss bankers. Levine's confidence, the ever-present impression that he knew what he was doing, had been a critical factor in the continued cooperation of Pletscher and Meier.

Levine had sensed from the start of the scheme that Pletscher was less committed to the cover-up than Meier. Levine and Meier had enjoyed a good rapport from the first, and he was sure that Meier would go along with the scheme. Meier had kept Levine up to date on the negotiations with the SEC, and he knew Meier might have to testify soon. He was sure the banker was charming and convincing enough to pull it off.

But Levine had often cautioned Wilkis that the insider chain was only as strong as its weakest link. In early November, he wanted to ensure that Pletscher, the possible weak link, did not deviate from the cover-up scheme. He also wanted to make certain Meier knew how to approach the SEC.

"You're still continuing with the plan?" he asked Pletscher.

"Yes, yes, we are," Pletscher replied. "We are going with it."

"Good. If you continue with this plan, then we won't have a problem. And Bernie, you just go and testify. You won't have a problem. You just have to go there relaxed. I told you before, you lie to the SEC and you get out of it. The whole thing will be over. The SEC does not have a single bit of evidence to prove the opposite."

As he had in previous meetings, Levine urged the bankers to destroy the withdrawal slips in his account. He repeated that the slips were the weak spot, the remaining link between his identity and the trading. Again, Levine relented in the face of Pletscher's stubborn refusal to destroy the slips.

Even the nagging worry over the withdrawal slips did not shake Levine's faith in his scheme. The plan he had laid out in September was progressing smoothly, and he had no reason to doubt its ultimate success. His faith was rooted partly in the ease with which he had deflected the Textron inquiry almost exactly a year before. The success of that lie had confirmed Levine's deeply held belief that not only was he smarter than the lawyers and bureaucrats at the SEC, he was smarter than anybody else on Wall Street. He was the guy who had fought his way to the top without a Harvard degree or the right social connections. He'd made it on brains and hustle. He was the guy with a million-dollar apartment and a new Ferrari, pulling down a million dollars a year at Drexel Burnham and amassing a hidden fortune that would soon bankroll his transformation from a paid adviser to a principal player.

As he sat in Bank Leu's office that day, Levine could see no reason why he shouldn't go back to trading. "I hate sitting tight and earning only bank-rate interest when I could easily be making a hundred percent profit by trading," Levine told the bankers.

Pletscher, who had been relieved when Levine halted his trading, was reluctant to permit a resumption. It was one less worry while he dealt with the pressures of the SEC inquiry. He told Levine he was concerned that trading would draw more attention to the bank's activities from the SEC, but Levine countered that the bank's failure to buy takeover stocks since the SEC inquiry started might indicate to the agency that the bank had something to hide. It was an argument that had become familiar to both Pletscher and Meier over the past few weeks, but Pletscher continued to refuse to allow Levine to trade.

The SEC's October deadline for Meier's testimony and records passed. Pitt and Rauch negotiated with the SEC throughout November over the wording of the agreement that would allow the agency to receive the redacted bank documents and the testimony of Meier. The lawyers kept the bankers informed of their progress and said they expected an agreement by the end of the month or early December.

In October, Meier had sent Pitt a draft copy of his explanations for the trades. Pitt had told him that the law firm's analysts had discovered no single source of information or pattern for all twenty-eight trades, such as the involvement of one investment bank or law firm in all twenty-eight transactions.

But as the possibility of his testimony neared, Meier began to worry. He was afraid he would be left standing alone before the agency after he perjured himself. His Bahamian work permit was about to expire and he was scheduled to be transferred back to Zurich before the end of the year. In his absence, the others at the bank could deny any knowledge that Meier had lied. They could claim they believed his story about being the smart guy who picked the stocks. If the others were not committed to the scheme, they could place all the blame on Meier after he lied to the U.S. government. He wanted a united front, in writing, as insurance against the risk he would be taking when he appeared before the SEC.

He appealed to Pletscher to help him convince Fraysse that, as the best course for the bank, they should sign an agreement supporting Meier's testimony. Pletscher finally agreed to help, and he and Meier went to Fraysse to explain the proposal.

The Central Bank of the Bahamas had been notified in writing on November 12 that Fraysse would be leaving Bank Leu and Pletscher would replace him as bank manager. The letter also said that Meier would be returning to Zurich for "other duties" with the bank. Fraysse had been at the bank little throughout the fall and he seemed to Pletscher to be more detached than ever from his responsibilities there.

When Meier and Pletscher asked him whether he would agree to sign a document supporting Meier's story, Fraysse agreed without complaint. He said he could draft a memo outlining their general agreement. They decided that they needed the assistance of Richard Coulson, the bank adviser who was also a lawyer, and he was invited to a meeting at 10:30 A.M. the following day, Thursday, November 21.

The three full-time bank employees had been drawn into Levine's illegal trading scheme and the subsequent cover-up through their own actions. Fraysse and Meier were sophisticated businessmen who had nonetheless copied Levine's trades. Pletscher had allowed his need for money to draw him into copying the trades, although he realized it was a "gray area." Fraysse, as the bank's general manager, had approved the original plan to lie to the SEC. Meier and Pletscher had destroyed evidence. Coulson was by far the least involved. He had not copied Levine's trades and he had never profited from the insider trading in any way.

Fraysse was an inveterate memo writer. He had written a memo on Levine's first visit to the bank and he had penned the "sailing a bit too close to the wind" memo in 1981. He memorialized the November 21 meeting in a nine-paragraph memo marked "secret" and captioned "S.E.C. CASE."

The memo was crafted cleverly. It placed Fraysse, Pletscher, and Coulson squarely behind Meier's story. Yet it avoided any indication that Meier's version of events was not true. It even created the false impression that the entire operation had been approved by Rauch and Pitt.

There were six points in the memo:

Item 1: The case is well known to all present and since the beginning of the affair Mr. B. Meier has punctually informed all present of its developments and the defensive action taken by our lawyers, in Washington, over the past few weeks. Our chairman, during his recent visit to Nassau, was given a full debriefing.

Item 2: Mr. B. Meier reported on a telephone conversation he had with Mr. Harvey Pitt, on 8th November 1985. The specialists employed by Mr. Pitt have detected no particular pattern in our dealings, no involvement of other investment banks in takeover situations, no industry pattern, etc.

Item 3: We maintain our position of an aggressive, imaginative and successful investment bank acting on a discretionary basis for its clients. Our Investment Department has been particularly astute in its selections.

Item 4: Mr. B. Meier has prepared an explanatory sheet, very well presented and documented, for every case listed by the SEC. These various documents were tabled. They have been submitted to our lawyers.

Item 5: Mr. B. Meier is still prepared to testify under subpoena (the SEC has not accepted to lift the subpoena for the testimony). This involves the presentation of various personal documents, including Mr. Meier's own bank account. Since this account has registered Mr. Meier's private dealings in various investment matters, including property in Europe, in association with European friends who could be victimized by the SEC, the statements to be produced should not include such names or destination of funds. They will be adjusted accordingly.

Item 6: All present took note of the latest developments and agreed unanimously to the procedure defined in Item 5 above, which will enable Mr. Meier to testify without exposing innocent parties, if our lawyers are still of the opinion that this is the right approach.

All four men signed the memo and each was given a copy. Pletscher placed the original in the bank's files. Meier's tensions were relieved, his confidence restored.

The Securities and Exchange Commission sponsors regular panel discussions on problems and issues confronting the industry. The discussions are conducted at the agency's headquarters in Washington and are called roundtables. The sometimes lively exchanges have brought the sessions a measure of prestige and attracted some of the leading minds in the securities business.

On November 26, 1985, the subject of the roundtable was recent takeover developments, and SEC chairman John Shad and two commissioners, Charles Cox and Aulana Peters, were on hand as hosts. The list of participants included many of the luminaries in the field, such as lawyers Arthur Fleischer from Fried, Frank; Martin Lipton from Wachtell, Lipton; and New York City comptroller Harrison Goldin. Eric Gleacher, the former Lehman Brothers partner who headed mergers and acquisitions at Morgan Stanley, was on the panel and so was his former associate, Dennis Levine.

David Kay, the head of mergers at Drexel Burnham, had been invited to the roundtable, but he had backed out earlier in the week and Levine had been selected as his substitute. As he shook hands that morning with Shad and the other commissioners, Levine knew that he would not be there if the SEC had the slightest suspicion of his involvement with Bank Leu. It was an irony he relished.

The meeting was called for 10:00 A.M. and the first topic was whether additional laws were necessary to regulate trading in the shares of target companies once a tender offer was under way. But the discussion eventually turned to the broader question of whether the wave of takeovers that was restructuring America was good for the economy.

Not surprisingly, Levine was a strong advocate of takeovers as a vehicle for streamlining American business and contributing to the general well-being of the economy.

"We do believe that these activities create wealth in the economy," he said. "There is clearly a flow of funds into the hands of shareholders and institutions which by and large is reinvested in the secondary market and many times invested in consumption and thereby stimulates spending and production."

Toward the end of the day, the discussion turned to evidence of possible stock manipulation in recent takeovers and to attempts by raiders and corporations to avoid the commission's regulations requiring a buyer acquiring more than 5 percent of a company's stock to notify the SEC. The written notice, which must be filed within ten days, must declare whether there is any intention to seek additional stock and control of the company.

In recent years, there had been allegations of collaborative efforts to buy up large blocks of stock in a target company, keeping the purchases under 5 percent to avoid the notice requirement. Shad said the commission was "aggressively pursuing" investigations into various stock manipulation cases, but Marty Lipton urged him to push harder.

"I think it would be worth the commission's while to look at the trading in some of the more notorious takeovers of the past two years," said Lipton. "Look at the trading pattern in the half dozen or so where there were no five percent filings but a series of rumors, very, very high trading in the securities of the company, and then the trading would drop off again and there would be another burst of trading and stories day after day that the company was a target, was going to be the subject of an offer. Only the commission has the power to get at the facts behind this, but I think there are enough instances—[this] is a fairly new phenomenon, I would say within the last year, eighteen months, but there are enough instances of it that it is something that ought to be looked at very closely."

Levine then offered Shad his advice: "The other thing is I don't think you should limit your analysis of that phenomenon to the corporations' activities. If you look at some of the other major transactions that took place, Nabisco Brands, for instance, General Foods, both of which had significant run-ups in the stock, raiders presumably were not involved. It's an isolated pattern that develops from time to time with certain transactions not always precipitated by raiders."

Levine flew back to New York that night on the New York Air shuttle flight. He felt he was at the height of his prestige and power—and cleverness.

Three days later, the Friday after Thanksgiving, Levine returned to Bank Leu determined to shake off the enervating effects of the SEC inquiry. Having just confirmed that the SEC knew nothing of his scheme, he was fed up with sitting back waiting until the investigation disappeared. He wanted to trade, make money. And he wanted to get some money.

Using the system he had designed in September, Levine got $100,000 in cash out of his account on November 29. Meier actually signed the official bank form and handed the cash to Levine in return for Levine's signature on a blank piece of paper. It was his first withdrawal since the SEC inquiry had started and his first withdrawal from his new account.

More than $10 million had been transferred into his International Gold account through the circuitous process designed by Pletscher. Levine wanted to use it to begin trading. He had not bought or sold a stock since August and his frustration had become too much to contain. Each day seemed to bring a new spate of tips that he could have transformed into profitable trades.

With typical bravado, he insisted that he must be allowed to resume trading immediately. He promised that he would be extremely careful in selecting stocks, avoiding big purchases that might create a stir in the market. But he was tired of being constrained by what he viewed as the bankers' unnecessary timidity.

"We wouldn't like any situations where we are participating in securities trades that are subject to takeovers within a short period after purchasing," Pletscher cautioned.

Levine said he could limit his trading to takeover stocks in which public information justified the purchases. He said he would trade on his own confidential information, but when he made a purchase he would tell Meier where he could find enough public information to support the trade if the SEC or the bank's lawyers questioned the transaction. The plan sounded reasonable to Pletscher and Meier, and they agreed that Levine could resume trading on a selective basis with the bank's discretion to cut down the size of his orders.

Levine was again rebuffed in his attempt to persuade Pletscher to destroy the withdrawal slips from his Diamond and Diamond International accounts. But he had another plan for distancing himself from the earlier accounts.

He told the two bankers he wanted to change his code name. He would no longer be Mr. Diamond. From that point on, he would telephone the bank under the name "Mr. Gold." Pletscher and Meier balked at the use of "gold," explaining that it might cause his account to be confused with the bank's gold trading. They suggested that Levine choose the name of another commodity, and he settled on "Mr. Wheat."

Despite Levine's attempt to erase the alias that tied him to the previous accounts, however, "Mr. Wheat" never stuck and the bank employees continued to refer to him as "Diamond."

On December 3, Levine telephoned the bank from New York to place his first order in months. Drexel Burnham had been hired by GAF Corporation, a large chemical and building supplies firm, to arrange financing for a hostile takeover bid for Union Carbide Corporation, a chemical industry giant ten times the size of GAF. Union Carbide stock appeared to be a bargain because the price had dropped after a December 1984 leak of poison gas from a Carbide plant in Bhopal, India, killed more than 2,000 people. GAF had already acquired 10 percent of Carbide's stock, and Drexel was preparing a letter stating the firm was "highly confident" it could raise $1.5 billion to finance GAF's bid for control.

Pletscher took Levine's call and listened as he explained: "This won't draw any attention to the bank's account because there's enough public information that a portfolio manager could buy Union Carbide on his own judgment. I know more, but there's enough public stuff out there that this won't cause you any problems with the SEC. If a question comes up, you can point to the public information."

Levine bought 100,000 shares of Union Carbide at a total cost of $6.3 million. Pletscher bought 300 shares for his own account, but Meier, because of his pending departure from Nassau, did not purchase any stock. After the bid for Carbide was announced, the stock did not run up as quickly as Levine had expected. The market was wary of the deal, partly because of concerns about Carbide's enormous liabilities from Bhopal and partly because the firm appeared prepared to go to great lengths to fight the bid. It would take awhile, but Levine was prepared to wait.

In the meantime, Levine bought a large stake in RCA Corporation after learning of a pending takeover bid for the giant electronics firm.

On Monday, December 9, Levine called to place an order for a purchase of stock in MidCon Corporation, a natural gas pipeline company. Since most of his account was tied up in Carbide and RCA, the purchase would have to be small, but Levine was eager to invest something in what he viewed as another sure winner. MidCon was a Drexel client involved in the acquisition of another energy company. Levine had learned MidCon would announce a dividend increase on Tuesday, a disclosure certain to send the price of the company's stock up.

Meier took the call, but asked Levine to talk to Pletscher. When Pletscher came on the line, he explained to Levine that the lawyers were insisting that the bank halt all transactions in takeover stocks until the SEC inquiry was finished.

"We'd like for you to liquidate your positions in Union Carbide and RCA and stop trading for the time being," Pletscher told Levine. "We want to sell your stocks and just maintain the cash on a deposit basis."

Levine complained, saying the deals hadn't started to roll yet and he would lose money on the RCA stock and barely break even on Union Carbide if he were forced to sell this early. When Pletscher persisted, Levine recognized he could not afford to antagonize the bank and said: "It's a shame to do it, but I guess I understand. Go ahead and sell them both."

As a means for recouping some of his RCA losses, however, Levine insisted on going ahead with the MidCon purchase because it was not a takeover deal. He said the bank could sell MidCon the next day when a dividend increase was announced.

The Union Carbide stock was sold and Levine's profit was only $127,062. Pletscher also sold his Carbide holdings and broke even. Selling early on RCA cost Levine $244,815, the second-largest loss of his trading career. The same day, the bank bought 10,000 shares of MidCon for Levine's account and sold it Tuesday for a profit of $64,033, a tidy amount for an overnight investment, but not enough to offset the RCA loss.

Although Levine had no idea MidCon was his last trade, he was concerned about the bank's decision to halt his trading again and decided to make a weekend trip to Nassau to survey the situation. What Levine had no way of knowing, of course, was that the liquidation of his stock positions was part of the new strategy for handling the SEC investigation, the strategy demanded by Rauch and Pitt.

16.

No Longer Valid

December 2 was a Monday, and when Michael Rauch arrived at his office in New York he told the chief of paralegals he needed someone to accompany him to Nassau on Wednesday to copy some records. He suggested picking a bright hard worker who deserved a leisurely trip to the Bahamas. The work would probably be finished Friday and the paralegal could enjoy a weekend of sunshine before returning to New York. Two hundred miles away in Fried, Frank's Washington office, Harvey Pitt was arranging for a paralegal to go with him on the same trip.

Meier had told Pitt that the twenty-eight stocks had been divided among forty to fifty individual and corporate accounts that he managed. The paralegals would "redact" the statements for each account, using special masking tape to cover information that might identify the name of the client to the government. The documents would then be copied for the lawyers to review and eventually submit to the SEC.

After weeks of negotiations with the SEC, Pitt and Rauch had reached a tentative compromise that allowed the case to move forward without either side conceding a legal principle. Several drafts of the agreement had been sent back and forth and the fine points were still being worked out. Under the tentative agreement, the bank would provide redacted versions of its records to show that the trades had been spread among many accounts. Meier would furnish his personal trading and business records and, after the SEC lawyers reviewed the material, he would be available for testimony. In return, the SEC would withhold its demand for the complete bank records and the names of the customers who held the managed accounts.

Paul Fischer and Leo Wang remained suspicious of the bank's story. They insisted on reserving the right to renew the full demand if they determined that the records and Meier's testimony did not verify the managed-accounts theory. Rauch and Pitt responded that the SEC would have to obtain a court order to get any additional information from the bank.

Attorneys in the enforcement division at the SEC frequently juggle a dozen or more complicated investigations at one time. Each one can be demanding and time-consuming. Sonnenthal's exclusive commitment to the Bank Leu investigation was creating a burden on other lawyers in the division, and Fischer was under pressure to show progress on the inquiry.

"Where is the agreement?" Fischer demanded Monday morning when he telephoned Pitt. "Where are the trading records? Let's get going. This thing has been dragging out."

Pitt tried to be soothing. He assured Fischer that he and the bank were moving as fast as possible. He said he and Rauch were taking a team of paralegals to Nassau in the middle of the week. He expected to have the records by the following week.

On Wednesday, Pitt and Rauch flew to Nassau. Accompanying them were two paralegals, Amy Jedlicka from the New York office and Dede Dunegan from the Washington office. They had reservations at the Cable Beach Hotel, a sparkling new $100-million complex on the ocean which included a 20,000-square-foot casino.

The women checked into their separate rooms and Rauch and Pitt moved into a two-bedroom suite with a stunning view of the ocean. They set up a mini-office in the living room of the suite and awaited the arrival of Bernie Meier, who was supposed to bring them the records that the bank had been assembling over the past few weeks.

From the start, Meier had resisted producing any records for the American lawyers. He argued many times with Pletscher and Coulson that the lawyers represented the bank and they should accept the bank's story and relay it to the SEC. As a Swiss bank operating in the Bahamas, he said, Bank Leu had no business providing its lawyers with the records of any customer accounts.

The sentiments of the other bank officials were against Meier, but he argued that presenting the bank's omnibus account should be enough. The omnibus account contained the overall numbers regarding the bank's stock purchases, but it did not reflect the allocation of purchases to individual accounts. Now, facing the possibility that the entire artifice would collapse if he refused to provide some documentation for his story, Meier tried to satisfy the lawyers with a rather paltry collection of documents.

He arrived at the hotel shortly after lunch, carrying several fancy binders under his arm. Meier told Pitt and Rauch that the binders contained his personal records—travel and entertainment receipts, the statement from his trading account. Opening the binders, Pitt found only three or four sheets of paper in each one. He looked at Meier with a puzzled expression, and the banker smiled and shrugged.

"Where are the trading records from the managed accounts?" asked Pitt. "This is not enough."

The question appeared to wound Meier. The banker said he would have to consult with Pletscher before he provided any additional records. He then left for the bank.

"Where are the other documents?" Pitt demanded when Meier returned later in the afternoon with Pletscher.

At the bank, replied Pletscher. He explained that he did not have the authority to give the lawyers access to the managed-account records because they would see the names of the clients. Disclosure of the names, even to the lawyers, Pletscher said, would violate Bahamian secrecy laws. The two Swiss bankers did not even want the lawyers near the bank.

Suddenly the idea of an easy trip was gone. Pitt and Rauch had flown to Nassau with their paralegals in anticipation of copying the records and returning quickly to the United States. The pressure from the SEC was growing and they had to provide the limited disclosure of documents to the agency soon or risk the collapse of their agreement.

Maintaining the agreement depended upon immediate access to the bank's records. Rauch urged Pletscher to allow the paralegals to accompany him to the bank. He explained that the paralegals had brought special masking tape to conceal the identifying information in the records, and proposed that bank employees use the tape to cover anything that might identify a client on the original statements. Pletscher then could provide the documents to the paralegals for copying. Neither the paralegals nor the attorneys would see the names on the records.

Stepping into one of the bedrooms, Pletscher and Meier held a brief discussion. They decided to let the paralegals copy redacted versions of the bank's managed accounts, with an important exception. They would withhold all documents related to the Diamond and International Gold accounts. Returning to the living room, Pletscher told the lawyers they had accepted Rauch's proposal. He arranged to meet the paralegals at the bank, but he insisted that they not come until nine o'clock that night. Meier agreed to return to the suite the following morning so he could review the records with the lawyers.

"We're going to dinner and the casino," Rauch told Jedlicka and Dunegan. "Leave the documents you copy on the table in the living room when you're done tonight."

The casino at the Cable Beach Hotel is a glittering half-acre of slot machines, craps tables, and blackjack dealers. Nassau doesn't attract the droves of hard-core gamblers who habituate its American counterparts, Las Vegas and Atlantic City. The average bettor at the Cable Beach casino tends to be a sunburned tourist willing to throw away a limited amount of money as part of the entertainment on vacation. There are exceptions, of course, and any afternoon finds a handful of players seated at the blackjack tables where the minimum bet is $100 a hand.

But Pitt and Rauch clearly fit the category of recreational gamblers. If they were going to be too wrapped up in meetings during the daylight to enjoy the beach that tantalized them outside the sliding-glass doors of their suite, at least they could unwind at night. They sat down at the cheapest blackjack table, where the minimum bet was $5 a hand, and played cards until shortly after 11:00 P.M. They broke about even for the night. It was a pattern they would repeat often over the next few months as the stakes and pressures increased in the other game they were playing.

When they returned to their suite, there were no documents on the table and they went to bed, assuming the paralegals were still at work. The next morning a small stack of papers sat on the table. They divided the papers in half and each lawyer began reviewing the documents.

It looked promising at first. The records were copies of actual statements from about twenty-five accounts managed by the bank on behalf of individual investors and they covered hundreds of trades. The names and other identifying information had been eliminated. It took Pitt and Rauch only minutes to discover that the records did not support the bank's defense. There were numerous trades all right, but only a handful involved the twenty-eight stocks on the SEC list. The records were not consistent with Meier's story. A major piece of the puzzle was still missing.

Meier had not really expected the material to fool the lawyers, and he had spent a fitful night preparing for the inevitable confrontation with Pitt and Rauch. When he returned to the suite that morning, Meier was greeted by two attorneys who were puzzled and very close to anger.

"Well, there are two possibilities," Pitt said. "One possibility is that these are the wrong pieces of paper. The second possibility is that we got the wrong story from the start."

Faced with Pitt's bluntness, Meier's composure evaporated and he became agitated. His face reddened, he sputtered about confidentiality and stupid American laws. His slight frame shook with anger as he stalked over to a telephone in the corner of the living room, dialed a number and got Pletscher on the line. As inevitably happened on the rare occasions when he lost control, Meier fell into Swiss-German as he shouted into the telephone. Neither Pitt nor Rauch spoke the language, but it was clear that Meier was chewing out Pletscher, somewhat surprising since Pletscher was Meier's boss.

After several minutes of heated conversation, Meier slammed down the receiver and turned to his lawyers: "You wait here. I'll be back." And he left the room.

As they had several other times during their visit to Nassau, Rauch and Pitt had the sense they were under "house arrest," confined to their hotel and definitely not wanted at the bank, where their presence might raise questions among employees.

When Pletscher heard the first words in Swiss-German on the telephone, he knew that Meier was very upset. But Meier was not berating Pletscher. He was furious about the American lawyers and their incessant demands for records.

"I'm not of a mind to produce any more documents," he had shouted at Pletscher over the phone. "Next thing you know, I'll have to give Harvey Pitt my underpants. We should give them only the omnibus account and nothing else. No allocation of trades."

Pletscher tried to calm his associate, assuring him that they could work out some way to deal with the lawyers.

"Bernie, we have to take some time out and discuss this," Pletscher said. "This approach of withholding documents from the lawyers is not right. There are murderers who got away with a life sentence because their lawyers could use the right approach. We must tell them the truth so they can defend us."

Pletscher felt he did not have the authority to alter the approach they had settled on for dealing with the lawyers. He wanted to meet with Fraysse and get the bank manager's advice on what to do next. But Fraysse was off the island. So he telephoned Coulson, who agreed to come to the bank immediately to meet with Meier and Pletscher.

"This has such big consequences that I feel we have to have the head office decide it," Pletscher told Coulson and Meier. "I feel that we must get Zurich to come and advise us."

Coulson agreed. He said that Hans Peter Schaad, the bank's general counsel, was arriving Sunday night on other bank business. The six-hour time difference meant that it was too late in Zurich to call, but he promised to phone Schaad the following morning and tell him they would have another item on the agenda when he arrived.

Meier objected: "Why do you want to have Zurich involved? They can't help us anyway."

"This decision goes above our authority," Pletscher replied.

More immediate was the problem of how to deal with Pitt and Rauch, who were waiting for an explanation. It was decided that all three would go to the hotel, but that Coulson would do the talking. Coulson telephoned and told the lawyers they were on the way. About 3:00 P.M. they walked into the suite where Pitt and Rauch were waiting.

"Let me ask you this question," Coulson said to the lawyers. "What if, hypothetically, we had a smaller number of accounts that had traded in some of these stocks?"

"Depends on how much smaller," replied Pitt. "We thought it was forty to fifty. If it's thirty-seven, that's no problem. But there is an inverse ratio here. The closer you get to one, the more trouble you've got."

"There are certain sensitive accounts that we aren't able to tell you about without permission of the home office," said Coulson.

Rauch said: "If you're going to tell us there are twenty accounts, we may be able to continue the deal with the SEC. If you say five or fewer, there's a problem. How many accounts are involved?"

Coulson considered the question and nodded thoughtfully: "I need permission to disclose that. I've got to get in touch with bank officials in Zurich on this."

"Can't you even tell us how many accounts are involved?" Rauch asked Coulson. "If it's a small number, the information we've been working on is inconsistent with what we've told the commission and their interest will be intensified."

"The bank's general counsel is coming here this weekend," Coulson replied. "Why don't we just wait until then?"

The American lawyers were in no mood for waiting. The defense they had been working on for more than two months seemed to be less than firm. They didn't know what was going on, but they knew it would inflame the SEC if the agency discovered Pitt and Rauch could not provide the documentation to confirm the managed accounts story. Protecting the bank would become difficult, if not impossible. Delay would make the situation worse, particularly because Fischer had been telephoning Pitt's office almost daily to find out why the agreement had not been signed.

"We'll go to Zurich right now," Pitt said. "This is extremely important. We'll charter a jet to New York tonight and get on the Concorde for London and be in Zurich by Friday."

The extravagance and urgency of Pitt's plan stunned the Swiss bank officials. Coulson and Meier objected. Both said they preferred to wait until Schaad arrived in the Bahamas on Sunday. Neither bank official wanted the confrontation with the head-office officials to occur in Zurich. They would feel much safer if the potentially unpleasant meeting occurred in Nassau on their home turf. The bankers prevailed because they were, after all, the clients. The lawyers agreed to return on Monday, although Coulson said the meeting was likely to be cut short because he and Schaad had to make a business trip late in the day.

The exchange created more mystery than ever. The question of the number of "sensitive" accounts and of the necessity for consulting with Zurich officials created the possibility that Bank Leu had been concealing trades by officials of the parent bank back in Switzerland. With the unanswered questions piling up, the two lawyers packed their bags and took a taxi to the airport for a flight back to the United States.

On the way to the airport, they speculated for a second time since taking the case that the bank was going to fire them. They also discussed the fact that the bank records did not fit the story they had conveyed to the government.

The legal and ethical obligations confronting a lawyer who knows or suspects that a client has been lying are complex and subject to different interpretations. Under no circumstances can a lawyer lie to a court with impunity. As officers of the court, lawyers are sworn to uphold the truth in court. But some lawyers feel there is nothing unethical or illegal about lying to an adversary, whether it is in a civil lawsuit or a government investigation.

Pitt and Rauch had to be concerned that their clients were using them to commit a further fraud against the SEC. If they concluded that the managed-accounts story was false, they could not ethically continue to tell the SEC it was true. On the other hand, they could not return to the SEC and admit that the managed-accounts story was untrue without their client's permission. One alternative was to resign without further contact with the SEC. Another was to obtain the authorization of the client to tell the truth to the SEC.

At that point, Pitt and Rauch could not know what the truth was. They knew something was amiss and they recognized that events were about to take a major turn. But they were uncertain what that turn might be. They would ride it out for a few more days and talk to Schaad before reaching a decision about whether to resign from the case.

In the meantime, more questions than ever swirled around the twenty-eight stocks, and the answers to those questions lay solely with the people at Bank Leu, whose motives and inclinations varied considerably.

Pitt had an important oral argument scheduled for the following Thursday before the U.S. Court of Appeals in Washington, and he wanted to spend the first part of the week preparing for it. He told Rauch he did not think Monday's meeting would require both of them. It was likely to be more of a get-acquainted session, a short one at that if Schaad and Coulson had to leave. So he asked if his partner would mind taking it alone.

"I'm perfectly willing to meet with the general counsel myself," replied Rauch. "That's no problem. But I have a feeling this is going to be a watershed meeting. And I know you, Harvey. You're going to kick yourself if you miss it. But you do what you have to do."

"You're right," said Pitt after a few seconds. "I don't know what it's going to be either, but I certainly want to be there when it happens."

Pitt extracted a price from Rauch. Making connections to return to New York or Washington from Nassau at night is almost impossible by scheduled airline. Pitt said he would go to Nassau Monday morning, but he insisted on chartering a small jet, which would take them down and wait until they were done that evening so they could be whisked back to New York and Washington. That way he could get back and spend time on his oral arguments. Rauch acquiesced with considerable reluctance because he hates to fly in small planes.

Hans Peter Schaad arrived in Nassau as scheduled on Sunday night. Pletscher picked him up at the airport and they drove to the Royal Bahamian Hotel, where Meier and Coulson were waiting in the nearly empty hotel bar.

Schaad, a stiffly formal and taciturn man, listened without comment or expression as the three men explained the dilemma confronting them. They described the SEC's initial inquiry into the twenty-eight stocks. They said the stocks had been purchased through a single account, but that they had decided to say the bank had bought the shares on its own judgment. Two American lawyers had been hired to convey the story to the U.S. government.

Schaad objected to hiring the American lawyers, saying, "Always get the legal office in Zurich."

"We asked and did not get any help," said Pletscher.

The comment surprised Schaad and he thought for a moment before responding: "Tell me everything now."

They continued with the story, explaining how the owner of the account had persuaded them to build up the false story and even recommended one of the lawyers, Harvey Pitt. They said the lawyers had been given documents from the bank's real managed accounts, but that they had quickly seen that the questioned stocks were not in those accounts in large numbers.

Meier then protested telling the lawyers the real story. "If we tell the lawyers, it may well be like talking to the SEC," he said. "If they know the story, they may have to tell it in court or to the American government. They would probably go straight to the SEC."

A few minutes later, Meier whispered to Pletscher, "How do you know Harvey doesn't *still* work for the SEC?"

"Why would Diamond recommend him?" asked Pletscher. The logic of the question stumped Meier and he said nothing more to Pletscher about Pitt's loyalties.

After listening to the complete story, including the involvement of bank employees in copying the trades, Schaad understood for the first time the dimensions of the problem. What angered him most was not the existence of the Diamond account or the trading by the bank employees. He was indignant that the bank officers had lied to their attorneys and he made up his mind quickly about the first step in dealing with the dilemma.

"Of course, we have to tell Mr. Pitt and Mr. Rauch the truth," he said. "You cannot deal with lawyers without telling them the truth. It is incomprehensible to me that you have lied to your lawyers. That is the worst course you could have taken."

The fears that Pletscher had from the start about the success of the cover-up had all been realized in the past few days. He had suspected it would not work and it obviously had not. He thought to himself that the cover-up would not have happened at all if they had gotten sound advice from Schaad at the start. He remembered his early attempts to persuade the lawyer to come to Nassau: the telephone call in late September. His insistence that the auditors alert the legal counsel. The meeting with Knopfli. If someone from Zurich with legal experience had been there at the start to tell them what was best, the basic decision on how to deal with the American government would have been dramatically different.

The leased jet carrying Rauch and Pitt landed at Nassau International Airport about mid-morning on Monday, December 9. The two men took a taxi to the hotel to meet with Schaad and the others in their suite. The bank was still off-limits.

The introductions were very formal, but Schaad wasted no time getting to the point.

"Nobody can deal with lawyers unless they tell them the truth," he said. "You have not been told the truth. It is my understanding that there is one account for all of this trading. What do we do?"

Pitt and Rauch were astute enough to have suspected insider trading. Those suspicions had grown over the weekend. But suspecting an insider was not the same as sitting in a hotel suite and hearing it virtually confirmed. Certainly, the deal that Pitt and Rauch had put together was dead. But there were other possibilities. Maybe a solution could be devised to protect the bank.

The long hours on the Bank Leu case had resulted in a close friendship and unique partnership between Pitt and Rauch, partly because they complement each other so well personally and professionally. Pitt is intense and aggressive. Rauch is laid-back and completely unflappable. Pitt has an intricate knowledge of securities law and the workings of the SEC. He is a top-notch negotiator who knows the players at the agency and speaks their language. He is also obsessed with thoroughness and perfection. Rauch is an experienced litigator, familiar with courtroom strategy and a sharp judge of character and legal theory. He can step back enough to keep the details in perspective and he never loses control of a situation. Like many first-tier lawyers, the two men enjoy the intellectual challenge of solving a difficult legal problem. They now faced a challenge that required their combined talents.

A solution would depend on many factors. The most critical was that the bank and its employees tell them the truth immediately. They had to know what they were confronting in order to craft a defense. The time for concealing information had ended.

"Anything that you need to know to do your job, you will have," Schaad said. "We will cooperate fully with you in this."

Equally vital, Rauch and Pitt would have to inform the SEC that the managed-accounts story was false. If the bank refused to authorize it, they would have to resign immediately. Schaad's decisiveness had impressed the American lawyers. Now he said he understood the situation and agreed that the SEC should be informed that the facts provided previously were no longer valid.

Schaad also agreed that the lawyers could draft a letter for the other bank officials to sign acknowledging that the cover-up scheme had been created and advanced by bank officials without the knowledge of their American lawyers.

Pitt and Rauch were still uncertain what they were dealing with, but they strongly suspected the case involved a large insider trading scheme. To limit any further damage to the bank, they now also insisted that the trading stop. "This whole deal may be illegal," Pitt said. "If so, it must stop at once. We cannot represent you if there is an ongoing fraud, so you must stop the customer from trading immediately. The second thing is that the money must be frozen informally. You cannot let the customer touch it."

Again, Schaad agreed.

Schaad and Coulson had to leave the island that afternoon on a previously scheduled business trip that could not be postponed. Schaad arranged to meet with the lawyers later in the week to discuss the options available to the bank. In the meantime, he instructed Pletscher and Meier to provide them with a complete and accurate description of what had occurred with the account.

For the remainder of the afternoon and into the evening, Pitt and Rauch met with Pletscher and Meier. It was a long and enlightening day for the lawyers. They questioned the two men separately and talked to them together. They listened carefully as the two bankers detailed the entire scheme, from the start of the trading to the conception and execution of the cover-up attempt at the insistence of the client they identified only as "Mr. X." And they learned that the customer had withdrawn almost $2 million in cash between 1981 and 1985.

The cash withdrawals were staggering. They drove home the possibility that this was a truly explosive case of insider trading. But the lawyers still did not know who the trader was, and therefore they could not be 100 percent certain that the trades were illegal. The chances of any other possibility were growing more remote by the minute, however, and they vanished almost entirely when the bankers disclosed that the customer was an investment banker at the New York firm of Drexel Burnham Lambert.

Pitt and Rauch were not certain they wanted to know the identity of Mr. X before they decided whether they would continue to represent the bank in the case. Virtually all communications between a lawyer and client are considered privileged, and the lawyer cannot be compelled to divulge their contents to legal authorities. But it was safer not to rely on the privilege covering the name of the client in this case.

When Meier and Pletscher told the lawyers that the client had telephoned the previous week with two large orders for takeover stocks, they were told that he must be made to sell the stocks and keep his money in the bank only on a cash-deposit basis. The bankers were instructed to explain to the customer that the lawyers had insisted the bank keep a low profile in its trading accounts until the SEC inquiry was cleared up.

It was late Monday night before the two attorneys walked up the

steps into the private jet. They were too tired and too numbed by
the day's events to discuss the case. What both men needed was
a rest and time to digest the information.

There was little calm. Tuesday afternoon, Rauch received a telephone call from Meier. Mr. X had telephoned and wanted to come
to Nassau to meet with Meier and Pletscher for a status report on
the inquiry. Meier feared that the demand that he sell off his stocks
had made the customer suspicious.

Meier faced a dilemma. He was a Swiss banker who firmly believed that the customer had a legitimate right to know that the
bank was on the verge of changing its story to the SEC. He disa-
greed with the bank's switch in strategy. But he had been virtually
ordered not to divulge any information about the change to the
client. He had also been told to stop the customer's trading. How
could he withhold vital information from Levine? How could he
enforce the order to stop trading without alerting the customer to
the change in tactics? He put the questions to Rauch, who told
Meier that he would have to delay any meeting with the customer
and avoid executing any further trades. He reinforced the notion
that Meier should explain that the lawyers had advised against
allowing any more trades. Under no circumstances, however, was
he to disclose that the lawyers had been told the managed-accounts
story was a sham.

On Wednesday, Pitt and Rauch spent several hours discussing
the various options for Bank Leu. The first option was an all-out
legal battle in the name of bank secrecy. The bank could fight the
subpoenas for its records and for Meier's testimony and records,
demanding that the SEC go to court to obtain any scrap of information. The bank would have both Swiss and Bahamian bank secrecy laws on its side. If it lost in the courts, it could still refuse to
turn over the information and risk having its U.S. assets frozen.

The second option also was predicated on a tough legal fight.
The difference was that it would be carried out with the under-

standing among the bank's lawyers that the client information would be turned over to the SEC if the bank lost in the U.S. courts.

A third option was a modified legal fight, rattling the saber of privacy and customer secrecy while trying to negotiate an agreement to provide limited documents to the SEC.

Finally, the bank could try to cut a deal with the SEC: tell the truth about the trading and provide the documentation for it. Trade the name of the client for total civil and criminal immunity for the bank and its employees.

Attorneys are paid great sums of money to advise clients on the best course of conduct. But sometimes the most they can do is propose the options and insist that the client choose one. What cautious lawyers want to avoid is a situation where, six months later, the client complains that he was forced to follow the wrong course.

That doesn't mean the lawyers don't develop a definite preference for a particular course, and both American lawyers believed that the option of a negotiated deal with the SEC offered the best chance of protecting the bank. If Pitt and Rauch had learned the truth at the start, they might have been able to craft a stronger defense against any disclosure. But the weeks of lying to the SEC had likely eroded some of their legal standing. Cutting a deal with the agency would be tough, in light of the lies, but it still offered the best avenue for extricating the bank.

In the meantime, Pitt's wife, Saree, flew to New York from Washington and Rauch was joined by his wife, Betty; together, they attended the annual party that Fried, Frank sponsored for its partners. It was a glitzy affair, dubbed the "senior prom" because formal dress was required, and normally Pitt enjoyed it tremendously. But that night he was poor company. He was distracted by his worries over the bank's options. Were they the right ones? Had they forgotten something? Were all the advantages and disadvantages weighed?

When he and his wife returned to their suite at the Westbury Hotel that night, Pitt found a copy of the options waiting for him.

He stayed up the remainder of the night going over them and penciling in his changes and questions.

Early the next morning, Pitt flew back to Washington. He completed his oral arguments and walked out of the ornate courtroom into a waiting car, heading for the airport. On the flight to Nassau, he reviewed the changes he had suggested in the options, but the substance of the four alternatives remained the same.

Late on the afternoon of December 12, Pitt and Rauch were back at the Cable Beach Hotel meeting with Schaad and the other bankers. Pitt and Rauch outlined the options and walked Schaad through the potential advantages and disadvantages of each.

"None of these alternatives sounds very attractive," the Swiss lawyer said dryly.

"That's because this is not a very attractive situation," said Rauch. "Three months ago there might have been some different alternatives, but this is what we have to deal with now."

"We'll do whatever you tell us to do," said Schaad.

Rauch explained to Schaad that this was a special situation and he and Pitt had agreed that the bank would have to choose the path to follow. The banker understood and said he would prefer attempting a trade with the SEC, the name of the client in exchange for immunity for the bank and its employees.

The discussion extended well into the evening before they decided to break until the following day, when Meier and Pletscher were to provide the lawyers with more details about the mysterious Mr. X.

The decision to abandon the cover-up fueled Meier's resentments. "We signed an agreement to do this," he complained to Pletscher late that day. "You said you would follow through with this plan and now you want to turn back and go in the opposite direction."

That night Pletscher telephoned Fraysse, who was traveling, to inform him of the new developments.

"I thought we had a plan," Fraysse said. "Why did it change?"

"What we gave our lawyers was not sufficient," explained Pletscher. "I was convinced that we should change the story."

Customer privacy is the cornerstone of seven centuries of banking tradition in Switzerland. The Bahamas also has strict laws against divulging the name of a client to anyone outside the bank without an order from a Bahamian court or the proper authorities or without the client's consent. The law and the tradition combined in a way that made it impossible for either Bruno Pletscher or Bernie Meier to name the customer. They could not bring themselves to do it. But the lawyers found a way around that reluctance that Thursday night.

Meier had invited Pitt and Rauch to join him for dinner at Lyford Cay Club. Meier had been strict in his refusal to allow the lawyers to visit the bank, and he had avoided being seen with them in public. The invitation to dinner at his home club was a surprise.

Meier explained that he had kept the inquiry from his wife. Now that the strategy had been changed and he was leaving the Bahamas, he had told her the situation and she was anxious about the possible consequences. He wondered if Pitt and Rauch, as friends and lawyers, would agree to have dinner with them and explain to his wife what was going to happen. They agreed and joined Meier for the fifteen-minute drive to Lyford Cay Club, a guarded compound along the ocean.

On the drive out, Meier tried to explain his position to the lawyers: "You must know that all of us at the bank agreed upon the first plan. It wasn't just me. I don't want you to think worse of me. I was following along with the others."

Pitt used the opportunity to question Meier about the identity of the customer.

"You're going to have to tell us," Pitt said. "We know that none of you wants to say his name, but we have to know it."

"You know which firm it is," said Meier. "Do you know any people at that firm?"

The lawyers said they knew the firm was Drexel Burnham. Meier again asked, "Who do you know?"

The lawyers caught on to his game. Pitt offered a name and Meier shook his head no. Rauch offered another name and again Meier shook his head no.

"How about Dennis Levine?" Pitt asked.

"That's it," responded Meier. Unable to say the name himself, Meier had nonetheless confirmed the identity of Diamond to the lawyers.

The October dinner came flooding back to Pitt. He had sat across the table from Levine for an entire evening, and Levine had known what was going on and smiled contentedly at him. Pitt tried to recall what Levine had looked like and what he had said during dinner, but his recollections were vague. The guy had not made much of an impression. Amazing, he thought, simply amazing.

The lawyers met Helene Meier at the club's restaurant, and the four of them sat down to dinner at a waterfront table. The lawyers acknowledged that they were uncertain what the government reaction would be to the new disclosure. They were optimistic that an agreement could be reached to avoid any penalty for the bank or its employees, but they were also realistic, explaining that nothing was certain. Meier's wife nodded occasionally and said little. She appeared to have decided to stand by her husband, regardless of the outcome.

Throughout dinner, Pitt was nagged by a question that might not have occurred to another lawyer. If the bank had intended to cover up its scheme from the start, as they obviously had, why had they hired Pitt to represent them? While he certainly negotiated frequently with the SEC on sensitive matters, Pitt prided himself on having a reputation as someone who would demand a full accounting from his clients. He was not a lawyer who would swallow a lie and eagerly convey it to the government. Why not use someone less likely to question the fabrication?

As he sat through dinner, the question assumed monumental

importance to Pitt. As soon as they got in the car to return to the hotel he confronted Meier with it.

"Why did you hire me?"

"Levine recommended you," Meier said flatly.

On Friday, December 13, Meier and Pletscher returned to the hotel suite. When Pletscher was asked by the lawyers to confirm the identity of the customer, he could not remember Levine's first name because he was so accustomed to referring to him only by the code name Diamond.

The bankers spent the day detailing the extent of the trading in takeover stocks. The list was too long to review in its entirety, but Meier described the largest trades made by Levine and the size of his profits. Nabisco, $2.7 million. American Natural Resources, $1.4 million. Jewel Companies, $1.2 million. They also described the piggybacking by bank employees and said that Levine had more than $10 million remaining in his account at Bank Leu. The magnitude of the profits was stunning. Levine was clearly tapping into a golden vein of information.

About midday, Pitt went into his bedroom, closed the door, and telephoned Paul Fischer in Washington. The SEC attorney had been leaving daily messages with Pitt's office and he had ignored them. There was no point in returning a telephone call until he had something to tell the SEC lawyer.

"Where are you?" demanded Fischer, whose patience was gone. "We've been waiting for that agreement and the documents."

"We want to come in and talk to you about the agreement and the documents," said Pitt. "We have a lot to discuss. I want Gary to be there."

Fischer demanded to know why Gary Lynch, the enforcement director, needed to be present.

"He should be there. Believe me," said Pitt.

"I'll have to check his schedule and get back to you."

"No, I'll call you back later."

Later that afternoon, Pitt contacted Fischer and agreed to come to SEC headquarters in Washington at 10:00 A.M. on Tuesday, December 17.

On the way to the airport that weekend to return to the United States, Pitt and Rauch mused about how different the bank's dilemma might have been if Levine had not persuaded Meier and Pletscher to lie. If Pletscher and Meier had told the truth about the American customer back in September, the lawyers could have gone to court to protect the bank's interests by citing the Bahamian laws against revealing customer information. Even if the SEC prevailed in court and the bank were ordered to disclose the name, the process would have been orderly and legal. The stakes had risen enormously because of the lies to the SEC.

Turning to Rauch, Pitt shook his head and said, "You know, Michael, Levine really took them down the absolute worst path."

17.

Moby Dick

A measure of Levine's success as an investment banker was owed to his keen instinct for how a transaction was progressing. It was a talent his boss at Drexel Burnham, David Kay, described as a "good feel for the deal."

In early December, Levine began to sense a change in the climate at Bank Leu. His concern had been triggered when Pletscher demanded that he sell his stocks, even though it involved taking a loss on RCA. He noted, too, a certain coolness in the way Meier and Pletscher were treating him, even discouraging him from coming to Nassau. Levine, however, couldn't sit idly by in New York. On December 14, he flew to Nassau. Meeting Pletscher and Meier at the bank, he demanded an update on the inquiry.

Against their professional instincts and natural inclinations, the two bankers lied to their customer, assuring him that the plan was going according to schedule and there was nothing to worry about. The American lawyers wanted the bank to stop trading in takeover stocks until the inquiry ended simply to avoid inflaming the SEC, they repeated, but that was only prudence and not the fruit of a major shift in strategy.

Bernie Meier disliked the lying and was glad that he would be leaving Nassau for good in two days. Right to the end, he was ambivalent about his own actions. And he had long ago formulated a comforting rationalization, telling himself that Levine might not be an actual insider—after all, Diamond hadn't always picked winners.

"Diamond wasn't right one hundred percent of the time," Meier would later recall. "He lost about two million dollars. It wasn't clear that it was all insider information. If he had been one hundred percent successful, maybe yes. But even then, there was talk and rumors about the stocks."

Even after the cover-up was abandoned and the lawyers were preparing to make a new deal with the SEC, Meier believed that Levine's scheme would have succeeded. The fake stories for buying the twenty-eight stocks were nearly complete; only five stocks were left unaccounted for by the vast mass of documents Meier and Levine had assembled. That very day Levine had brought more material to Nassau to back up the story.

On a deeper level, Meier recognized that Bank Leu had earned millions of Swiss francs in brokerage commissions from the trades it executed for Levine. Indeed, in the days soon after Meier's arrival, the bank was struggling to make a profit and it had lived off Levine's commissions for many months. In 1984, commission income at Bank Leu international rose 71 percent, primarily as a result of Levine's heavy trading.

Now that the going was getting tough, Meier thought, the bank was abandoning Levine. Worst of all, in Meier's view, they were doing so without giving the customer a chance to defend himself. They were trading Levine for their own freedom.

So on December 14, when Levine demanded to know what documents had been turned over to the lawyers, Meier acknowledged that the bank had provided the lawyers with records allocating trades to some of the managed accounts in an attempt to persuade them to accept the story.

"That was the stupidest thing you could have done," Levine snapped. "Do they know who I am now?"

Pletscher and Meier assured him that they had not divulged his name to the lawyers and none of the records involved his account. But they said Levine's name had been mentioned among many others as a possible source of information on the stocks.

"That's no surprise," said Levine. "My name gets mentioned regularly among the thirty top people involved in takeovers."

Turning over the records angered and concerned Levine because it could be the first step toward divulging his trading records. He told the bankers that his Bahamian lawyers had explained to him that the bank would breach Bahamian bank secrecy statutes if it provided any individual account information to the lawyers or the American government. He insisted that Pletscher and Meier demand the return of the documents and ensure that none of them was passed to the SEC.

"You have the best lawyers possible," he said. "But you've hired these lawyers and you should tell your lawyers what to do. You should control your lawyers and not let them control you."

If they adhered to his plan, Levine assured the bankers there was nothing to worry about; the SEC was on a fishing expedition. He said he understood the need to keep his account inactive for a few more weeks, but he complained that he would lose millions, just as he had during the fall months when he was not trading.

Before Levine left, Meier told him that he was returning to Switzerland because his work permit was expiring. Richard Coulson would assume Meier's duties until a full-time replacement was found, Levine was told. Levine was not told that Coulson's involvement was an accommodation to the lawyers, who wanted two witnesses to every future meeting.

Often the most crucial moment in a civil or criminal case occurs in a roomful of lawyers, outside the hearing of the judge, jury, or defendants. As a result, the private, high-stakes negotiating sessions are scripted and rehearsed as carefully as any courtroom drama.

Harvey Pitt is a master of these situations, a skillful negotiator who made his professional reputation not through courtroom preeminence, rarely in fact setting foot in court. His mind is agile and creative, capable of shifting from tiny details to broad concepts with ease. And he has consummated deals from both sides of the table.

Rauch and Pitt had been meeting regularly with the mid-level SEC staffers, but Pitt's insistence on a session with Gary Lynch was intended to send a signal to the agency: this was to be an unusual session, not just another round in the long process of reaching an agreement to provide bank records. He had heightened the expectations of the SEC, forewarning them of the possibility of a dramatic shift in the inquiry.

Over the weekend, he and Rauch had prepared for Tuesday's encounter as thoroughly as if it were the final argument in a murder case. They wrote an agenda for their own use during the meeting, outlining the subjects they wanted to cover, the order in which they would cover them, and the way in which the most sensitive points would be phrased. Style was as important as substance. The language had to be precise without being blunt. The tone had to be just right, low-key and casual so as not to create too much alarm, but not so soft that it detracted from the significance of the offer to the government.

Gary Lynch's position as a senior government official is reflected by his corner office on the fourth floor of SEC headquarters in Washington. It is spacious and comfortable, with windows along two walls providing views of District of Columbia courthouses and other government buildings. There is room for a conference table, a couch, and several chairs in addition to Lynch's desk.

When Pitt and Rauch were ushered in promptly at 10:00 A.M.

on December 17, they found six SEC attorneys waiting for them. Pitt had an audience for his performance.

John Sturc, the associate director, had walked across the hall from his office to join Lynch and, as the three attorneys most intimately involved in the Bank Leu investigation, Fischer, Wang, and Sonnenthal were also present. They had been joined by Michael Mann, chief of the SEC's international legal office and an expert on laws covering foreign financial institutions.

Since Fischer had told him of Pitt's telephone call Friday, Sturc had been contemplating the possibilities that might unfold at Tuesday's meeting. As the division executive responsible for supervising the Bank Leu inquiry, he had been briefed regularly on the progress of the investigation. The request to meet with Lynch was unusual enough to indicate something important was about to occur in the slow-moving case.

True to his cautious nature, which he had developed over eight years as a government lawyer, Sturc had never drawn any conclusions about where the evidence pointed. An interesting pattern had emerged from the brokerage records obtained by the agency. It might or might not lead anywhere. The story about the managed accounts was not the kind of representation that a government attorney would accept at face value. Yet it could be true. The SEC attorneys would have to see the documents and judge for themselves.

Lynch and Pitt were former colleagues and friendly adversaries. Some attorneys might have been directed to the office couch, where, sinking into the cushions, they would be forced to look up at the government attorneys arrayed around them in straight-backed chairs. But Rauch and Pitt were invited to the conference table next to one of the large windows.

Pitt opened the green composition notebook in which he had written the agenda and extensive notes he and Rauch had prepared. They had agreed that a "we're-all-in-this-together" approach might best set the stage for their disclosure.

"Look," Pitt said, referring to his notes, "we've been working with you guys and it's taken a fair amount of time. The last week of delay, which we know was frustrating for the staff, has really been our fault. We had an opportunity to review the redacted documents and we think it is appropriate to sit down with the staff before any agreement is executed, more from the staff's perspective than ours. We want to deal first with the things we feel we are ethically obliged to discuss. Then we'd like to engage in what I would refer to as an off-the-record discussion."

Lynch, rail thin and poker-faced, raised his eyebrows slightly and asked, "What do you mean by 'off the record'?"

"Basically, you'll see when we get to that point," said Pitt. "I can't help your knowing what I've told you, once I've told it to you, but I don't want you to ever attribute what has been said here either to my client or to my client's lawyers. That is, you can use whatever I tell you for what you think it's worth. That is what I mean by off the record."

Pitt wanted to make his point before another interruption threatened his control of the situation, so he continued without pausing.

"The ethical obligations are that we have negotiated, you know, with the staff to avoid a confrontation, which is what we all desired to avoid," he said. "Among other things, however, we have made certain factual representations based upon what our clients told us were the true facts. Based upon our actual review of the documents and recent discussions with our clients, we are now obliged to tell the staff that you should not rely upon our prior factual representations."

Paul Fischer erupted into angry shouting: "What? Listen, we have negotiated these agreements based upon specific representations that these were all, that the trading was done all in managed accounts."

"That is why we are here," Pitt replied calmly. "Without going into what factual representations you can or can't rely on, we didn't think it was appropriate to pursue our agreement any further until we had communicated that information to you. Now, we'd like to go off the record."

The mood in the room had shifted from mild curiosity to genuine anticipation, although Fischer was the only person who had responded overtly to Pitt's news. Pitt had now come to the most delicate part. He had to lay out the new facts without revealing too much about what had actually gone on at Bank Leu. It ended up sounding extremely convoluted.

"If you assume that the trading that the commission has been concerned with should be explored by the commission staff, and if you assume that it would be worth the staff's while to ascertain for whom the trades were effected, and assume further that the bank would agree to expend all energies to facilitate the commission's ability to get to the bottom of things, would the commission be willing to focus its enforcement efforts, if any were required, solely on the person or persons who initiated the trading in question, particularly if the bank and any other persons who may have piggybacked on such trades disgorged any profits they may have made in connection with any wrongdoing by those who were behind the orders?"

Despite the purposely convoluted language, Pitt had put the deal on the table: if Bank Leu gave up the person or persons behind the trades, would the SEC agree not to bring any civil actions against the bank or any employees?

The basic advantages of the deal for the agency were cooperation and expedition. The SEC had never encountered a foreign case where they might actually discover the source of the trading so quickly. The Santa Fe and St. Joe Minerals cases had taken years. This agreement could compress all that time into a matter of weeks. Further, the commission eliminated the risk of losing a lengthy court battle, which would not only delay or end the case but set a terrible precedent. Finally, there was the hint at the chance to bring a major case against what Pitt described as a "status player" on Wall Street.

Regardless of the commission's decision, Rauch added, the deal would collapse if the Justice Department refused to grant similar blanket criminal immunity to the bank and its employees.

Lynch, too, is a shrewd negotiator. He said little in response to the deal proposed by Pitt and Rauch. He simply listened and then asked them to step into the anteroom outside his office while he discussed their interesting proposal with his colleagues.

When the two attorneys were invited back less than half an hour later, Lynch said that the deal might work, although he did not like the inclusion of Bernhard Meier, the bank's portfolio manager.

Meier was really the only bank employee whose name meant anything to the SEC attorneys, and they had focused their inquiry on his activities. They had heard about him from Brian Campbell and they knew he had placed the trades. Since he was well versed in American securities laws, it would be hard for Meier to claim ignorance in the face of an insider trading allegation.

Rauch and Pitt insisted that the deal had to cover all bank employees, including Meier, or they could not proceed. Lynch agreed and, suddenly, Meier went from potential defendant to potential star witness. As the bank official who took the orders and executed the trades, he could provide vital testimony linking the unknown person or persons to the trading. He also could describe meetings with the customer and any of the reasons the customer might have given for buying particular stocks.

"Obviously, I can't commit the commission to this," Lynch told the bank's lawyers. "I'll have to talk to them. But I'll recommend we go for it."

As for the criminal matters, Lynch suggested the lawyers discuss the issue with the U.S. Attorney's Office in Manhattan, where the commission directed the majority of the criminal cases arising from its insider trading investigations. He agreed to recommend that the deal be accepted and said he and Sturc would go along for the meeting with the prosecutors in New York.

With the cards on the table, Wang and Fischer pressed for the identity of the trader. When that failed, as they expected it would, they sought his title or the name of his firm. Again they were rebuffed, but along the way either Pitt or Rauch described the trader as "a big fish."

"For what you're asking, he'd damn well better be Moby Dick," said Sturc.

The chairman and the four commissioners of the Securities and Exchange Commission conduct regular public meetings. But the agenda for enforcement matters is always heard behind closed doors because of the sensitive nature of the subject matter. Later that week, Lynch and Sturc outlined the deal offered by Bank Leu to the commissioners and received approval to proceed with negotiations. A final agreement would have to be brought back to the commission for an okay, but that was little more than a formality. It was up to Lynch and the enforcement division to arrive at the best compromise.

On Friday, Fischer telephoned Pitt and said Lynch wanted a meeting as soon as possible. Pitt planned to spend the Christmas holidays with his wife and her family in Winston-Salem, North Carolina, but he agreed to cut the holiday short and return to Washington on December 26. He contacted Rauch and arranged to have his partner accompany him to the meeting.

Pitt had been trying to secure Meier's promise of cooperation for several days and on Christmas Eve, his last opportunity before the meeting in Washington, Pitt telephoned Meier at his home in an upper-class suburb of Zurich. It was 8:00 P.M. and Meier was preparing to leave with his wife for dinner at his in-laws. The call annoyed him. The last thing he wanted was a reminder of the awful business with the American government. But Pitt insisted that his business was urgent. He needed to explain the agreement being worked out with the SEC and secure Meier's promise of testimony.

Meier resisted making any commitment. Now that he was in Switzerland, he explained, he had hired a Swiss attorney who was reviewing the case. Pitt stressed the urgency, saying that he had an important meeting with the SEC the day after Christmas and he had to have his end of the bargain worked out. Meier said he would think about it, and Pitt said he would call back later that night. At 11:00 P.M. Pitt phoned again. Meier told him he had not made a final decision, but he would probably go along with the deal and testify. Pitt felt he had extracted enough of a promise from Meier to proceed with the negotiations with the SEC on December 26.

December 26 was a bitterly cold day in Washington. The temperature was in the low teens, and a strong wind swept between the nearly empty government buildings as Harvey Pitt and Michael Rauch headed for the SEC offices. With the exception of Wang, the entire cast was reassembled in Lynch's office to hear Lynch explain that the commission had approved proceeding with negotiations along the lines outlined the week before by Pitt. The enforcement chief suggested that the meeting with the U.S. Attorney's Office in New York be arranged as soon as possible, and Pitt and Rauch said their paralegals were already copying documents at the bank for eventual delivery to the SEC.

The documents, of course, would still be redacted. The bank and its lawyers faced another enormous hurdle—persuading the Bahamian government to allow the bank to divulge the name of its client. Meanwhile, if the first step had been to reach an agreement in principle with the SEC, a delicate task, the second step was negotiating similar criminal immunity with the Justice Department. Given Lynch's promise of support, that hurdle seemed to the lawyers less formidable than the first, but it would be no cinch.

The third step, however, was no less crucial than the first two, because Lynch had made it clear that the deal would collapse if the bank did not provide the name of the trader. And that might be far more difficult. Delivering the name would depend on convincing the unpredictable Bahamian authorities that it was in their best interest to allow Bank Leu to breach the secrecy laws that had transformed the tiny nation into an offshore financial haven. Any attack on the sanctity of those laws might shake the confidence of

the institutions and investors that relied on them and thereby threaten
the nation's second-largest industry.

As the new year began, Bruno Pletscher officially took over as
general manager of Bank Leu International. He had been handling
the duties for several months and finally had the title. But the job
he had once coveted seemed to be just another burden. The secret
effort to mislead the lawyers and the American government had
taken a toll on Pletscher, robbed him of his good nature, and sapped
his self-esteem. Last summer's problem had grown into a crisis that
now carried on into another year.

With the abandonment of Levine's cover-up scheme came new
strains and pressures, not the least of which was lying to a customer.
Meier wasn't even around to share his apprehension. Hans Schaad,
the bank's counsel, and Pitt had assured him the new course was
the proper one. The bank would stand behind him. But in dark
moments, it seemed to Pletscher that he had swapped one set of
lies for another. A time that should have represented the culmi-
nation of nineteen years of dedication and hard work in banking
was ruined by lies and anxiety.

Shortly before noon on January 2, the receptionist buzzed
Pletscher's phone and said "Mr. Diamond" was there to see him.
Pletscher balked. He hadn't expected Levine. He couldn't remember whether Levine had even told him he was coming. Coulson
was off somewhere for the holiday. The lawyers had told Pletscher
he was not to meet with Levine alone. Who could he get to join
them? No one. What if Levine wanted to withdraw money? On
December 30, Schaad had authorized the entry of an official notice
in Levine's International Gold file that interdicted cash withdrawals
and directed inquiries about the account to Pletscher.

What could Levine want? It was his second visit in as many
weeks, his third since the bank had begun telling the truth to the
lawyers. Each encounter with Levine made the situation more un-
bearable for Pletscher, the pretense more difficult to maintain.

Levine also disliked the frequent trips to Nassau. They were time-consuming and risky. But he was worried that the cover-up might come unraveled without his personal influence. Even as his sense of danger from the SEC inquiry heightened, he remained frustrated that he was unable to resume trading at Bank Leu. The juxtaposition of the two concepts—increasing danger and rising frustration over the trading ban—was something that would continue for months for Levine.

Two weeks before, on December 20, he had gone to the bank to reinforce his view that the SEC was impotent. And he had a letter to prove it. As he sat at the conference room table with Richard Coulson and Pletscher that day, Levine pulled from his pocket a piece of paper, unfolded it, and held it out. It was a letter from which Levine's name had been clipped as part of his penchant for theatricality and games, as if the men in that room did not know his true identity.

"It was sent to me," he said. "You must understand that for obvious reasons I have cut off my name. But it should give you comfort. The SEC doesn't have any suspicion I'm involved in this investigation. It has nothing to do with me. They haven't the slightest clue, or they wouldn't have sent me this letter."

He handed the letter over to Coulson and Pletscher. It was from John Shad, chairman of the Securities and Exchange Commission, who had written to thank Levine for participating in the commission's roundtable discussion on recent takeover developments on November 26, 1985. Coulson and Pletscher nodded as Levine took the letter back, refolded it, and tucked it into his pocket.

Now, on the first business day of 1986, Pletscher greeted Levine in the foyer and took him to the conference room. If he couldn't have a witness, at least Pletscher would take notes of the meeting for the lawyers, and he placed a pad of paper on the table in front of him.

Levine asked whether the lawyers still had the allocation records for the managed accounts. When Pletscher replied that they did,

Levine said the lawyers might be subpoenaed and forced to turn over the documents in their possession. Attorney-client privilege made it highly unlikely that the SEC could ever obtain documents from Pitt and Rauch, but Pletscher did not understand enough American law to know that. He nodded silently as Levine said he would "strongly recommend" that the lawyers be asked to return the documents to the bank.

What was really bothering Levine, however, were the withdrawal slips he had signed for his cash over the years. In his view, the slips were the only documentary evidence linking him to the trading.

"Hypothetically, couldn't the bank lose a file, a whole file, or part of a file?" Levine asked.

"Theoretically yes, we can lose a file," said Pletscher.

"The withdrawal slips with my signature," said Levine. "I really feel that we should destroy them or lose them. They are the only remaining documents that could lead to me. After destroying those old signature cards there would be nothing in the files to prove a connection to me."

"I see your point and I will think about it," said Pletscher.

"As far as this trading goes, only four people know that I exist," Levine told Pletscher. "You, Bernie, Jean-Pierre Fraysse, and Coulson. In an emergency, it couldn't be proved that I had any connection to the bank or the trading. Having bearer shares in the Panamanian company is not a direct link to my identity. I have control over those shares, but I have an emergency plan in case the SEC finds out about the International Gold account."

Levine explained his plan: "I would deny any link to the account or the trading. And I have a person who will stand up and say, 'I am the beneficial owner of this company. I hold the bearer shares.' This is someone who is not an American citizen, someone who would not have to worry about the SEC and American laws. I also have a Liechtenstein entity that will play a role."

Levine saw no reason to provide more details. Pletscher didn't need to know the name of the person or the Liechtenstein company. All he needed to know was what to say in the unlikely event that the government asked who controlled International Gold.

"You should say that the ultimate beneficial owner is a non-American," Levine instructed Pletscher. "The bank should be ready to go along with this strategy. This is the hard way. It would be much easier if you didn't give the lawyers any records allocating trades to my account. That is against the Bahamian secrecy laws."

Levine shrugged and smiled. Probably it was all for nothing, he told Pletscher. The SEC didn't have a clue to his identity and he had needlessly missed opportunities for trading.

"Damn," he complained. "The information I've wasted in the last four months could have made me another $15 million."

Pitt was nearly apoplectic. He was getting ready to try to cut a deal with the federal prosecutors in New York and suddenly he was unsure about what he had to offer. What if the guy behind the trading wasn't Levine? What if someone else had used the investment banker's name in dealing with Bank Leu? Some junior analyst or copy machine operator? Even another investment banker? Meier and Pletscher had only seen the passport once and the photocopy had been destroyed. The man claimed to travel under a false name and use fake identification. The bankers had never tried to call him. The customer had refused to provide a number, and they had never even thought to check directory assistance in New York for a way to contact him. His withdrawals had all been in cash, so the bank had never even issued a check that would require some identification for cashing.

Pitt telephoned Rauch and shared his fears. What should they do? The whole deal could collapse if the bank delivered Dennis Levine and he turned out to be somebody else. Rauch came up with the solution: they would simply get a photograph of Dennis Levine and show it to Pletscher and other employees at the bank who had seen the client regularly. They could even wire a copy to

Meier in Switzerland. But finding a photograph turned out to be difficult. Obviously, they couldn't ask Levine for a recent snapshot, but contacting the newspapers or photoagencies was also out because it might stir someone's curiosity.

Then they hit on it. Investment banking houses put out annual reports in which they glorify their accomplishments. Much like high school yearbooks, the reports contain candid shots of principal players. All they had to do was get a book with Levine's picture in it. But the lawyers feared contacting Drexel Burnham for the same reasons they didn't want to contact the press. Eventually, a paralegal in Fried, Frank's Washington office said he had a friend at Shearson Lehman Brothers. He obtained the firm's 1983 yearbook, and a professional photographer was hired to rephotograph several candid shots of Levine individually and in a group of people.

Several sets of the photographs were made and taken to Nassau. In a tactic reminiscent of a police lineup, the bank employees who had had contact with the customer were first shown a group shot and asked to pick out "Mr. Diamond." They were then shown individual photographs to confirm the identification. Pitt's fears were dissipated. The customer was Dennis Levine.

Peter Romatowski was chief of the securities fraud division of the U.S. Attorney's Office in Manhattan. He had been the lead prosecutor in the case against R. Foster Winans, a former *Wall Street Journal* reporter convicted of securities fraud and other charges in one of the most widely publicized and controversial insider trading cases. In 1983 and early 1984, Winans had been one of two principal writers of the paper's "Heard on the Street" column, an influential source of tips and rumors about stocks and the stock market. Often news about a company in the column had an immediate effect on the price of its stock. In exchange for a small share of the profits, Winans had leaked sensitive information about upcoming columns to two stockbrokers, who then traded on the information. It was not a classic insider case, but in 1985 Romatowski won convictions of Winans and two others by arguing, in part, that Winans had misappropriated information that belonged to his employer.

At 2:30 on the afternoon of January 16, 1986, Romatowski played host to an impressive gathering of lawyers. Crammed into his scruffy federal office were Harvey Pitt, Michael Rauch, Richard Sauber—a Fried, Frank lawyer and former federal prosecutor—and Amy Jedlicka, one of the firm's paralegals. On the government's side of the table, in addition to Romatowski, were John Sturc, Michael Mann, and Gary Lynch from the SEC, and Charles Carberry, a federal prosecutor who had handled many celebrated white-collar crime cases.

Up until that meeting, only slightly more than a dozen enforcement division attorneys at the SEC, as well as the agency's commissioners, knew about the investigation into suspicious trading at Bank Leu. Until the need arose as part of the compromise with the bank, there had been no reason to bring in the Justice Department or the U.S. Attorney's Office. But the SEC has no power to grant immunity to a witness and no authority over potential criminal charges arising from information it uncovers. So the blessing of the U.S. Attorney's Office in Manhattan was critical to keeping the deal alive.

The threshold decision of whether the prosecutors would accept the deal depended on their subjective judgment. While it was unlikely that they would overrule Lynch's recommendation, the SEC enforcement boss carried no official weight within the Justice Department. Romatowski and Carberry would have to be convinced that the agreement was not too lenient, and that the government's part of the deal was a significant enough case to justify a blanket pass for the bank. If they liked it, the prosecutors would have to persuade their boss, U.S. Attorney Rudolph Giuliani, to approve the agreement.

There was no percentage in dwelling on the leniency problem, so Pitt and Rauch concentrated on the advantages for the government. They repeated the arguments presented a month earlier to the SEC—expediency, full bank cooperation, testimony from Meier, and the identity of the person behind the trading.

Sturc's quip about "Moby Dick," made at the December meeting, had stuck with the bank's lawyers. Because of the secrecy that still shrouded the identity of the trader, they had begun to refer to him among themselves and the bank employees as "Moby Dick." They also liked the impression of size the name implied, so they used it repeatedly in their presentation to the prosecutors.

After listening attentively to the deal Pitt and Rauch sought, which included complete criminal immunity for the bank and all of its employees, Romatowski's face grew stern as he addressed the bank's lawyers.

"You know," he said, "it occurs to me that there are two things you haven't asked for on behalf of your client."

Pitt, who prides himself on thoroughness, was stunned. "Gee, if we've left something out, that would be troublesome. Why don't you tell me what it is?"

"You haven't asked for a cash award and an apology," Romatowski said with a grin.

18.

Maneuvers

Down the hall, in another room, two toddlers were engaged in a loud struggle over a toy. The noise distracted Ilan Reich momentarily, but he quickly returned his attention to the man seated next to him.

It was a Sunday in February 1986. Dennis Levine, his wife, Laurie, and their four-year-old son had been invited to brunch at Reich's apartment in a brownstone on the Upper West Side. Reich's wife, Diane, and Laurie Levine were off in the kitchen cleaning up from a meal of lox and bagels. In his room, Reich's three-year-old son was tussling harmlessly with Levine's son.

Although Reich had firmly refused to provide Levine with information for more than a year and a half, he and the investment banker had remained friendly, getting together occasionally for lunch. This was the first time Reich had invited Levine to his home, however, and the first time their families had socialized.

Now, in Reich's living room, Levine was telling the young lawyer how smart he had been to get out of their little scheme and how he, Levine, wasn't really "doing it" anymore either.

"I'm doing so well at Drexel," he said with a laugh, "it's enough to make an honest man out of me. With all these insider investigations by the SEC, somebody would have to be crazy to be doing it. There's really no reason to pursue anything that reckless."

Caution had never been one of Levine's personality traits and his remarks surprised Reich. He remembered his own fears of exposure each time he learned of an SEC investigation or insider trading arrest when he was providing information to Levine. He had been particularly unnerved in 1982 by the arrest of Carlo Florentino, a young partner at Wachtell, Lipton whom Reich had known casually. Reich had told Levine at the time, "I'm not going to be another Carlo Florentino."

Levine, as usual, had been persuasive in convincing Reich not to worry. He had always managed to sound self-assured and unconcerned as he explained where the people who got caught had been careless or stupid.

Such worries were long behind Reich in February 1986. He had been named a partner at Wachtell, Lipton in November 1984, and he was handling key deals and making important presentations to corporate boards by himself. He had developed a "father-son" relationship with Marty Lipton as they created new strategies for defending clients from raiders financed with Drexel's junk bonds. They thought alike and even doodled alike on yellow legal pads at meetings. His relationship with his wife had improved enormously over the last year and a half. His involvement in Levine's insider trading operation was a skeleton hidden away in a closet of his life that no one knew about. Except the man sitting next to him in his apartment that Sunday.

As Levine talked about the recklessness of insider trading as though it were a distant and foreign concept, Reich had the sense that his friend was making a clumsy if unmistakable attempt to cover his tracks.

It was an impression shared by Richard Coulson, who had been handling as many of Levine's telephone calls as possible at the bank in recent weeks in order to minimize the customer's contact with Pletscher.

On January 16, Levine telephoned collect for Pletscher. The call was routed to Coulson, who explained that Pletscher was busy. Levine told Coulson he had asked a Swiss lawyer and his lawyers in Nassau about the legality of the bank's action in providing account records to the American government even without the names of the customers. He said the lawyers in both countries agreed that even providing anonymous account records to the authorities violated the law unless the customer gave permission.

"Other account holders could sue the bank," Levine warned in advising Coulson that the bank should demand the return of its records. "You should talk to my lawyer in Nassau, Hartis Pinder, and see if he can give you a legal opinion that you can use to get the records back. I'm trying to help you."

The threat of a lawsuit was one of several recurrent themes in conversations between Levine and the bankers. It was calculated, of course, to provide a strong motive to maintain the cover-up and keep his records from both the bank's lawyers and the SEC. Coulson viewed Levine's reference to other account holders as a thinly disguised warning. In his notes of the conversation, Coulson wrote: "Wants to help us!! HAH."

Another of Levine's tactics was to pretend that, through high-level sources, he knew what was going on at the SEC. He thought this both reassured the bankers that he was well informed when he downplayed the progress of the investigation and encouraged them to tell him the truth about what was going on lest he find out from sources within the agency.

On January 27, Levine's collect call was again put through to Coulson.

"Has anything new happened?" Levine asked.

"Our lawyers are still negotiating and discussing things with the SEC," replied Coulson.

"For your information, on my recent trip to Washington, during my usual high-level talks with the SEC, I had the impression that all the investigations into stocks that started last summer and fall had died down and were dormant."

"That's interesting," said Coulson.

"I'd like to come down and talk to you and Bruno next week about new ways to trade. I've got some more secure ways. And I could keep on doing business with your bank."

"I see," said Coulson.

Coulson would not be careless. As a lawyer and former investment banker himself, Coulson was a good negotiator and the last thing he wanted was to precipitate a confrontation by alarming Levine. He continued to caution the customer against any resumption of trading, stressing that the bank's attorneys were insisting on a low profile while they tried to stop the SEC investigation with the managed-accounts story.

To keep Levine away from the bank, Coulson had built a web of excuses and half-truths. With the departure of Fraysse and Meier's return to Zurich, he said, he and Pletscher were extremely busy running the operation. In addition, every trip to Nassau posed a risk for Levine. Now he urged that, unless the business were urgent, Levine put off his visit. Reluctantly, Levine agreed.

Despite Coulson's words of warning, Levine's desire to trade remained strong. Less than a month later, he telephoned Coulson and repeated that he wanted to begin buying and selling stocks again. In a potentially ominous development, he told Coulson that his Nassau lawyer was helping him develop a legal method for buying and selling stocks through Bank Leu, but he did not describe the scheme. Coulson knew he would have a much harder time stopping Levine if he were to concoct some new scheme for employing his inside information.

On this call, Levine once again told Coulson that his government sources said the SEC investigation was "petering out." Neither Bank Leu officials nor Pitt and Rauch had any idea whether Levine really had sources within the SEC. If he did, the sources were not particularly accurate because he had received no indication of the change in strategy. A far more likely possibility was that the Wall

Street rumor mill, which Levine had played so well for so many years, was generating gossip about the SEC inquiries at the various brokerage houses. But the lawyers and the bank officials could not afford to discount the possibility that Levine also received information from someone inside the agency, someone who had not yet received an accurate picture of the Bank Leu inquiry.

At 10:30 A.M. on February 26, Dennis Levine had an appointment to see Ivan Boesky in the arbitrager's thirty-fifth-floor office at 650 Fifth Avenue. Bank Leu had forced Levine to stop trading, but the investment banker was by no means allowing all of his valuable information to lie fallow. His insider ring was still functioning and he had supplied Boesky with several tips. The most recent had been on plans for a financial restructuring by FMC Corporation, the machinery and defense equipment giant headquartered in Chicago.

FMC's management had held several meetings with its investment bankers at Goldman, Sachs & Co. in late 1985 to explore the possibility of a financial restructuring that would make the company a tougher target for a hostile takeover bid. In January, through his job at the investment bank, David Brown had learned confidential details of FMC's contemplated plan to recapitalize by purchasing stock from outside shareholders at a premium price and giving more stock to FMC employees. Brown passed the information to his friend at Shearson Lehman Brothers, Ira Sokolow, who in turn passed it to Levine.

By the middle of February, the deal was solid enough that Levine provided the information to Boesky, telling him that FMC intended to buy back stock from shareholders at a premium price. Boesky purchased 95,300 shares of FMC stock between February 18 and 21, the latter the day the company's board of directors announced it was considering a recapitalization plan. When Boesky sold the stock that day, its price had risen almost $11 a share and his profit was $975,000.

The increase in the price of its stock over that three-day period was not just the result of Boesky's buying, because others had started to buy FMC also. The run-up forced FMC to sweeten the terms of its recapitalization plan: outside shareholders were offered $80 cash for each common share instead of the intended $70. The company announced later that spring that it would have to raise an additional $225 million to cover the sweetened terms.

Under the formula they had negotiated, Boesky owed Levine 5 percent of his profits from the FMC deal, or slightly less than $50,000. That was small change to Levine. And he had to pay a portion of it in cash to Sokolow who, in turn, would share it with Brown. Levine knew he could have made twenty times that much buying FMC through his trading account at Bank Leu. The more Levine dwelled on it, the stronger his resolve became to resume trading again despite the opinion he had expressed to Reich about the recklessness of insider trading. Levine had been working on two new plans to get back in the game. One would involve Bank Leu; the other would involve Ivan Boesky.

The compulsion to trade overcame the instinct to be cautious. And Levine had had ample reason for caution that winter. He had told Wilkis in February that Pletscher had slipped during one of their conversations and mentioned the word "immunity." Levine suspected that the bank was trying to cut its own deal with the SEC, or at least that the possibility of a deal had been mentioned by the lawyers. Levine repeated to Wilkis the need for "getaway money," and he tossed out another option for dealing with the problem.

"I might go over to Switzerland and make sure Bernie Meier keeps this quiet," Levine told Wilkis one night in February. "I've thought about getting a contract on him."

Wilkis was dumbfounded. Even though he felt certain his friend was joking, the talk of violence terrified him and he said sharply: "I don't want to hear about that. Don't talk about anything like that."

Yet, despite his apprehension over the course of the SEC inquiry, Levine couldn't control his need to trade. Clearly he was driven by greed for what money could buy. He had grown used to eating in the most expensive restaurants, spending extravagantly on his apartment, sending his son, Adam, to the city's top nursery school. But there was also a strong streak of arrogance. Levine believed he was smarter than the SEC lawyers who had been on his trail since the end of August. The rush his secret triumphs brought him and the prospect of outfoxing the SEC might have displaced his continuing fears about not making it in the real world because, in spite of his bravura, Levine was not a creative force in investment banking and his hold on stardom was precarious. In early February, his confidence had been dealt a severe jolt when he heard that Martin Siegel, a principal architect of modern takeover strategies, was joining Drexel Burnham. Levine was devastated. Siegel was blessed with every attribute necessary for success, attributes that had made him a genuine star. Indeed, Siegel had been on Drexel's list of "stars" back in the summer of 1984 when they had hired Levine instead. Hiring Siegel away from Kidder, Peabody & Co. was viewed as a major coup at Drexel, and a major threat by Levine.

It wasn't that Levine had disappointed his employers. Executives at Drexel remained high on his contribution to the firm. But the chance to wed Siegel's reputation as a dealmaker with the firm's legendary expertise in raising financing was irresistible to Fred Joseph and the other executives at the investment banking firm.

In fifteen years at Kidder, Peabody, Marty Siegel had become known as a skillful protector of corporations that did not want to be taken over. It was an arena that Dennis Levine regarded as his preserve at Drexel. Even worse from Levine's point of view, Siegel was coming aboard as co-head of the mergers and acquisitions division, which meant he would share the top spot with David Kay and Leon Black. Office gossip was that Siegel's combined salary and first-year bonus would exceed $2 million.

Since moving to Drexel a year before, Levine had viewed himself as the equal of the big names in M&A on Wall Street. As confirmation of that standing, he was scheduled to appear at a two-day seminar in March with Siegel and Bruce Wasserstein, the chief mergers specialist at First Boston. Now Siegel would be there not as an equal but as Levine's boss. Just as Levine had feared being overshadowed at Lehman Brothers when Tom Hill arrived, he now told Wilkis and Reich of his worries that Siegel would grab the limelight at Drexel and all the blue-chip clients, too.

February also brought frustrations for Harvey Pitt and Michael Rauch. Negotiations over the written agreement with the SEC proved difficult and time-consuming, and the main question looming over them remained unanswered: would the Bahamian government allow the bank to reveal the name of its client?

The bank had hired two Nassau lawyers, Michael Barnett and Claire Hepburn, to research Bahamian law and work with Pitt and Rauch in deciding the best approach to the government in Nassau on the issue of naming a bank customer. The bank secrecy act seemed to prohibit any such disclosure, but one of the jobs of a smart lawyer is devising exceptions to the law.

The SEC staff insisted that the written agreement contain a clause that allowed the agency to call off the whole arrangement if the bank did not divulge the name of the client. Because of the uncertainty of the legal situation in Nassau, Pitt and Rauch argued that the bank should retain its immunity if it made a good-faith effort to obtain approval from the Bahamian government. Various drafts of the agreement were written in late January and early February; some contained the cancellation clause, others did not.

By the end of January, the statements from Levine's three trading accounts had been assembled and analyzed. The results were compiled in a remarkable eight-page document. It listed the name of every stock he had bought, the number and cost of the shares purchased, and the sale price and profit or loss.

For security reasons, the bankers, lawyers, and their staffs still did not refer to Levine by his name. Since the December 17th meeting with the SEC, Moby Dick had replaced Diamond and Mr. X as Levine's nickname among the people who were dissecting his hidden life. The compilation of his trades bore the headline PROFITS MOBY DICK.

In all, Levine had purchased stock or options in 114 different companies—from Dart Industries on June 5, 1980, to MidCon Corporation on December 9, 1985. He had earned $13,610,897.49 in profits on seventy-one winners. The bulk of his profits came in the last twelve months of trading, and the biggest jackpot was $2,694,421.26 on Nabisco Brands.

He lost money on forty-three stocks when deals collapsed or his information was imperfect. The amounts of the losses were minor—$2,052,300.52. The biggest loss, $274,718.74, came when a bid to acquire Southland Corporation was dropped in 1984. His net profit on the 114 stocks had been $11,558,596.97.

The addition of routine bank interest over the years had raised the total return on his original investment of $168,900 at Bank Leu to a staggering $12.6 million.

Analyzing and listing the trades from the statements was the easy part. The tradings slips and confirmations from each purchase and sale then had to be redacted and copied. A single stock might generate ten or more slips, since Meier had spread them among many different brokers. In addition, the trading records of Pletscher, Meier, and Fraysse had to be copied and nearly six years of bank files had to be combed for any documents relating to the investigation.

The team of paralegals in Nassau had been expanded to four with the addition of Erna Bongers from Fried, Frank's New York office and Allison Fraser from the Washington office. David Hardison, a bright first-year lawyer at the firm, had gone down to supervise the task. The living room of the two-bedroom suite reserved for Pitt and Rauch was transformed into a small office, complete with a copying machine and cluttered with boxes of documents.

Meanwhile, with the assistance of Schaad and other officials of the Bank Leu parent company, Pitt and Rauch were still trying to persuade Meier to sign a written promise that he would testify before the SEC. The testimony was an essential ingredient of the deal, but Meier, citing the advice of his Swiss attorney, was balking.

Meier distrusted the entire process of negotiating with the American government. He did not believe that he would be treated fairly by the SEC or the bank even if he agreed to testify. And he retained a deep distaste for the idea of turning in a client.

In mid-January, he had telephoned Pletscher in Nassau and urged him to hire a lawyer to represent only him, warning: "You will lose your job and career. Bank Leu International will fire you. You should get legal advice from a third party, someone who represents you."

"The head office assured me I will be treated all right and I will not be dropped," Pletscher replied. They had told him, he said, that if he cooperated, they would support him.

"You are a fool," snapped Meier. "You must get your own lawyer and get a promise from the bank in writing."

"After nineteen years, I believe the head office," Pletscher said.

By the middle of February, Meier's written pledge to cooperate had become essential to moving forward in the talks with the SEC. Bank officials in Zurich promised Meier that his job and career would be safeguarded if he cooperated. If he did not cooperate, Meier was told that the American government would refuse to grant him immunity and he was likely to be sued by the SEC for insider trading. It mattered not: Meier refused to cooperate.

The trading records and name of the customer would be insufficient for the open-and-shut case demanded by the SEC and the U.S. Attorney's Office. The government needed an articulate witness with a good memory who could explain how the customer had placed the trades and what indications might have existed that the trades were based on inside information, a witness who could transform the raw data into a compelling story for a judge and jury, if it came to that. Meier fit the bill, but someone else would have to be found.

The logical substitute was Bruno Pletscher. Jean-Pierre Fraysse no longer worked for the bank and his personal contact with Levine had, in any case, been minimal. Richard Coulson had no firsthand knowledge of Levine's trading. Pletscher, on the other hand, helped Levine open his account and had executed his trades in the early days. In recent years, he had substituted for Meier on many occasions. Further, he had been involved intimately in the cover-up scheme.

But, chiefly because he had remained in the background in dealing with the lawyers, no one knew what sort of witness Pletscher would make or whether he could be persuaded to testify. Although undeniably bright, he lacked Meier's polish and charm. Gary Lynch, who had resisted including Meier in the deal, calling it a "bitter pill," was pleased that his withdrawal would allow the SEC to bring a case against the banker. But he was concerned about the loss of a key witness and he had no idea whether Pletscher could carry the burden.

On February 16, Pletscher had flown to Zurich for a one-week skiing holiday. He had gone with some friends to Davos in the Swiss Alps and it was there that Bank Leu located him. Pletscher was told that the bank's lawyers, including Hans Peter Schaad and Harvey Pitt, needed him immediately in London. Bernie Meier had dropped out of the deal and Pletscher would have to take his place as the chief witness, he was told.

Davos is about two hours from Zurich, and one of Pletscher's friends agreed to drive him to Zurich so he could catch a plane to London. It was snowing hard as they left the resort and, about halfway to Zurich, the snow turned into a raging storm. Six inches fell in two hours and traffic was stopped completely. Even for the Swiss, who are accustomed to heavy snowfalls, the storm was enormous, and it took Pletscher and his companion six and a half hours to get to Zurich.

Pletscher had missed the last plane to London, so he checked into a hotel for the night, planning to take the first available flight in the morning. He telephoned Meier at his suburban home.

"I heard you were not in the deal," Pletscher said.

"They forced me out," said Meier.

"What do you mean?"

"I didn't have enough time to decide what to do. They said that I would have to sign an agreement that I would testify. Harvey demanded it. I will not be rushed into this. I told them no."

Pletscher told Meier that the bank wanted him to sign the agreement in Meier's place. As he had a month before, Meier warned Pletscher he was making a mistake, risking his career on the advice of lawyers who had no interest in his future. The publicity would ensure that his career in the Bahamas and probably in banking anywhere would be finished, said Meier. But Pletscher repeated his belief in the promises made by the bank about his job security.

Unlike Meier, who had been preparing to return to Zurich when the inquiry broke, Pletscher wanted to remain in Nassau a few more years. He had earned the promotion he had sought for so long and he needed time to develop in the job. In addition, his relationship with Sherrill Caso had blossomed into a love affair and they planned to be married. She was a native of the Bahamas and was reluctant to leave.

There were other differences, too. Pletscher's rise within the system, from apprentice to bank manager, had imbued him with a deep sense of obligation and loyalty. He had no reason to think that he would not be protected by the system that had nurtured him, as long as he followed orders. When the head office assured him that his job was secure if he cooperated, he believed it.

But the telephone call with Meier planted new doubts in Pletscher's mind. He was frightened of being used and then sacrificed, if not to the SEC, then to the Bahamian banking authorities or the Swiss banking tribunal.

The snow from the day before remained and the next morning Pletscher took a small bus from downtown Zurich to the city's modern airport. He flew to London to meet with Pitt, Rauch, and Michael Barnett, the Bahamian lawyer. Winning Pletscher's agreement to testify was a delicate task. What the lawyers had going for them was his predisposition to accept the word of his superiors and his basic honesty. Working against them was Pletscher's distaste for revealing any details involving a client's account and his fear about the effects of publicity on his ability to remain in Nassau.

Pitt did most of the talking, patiently courting the Swiss banker with reassurances that the best course for the bank and Pletscher was to tell the truth and repeating to him the promises from the bank that, whatever happened in the aftermath of the case, the home office would help him land on his feet. Implicit in the bank's promise to help Pletscher if he cooperated was the warning that he would lose his job if he refused to testify.

"The publicity could be very terrible," Pitt said. "But we will do our best to keep it to a minimum."

In the end, Bruno Pletscher was persuaded by Harvey Pitt that his best chance for emerging from the investigation with his career and self-esteem intact was to cooperate with the bank's lawyers, the officials from the home office, and the American government.

Pletscher would make a far better witness than anyone imagined that day in London, and the impact of his decision would be felt in many quarters.

19.

"The Genius Plan"

"It's obvious that the SEC investigation isn't as quiet as I thought it was. And I'm down here to tell you it's not."

Levine sat hunched forward in his chair, elbows resting on the oak table, a serious expression on his pudgy face. Pletscher and Coulson were startled by his statement. For months, Levine had been predicting the imminent end of the inquiry, dismissing the abilities of the SEC to penetrate the curtain of lies, downplaying the danger of the situation. He had seemed oblivious to any threat. Suddenly, late on Friday afternoon, March 7, Levine was expressing concern about the inquiry.

In a telephone conversation just three days before, Levine had reported that the inquiry appeared to be at a standstill. "No news is good news," he had said heartily. Now the abrupt transformation troubled the bankers. Why, after all these months, was Levine changing his tactics? Did he really have a source inside the SEC who had told him what was going on? How would he react if he suspected how close the SEC was to nabbing him?

Levine's alarm threatened to break the status quo. As long as Levine felt the SEC was not a real threat, he had been satisfied with the lies and half-truths and had not asked to withdraw his money. As long as he didn't feel threatened by the inquiry, there was no reason to take his funds.

From the bank's perspective, a demand for the money was the one thing that might cause its deal to come unstuck, even though the account was not legally frozen. But if the bank refused to honor a Levine demand for a substantial portion of his account, it would in all likelihood expose its cooperation with the American government. Putting him off with stories that the lawyers wanted him to maintain a low profile by not trading while they were trying to kill the inquiry was one thing. Refusing a customer access to his own account was far more serious and could throw the issue into an entirely different arena.

Levine had already demonstrated a willingness to seek his own legal advice, and he might well file a lawsuit in the Bahamian courts to obtain his money. Under the bank secrecy laws, it was conceivable that Levine's lawyers could file a suit without identifying their client. In order to fight the lawsuit, Bank Leu would have to reveal its reasons for refusing to turn over the money. The secrecy essential to the SEC deal would be blown, and with it, any opportunity to approach the Bahamian authorities informally for permission to trade the name of their customer for immunity.

When he had telephoned on Tuesday to arrange Friday's meeting, Levine had said he wanted to explain his new plan to reactivate his trading account. He had described the plan on the telephone as "very clever." Pletscher had again demurred, arguing the necessity for caution.

When Levine had then inquired about the progress of the investigation and whether a date had been set for Meier's testimony, Pletscher told him, "The lawyers are still negotiating with the SEC. Everything is quiet. They may talk forever. The whole case may die a natural death."

"No news is good news," Levine had said. "But do you expect any answer from the SEC in the near future?"

"Our lawyers didn't give us any indications."

"Do you speak frequently to the lawyers? Do they talk frequently to the SEC?"

"No date has been set," Pletscher said. "I don't know when the lawyers spoke last with the SEC. But we will certainly contact the lawyers by the end of the week or early next week in order to find out where we stand. We don't like this situation. We hope we'll have a clearer idea what's going on by that time."

"I really feel it's a shame not to be trading, but I respect your views. Like I said, no news is good news. And as far as I can see up here in New York, it's absolutely quiet."

His decision to testify before the SEC in Meier's place had fed Pletscher's anxieties. Knowing that he would be the one telling the whole story of Diamond's account to the American government had made it more difficult than ever to lie to the customer.

Coulson had been listening on another telephone. After hanging up, Pletscher had turned to him and said: "This is very uncomfortable. It's entirely against our word to be telling a customer such bullshit and to lie this way." Coulson shook his head in agreement.

When he went over the conversation with Pitt later that day, Pletscher made his discomfort plain: "You'd better rush this thing. I'm getting sick and tired of being the buffer between you guys and Diamond."

Now, sitting in the bank's conference room three days later, Pletscher's distress increased as he listened to Levine describe what he had heard about the SEC investigation since their telephone conversation on Tuesday.

"My sources at the SEC tell me the investigators have expanded the list of takeover stocks to about forty," said Levine as he pulled out a scrap of paper from his pocket and read the names of several stocks that were on the new list. All were stocks Levine had bought heavily through Bank Leu.

"Along with adding stocks, they've expanded the time frame on this thing. They're going to go back a long way looking for information. The SEC has talked to lawyers, investment bankers, and brokers trying to get information about these stocks. This week they started pressing the brokerage houses for information on who bought all forty of these stocks.

"I know one of the brokers they've talked to is Brian Campbell," Levine continued. "That guy has been stupid enough to copy Bank Leu trades in large numbers. Interviewing brokers and lawyers means the SEC doesn't have a clue who is behind the trades.

"The time to end all this is now," Levine said emphatically. "You should have your lawyers arrange it so Bernie testifies very soon about the managed accounts. And the bank should stay silent about the truth because of the bank secrecy law. Your lawyers should stonewall the SEC. Don't give them any documents. Just have Bernie testify as we planned."

Pletscher and Coulson assured Levine that the bank's lawyers were moving as quickly as possible with the SEC. They said they hoped to have the testimony arranged within a matter of weeks.

Pletscher felt certain that Levine's new caution would lead him to abandon his plan to resume trading, but he was wrong. Despite the realization that the SEC inquiry was still a menace, the lure of trading had become almost palpable, a force Levine could no longer resist. If his position were precarious and he were still exposed to danger, it would be all the more satisfying to trade. It would prove that he was smarter, quicker, and more creative than the SEC attorneys he described to Pletscher and Wilkis as "dumb clerks." The same deep-seated craving for recognition that powered his career on Wall Street drove his illegal enterprise. If the risks were greater, so were the rewards.

Nothing better exemplified Levine's psychological makeup than the name he had given to his scheme to resume trading. He called it "the genius plan."

"There are so many opportunities to make money, and you can make money, too," Levine told Pletscher and Coulson. "What I'm going to do is start trading through a mutual fund. The bank will set it up and participate, too."

Although he said the final details were being worked out, Levine described a plan that was similar in theory to the managed-accounts story that had been fabricated for the SEC. His description was sketchy, and Pletscher had the sense that Levine himself understood little about how the concept would work.

According to Levine's scheme, Bank Leu would create a mutual fund and pool some bank funds with Levine's account. The bank also would invite some of its large customers to invest in the fund, but Levine would be the major investor and the principal beneficiary. Levine would supply information on which stocks to purchase, only instead of buying for Levine's Panamanian company, the purchases would be made through the mutual fund and profits allocated to its investors, with Levine taking the lion's share.

"The more clients you can bring into the fund, the more the whole thing would be spread over a lot of people," Levine explained.

Coulson recognized that the plan posed many dangers for the bank and sought to stall Levine, saying: "Now isn't the time to start a new mechanism for trading. There's too much attention from the SEC. We want to keep a low profile in the U.S. markets."

Levine was adamant. He had $10 million in his account but he wouldn't see $20 million unless he were allowed to resume trading on the sensitive information that was still flowing his way. If Bank Leu refused to go along with his genius plan, he threatened to withdraw some of his money—even all of it—and implement the scheme somewhere else, at least until the heat died down at Bank Leu.

As a calculated confirmation that his threat was real, Levine demanded a copy of the current statement for his International Gold account, the successor to the Diamond and Diamond International accounts. When Pletscher handed over a copy of the statement, he was amazed to see Levine fold it carefully and tuck it into a pocket. It was the first time in nearly six years that Levine had taken anything from Bank Leu except $100 bills. He said he would be back in a couple of weeks.

Pletscher and Coulson telephoned Michael Rauch in New York

and told him what had happened. Rauch agreed that there was reason for concern. Moreover, Rauch felt Levine could win if he sought his money in court, although he believed the bank would be entitled to disclose Levine's name as part of its defense, and that possibility might force Levine to rethink any threats of a lawsuit. But that was a confrontation no one connected with the bank wanted, and Pletscher and Coulson would have to find some way to stall Levine without touching off a dispute that would wind up in the Bahamian courts.

Meier's refusal to cooperate and the substitution of Pletscher as the bank's star witness had slowed down the process. The written drafts of the agreement itself had to be altered: Pletscher's name was inserted as witness, and Meier became a target of the SEC. The prosecutors in New York had to be informed of the change and a new agreement worked out with them. Under this new burden of cumbersome details, the negotiating process that had been moving slowly for weeks nearly came to a halt.

On March 10 or 11, Gary Lynch telephoned Pitt. Lynch had not been involved in the nitty-gritty of the talks, although he had signed off on the major issues as they arose. When he reached Pitt, Lynch said firmly that the commission had to have an agreement worked out by Sunday. He said he had informed his staff of that and he expected the talks to come to a rapid conclusion so the case could move ahead.

"The staff is too much into the negotiating process and they aren't focusing on getting the deal done," Lynch told Pitt. "I want to stop this fascination with the process and get the deal done by Sunday."

Coupled with the news Rauch had received from Nassau, Lynch's demand had the desired effect. The attorneys on both sides addressed the few substantive issues separating them and settled their remaining differences in a matter of days.

On Wednesday, March 19, Pitt joined the SEC attorneys for a

final session that lasted until 10:00 P.M. All copies of the agreement were signed, and Pitt accepted SEC subpoenas on behalf of the bank. The "Moby Dick" profit analysis had not been submitted to the SEC, but the government attorneys knew from their own investigation, and had gathered from their conversations with Pitt and Rauch over the weeks, that the scope of the inquiry would expand dramatically once the bank records were turned over.

Under the accord, Bank Leu would produce the complete records associated with the customer behind the trading, ranging from the customer's trading slips to internal bank documents relating to the account. The records, which would be redacted to eliminate any information that might identify the customer, were to be delivered to the SEC by April 7.

A week after the documents were due, the agreement required Pletscher to provide sworn testimony to the SEC lawyers. It stipulated that he would answer all questions except those dealing with identifying the customer. In order to limit the bank's exposure to U.S. laws in the event the deal collapsed and avoid angering Bahamian authorities by placing the bank in U.S. jurisdiction, Pletscher's statement would be taken in the Bahamas, Canada, or the United Kingdom.

For its part, the SEC agreed not to bring civil actions against the bank or any former and current employees, with the exception of Bernie Meier. The prediction Pitt had made in February had come true. The SEC was going after Meier as an accomplice in the insider trading scheme.

The bank and the employees covered by the agreement pledged to pay all profits made from their piggybacking on the customer's trades to the U.S. government. But the SEC agreed not to seek the triple damages allowed by the 1984 Insider Trading Sanctions Act.

In an attempt to keep the deal secret until the SEC was ready to move on the customer, Bank Leu agreed not to inform the customer of the compromise and to take steps to stop its employees from informing the customer.

298 / Mr Diamond

In the end, the SEC staff prevailed on the important issue of whether the bank would retain its immunity if it were unable to deliver the name of its customer, although weeks of wrangling and lawyering had laundered the directness out of the wording.

The final language in the agreement said "failure to comply" would render the deal "null and void." The agreement specified that it would be considered a failure on the bank's part if the institution refused to identify the customer after being ordered to do so by a United States court or receiving permission from proper Bahamian authorities.

Receiving approval from the Bahamian government to disclose the name was still questionable. But the language provided the SEC with insurance because the agency expected little difficulty persuading a U.S. court to order the bank to divulge the name of its client. The SEC had ample evidence that insider trading laws had been violated by a U.S. citizen in U.S. markets, and the government victories in the Santa Fe and St. Joe Minerals cases provided sufficient precedent. If Bank Leu refused to comply with an American court order, the deal would be off.

If the government in Nassau went along with the informal request, the process of identifying and apprehending the customer would be expedited. If Nassau rejected the proposal, the SEC would be free to go to court in the United States and obtain an order for the name. It would take longer, but the recent court precedents favored the SEC. Under an American court order to divulge the information, Bank Leu would have to decide whether to disobey Bahamian law and identify the client or lose the agreement and its immunity under U.S. law. In either case, the consequences for Bank Leu International could be serious.

Although the wording of the final agreement was neither more nor less than Pitt and Rauch had expected from the beginning, it became more important than ever that the government in Nassau be persuaded to cooperate so the bank could avoid legal troubles in both jurisdictions.

An old saw among lawyers is that a legal document should be read from the back forward, because the most substantive material is often at the end.

In the case of the March 19 agreement, an attachment to the document acknowledged that on May 27, 1980, an account had been opened at Bank Leu by "an American customer who is presently a managing director of a major investment banking firm located in the United States. It is believed that the customer resides and works in the Southern District of New York." The attachment listed nine cash withdrawals by the customer, ranging from $30,000 to $200,000, and totaling $1.3 million. It wasn't the total amount Levine had withdrawn, because not all of the withdrawal slips had been found in the records yet. But the figures were enough to sustain the interest of the SEC.

Leo Wang had kept the name "Dennis Levine" in a mental file of suspicious characters since the Textron investigation in the fall of 1984. The SEC attorneys involved in the Bank Leu case had batted around many names since the disclosure by Pitt and Rauch on December 17 that the trading had been conducted by a major player on Wall Street. The fact that no single investment bank or law firm was common to all twenty-eight stocks had left them puzzled and without a clear suspect.

After the disclosure attached to the March 19 agreement, however, Wang's suspicion that Levine was a possibility was strengthened. He was, after all, a managing director at Drexel Burnham, and a quick check of SEC registration forms showed that he had been in the investment banking profession prior to May 27, 1980. It was a long way from confirmation, nothing a good lawyer would take to court. But there was a possibility that Wang's skepticism from 1984 had been better founded than even he had imagined back then.

Playing a hunch, Wang asked Stuart Allen, a special investigator for the SEC, to contact the U.S. Customs Service and see if Levine had ever declared that he was entering the country carrying a substantial amount of cash. Allen, who represents the SEC's link to criminal investigative agencies, called an investigator in the Customs Service financial investigations division and requested a check on Dennis Levine in the service's computers. On April 1, he followed up the informal request with a formal letter to Bonnie Tischler, director of the division.

A few days later, Tischler responded with inconclusive results. Levine, "who may be the individual that your office is trying to identify," had declared on a Customs form in 1979 that he had more than $10,000 in a checking account in Paris. But the computer check did not turn up any evidence that Levine had ever entered the country carrying more than $10,000 in cash.

For Wang, the results were only a mild disappointment. He hadn't really expected someone operating an illegal insider trading operation to declare the cash he was carrying to avoid breaking another law. And the results did not rule out the possibility that Moby Dick was Dennis Levine.

On March 24, slightly more than two weeks after he first broached his genius plan with the bankers, Levine returned to Bank Leu. He had spent the Palm Sunday weekend in Florida with his family and wanted a short hop to Nassau to confer with the bank officials.

Pletscher twitched with tension as he headed for the conference room with Coulson. He hadn't made up his mind how to handle the situation if Levine demanded the transfer of his money to another bank. It was Pletscher who would have to confront the irate Levine. He had seen flashes of temper in the investment banker over the years and, while he had no rational basis for it, Pletscher was growing frightened of Levine. It was an emotional time, and under such stress, rational faculties are often overcome by irrational fears. It was a feeling that Pletscher hated, but that didn't mean it was one he could control.

Levine's first request threw Pletscher. Levine explained that he was leaving soon for a two-week business trip to Europe and he wanted to get in touch with Bernie Meier.

"I may have some free time on my trip and I'd just like to get in touch with him and see how it's going," Levine said casually.

Pletscher politely refused. He realized the potential for disaster if Levine sat down with Meier, who had backed out of the scheme and was openly unhappy with the decision to tell the truth to the American government. Claiming that Meier was traveling, staying with various friends and relatives, Pletscher said he didn't have any way to help Levine. The American did not press the point.

Levine's second reason for the trip was to raise again the matter of bank secrecy laws. For several weeks, he had been urging the bank to contact his Nassau lawyer, Hartis Pinder. Levine thought the bank could hire Pinder and use his analysis of the bank secrecy laws both to thwart further demands from the American lawyers for documents and to stop them before they provided any records to the SEC. Coulson had refused the offer repeatedly, so Levine had taken matters into his own hands and had Pinder write a letter outlining his interpretation of the laws.

On his way to Bank Leu that day, Levine had stopped by Pinder's office two blocks away and picked up a copy of the lawyer's opinion, which was addressed to Bank Leu. The bank officials were well aware of the bank secrecy requirements and, when Levine presented the letter to Coulson and Pletscher, they viewed it as a threat, rather than an offer of assistance.

As if to emphasize the importance of secrecy, Pinder did not identify Levine anywhere in the letter. Instead, he said he was writing on behalf of an unidentified client in response to a "hypothetical request" from a United States agency for bank information that would identify a customer. Pinder cited English common law and the 1965 Bahamas banking statute as precedents for refusing to turn over any information to any outside agency without permission from the customer or from proper Bahamian authorities.

The letter also referred to an opinion on a 1975 bank secrecy case, which was written by Sir Leonard Knowles, chief justice of the nation's highest court: "The secrecy provision is one of the pillars of this part (banking) of our economic structure, destruction of which would lead to the collapse of the whole structure which it supports."

The letter concluded by noting that there were various criminal penalties and civil remedies that could be imposed in the event a bank in the Bahamas wrongfully disclosed information about a "hypothetical" customer's identity or account.

After Pletscher and Coulson read the letter, Levine said: "This is just to help you, of course. If the bank gave out any account details, you could get sued." He paused before adding, "I'd probably have to sue you, too."

Something more sinister than the threat of a lawsuit frightened Bruno Pletscher and Sherrill Caso as they stood holding hands in the living room of their house in a quiet, middle-class neighborhood on the outskirts of Nassau.

Just a few days before, it had been a typical house in the tropics, open to the year-round sun and constant warmth through a giant, three-panel, sliding-glass door in the living room and a spacious sunroom, known as a Bahamas room, which was enclosed by walls of screens and two more sliding-glass doors. Before Pletscher moved in several months earlier, Caso had lived in the house alone without fear. As a native of the Bahamas, she knew Nassau had a problem with property crime, but she also knew physical violence was rare and she had never had any reason to fear someone cutting through the screens or shattering the glass in an attempt to harm her.

As they stood silently in the living room that day in late March, the house was dramatically different. A crew of carpenters had just finished replacing the three-panel door in the living room with a wall and two small windows. The screens and sliding doors in the Bahamas room were also gone, replaced by conventional walls, windows, and a single door.

The virtual fortification of their house reflected the fundamental shift their lives had undergone in recent months. The forces that had first buffeted Pletscher in late August and September now affected every facet of his life and, because they shared so much, Caso's life as well. Gone was the easy conviviality of life in the islands, where the heat seems to slow everything to a more civilized pace and work that isn't done today can be finished up tomorrow. In its place was a pressure-filled world where foreign laws and lawyers made the rules, and the lies and deceptions seemed to create an endless maze in which no turn offered a way out. The strains and frustrations and fears combined to forge a powerful paranoia that infected both of them.

For irrational fears to dominate the lives of two perfectly rational, intelligent people, the situation must contain several key ingredients. The all-important ingredient in this case, as in most, was a sizable dose of truth. Pletscher was indeed the critical link between Levine and the trading. Levine himself had stressed in recent meetings that only four people at the bank could tie him to the trading. Whether he knew it or not, two of them—Meier and Fraysse—were out of the picture, and the third—Coulson—had only a limited knowledge of Levine. That left Pletscher, and, given Levine's constant boasting about his sources inside the SEC, Pletscher feared these sources might learn what was going on in Nassau and tip Levine. If he could penetrate the government, where else did his influence reach?

Another ingredient contributing to his fear was the pressure, which twisted and exaggerated the truth into something more ominous. Pletscher felt as if he had traded one set of lies for another and piled pretense upon pretense over the months. He had lost his emotional bearings and, because he was adrift, he was less able to sort out the real from the surreal.

These fears, developing gradually over many weeks, were sharply accelerated by another ingredient—a catalyst, a particular event that magnified all that had gone before it. The catalyst was Pletscher's approaching date with the SEC.

Having agreed to provide testimony about Levine, Bruno Pletscher, along with Sherrill Caso, now became convinced that his life was in danger because he was the only person left who could link Dennis Levine to the illegal insider trading at Bank Leu. If Bruno were murdered, they reasoned, the American government would have no way to get to Levine.

Pletscher began looking over his shoulder as he walked the crowded streets in downtown Nassau. He slept poorly, tossing in bed during nightmares and awakening at the slightest sound in the house. The fears reached out to encompass concern over Caso's safety, too, and finally she confided to Pletscher that she no longer felt safe in her own house.

"I'm very, very uncomfortable with all these glass doors and screens," she told him. "There's a lot of lying going on and I'm afraid of where it might end up. Neither one of us may be safe before your testimony."

So they summoned a crew of carpenters and shuttered their house and waited for Pletscher's rendezvous with the SEC, which was scheduled for April 14 in London. They hoped it would be the first step on the path out of the maze and back to normal lives.

20.

A Sordid
Affair

Bruno Pletscher arrived in London from Nassau on Tuesday, April 8, and met Pitt and Rauch at the Savoy Hotel. It was a full week until his scheduled testimony before the SEC lawyers, but they would be seven of the most grueling and important days of Pletscher's life as he prepared for the confrontation with the American government.

Although he was to testify under an agreement reached after weeks of generally friendly negotiations, it would still be an interrogation, and the relationship between Pletscher and the government lawyers remained inescapably adversarial. Pitt and Rauch had explained to Pletscher that an incautious word or unguarded fact could have grave consequences. Responding to hostile questions in those circumstances is frightening for anyone. Distrust of an unfamiliar legal system made it particularly so in Pletscher's case.

To help him overcome the psychological barriers before the genuine grilling by the SEC, Pitt and Rauch had decided to bring Pletscher to London early for several days of informal questioning in their hands. Away from the distractions of Nassau, they could prepare him for his testimony in the setting where the event would actually take place.

The session also offered Rauch and Pitt an opportunity to evaluate Pletscher as a witness, for, because the rush of events had not allowed them to debrief him extensively, they remained unsure of how he would perform or what he would say. A good trial lawyer never asks a question in court unless he knows what the answer will be. Michael Rauch was determined that the SEC would not ask his client any questions unless he and Pitt knew what the answers were going to be. Between them, the two lawyers for the bank had enough government background and courtroom skills to anticipate every avenue the SEC was likely to explore, if not the specific questions they would ask.

Equally important, the two lawyers wanted the chance to ensure that Pletscher did not venture any facts that might identify the bank's customer and jeopardize the dealings with the Bahamian government, the next step in the process. It was not a matter of counseling evasiveness or lack of candor; it involved recognizing the dangers of accidental disclosure.

After a 7:00 A.M. breakfast Wednesday, Pletscher accompanied Rauch and Pitt to Fried, Frank's small law office at 3 King's Arms Yard in London's financial district. The questioning was planned for the conference room, where the actual deposition would occur the following week. It was a simple but effective technique that Rauch often employed in preparing witnesses. He wanted to make sure Pletscher was familiar with the setting, which would help him relax when he confronted the government attorneys. Government attorneys have their own version of the technique: they often seek an edge by interrogating unfriendly witnesses in surroundings that are unfamiliar and frightening for the witness.

Pletscher was drained from the sleepless nights and incessant worries. Moreover, he was still brooding about the propriety of testifying and uncertain about his ability to satisfy the demands of his own lawyers, much less the SEC. As he sat down to begin answering questions, there was still an unanswered question in Pletscher's own mind. "What am I doing this for?" he asked himself.

The three men sat at the large rectangular table in the center of the conference room. Pitt and Rauch had determined that they would lead Pletscher through his testimony chronologically, and so they began by questioning him about the series of documents Levine had signed when he first opened the Diamond account at Bank Leu. They pressed Pletscher about how Levine had identified himself the first day he showed up at the bank, what the banker understood Levine's position to be in New York, why Levine had refused to provide a telephone number where he could be contacted.

Throughout the questioning, Levine was never referred to by name. Pletscher had spent more than five years calling him "Diamond," and it was a hard habit to break. Indeed, it was one that the lawyers did not want Pletscher to break because they did not want to increase the risks that he would slip and use the name "Levine" during his interrogation by the SEC. In recent weeks, Pletscher also had begun referring to Levine as "Moby Dick," so the two pseudonyms were used interchangeably during the questioning.

Rauch and Pitt then went down a long list of questions, ranging from Levine's demeanor to what he said when buying specific stocks. How had Levine contacted the bank? What had he said about why he was buying Dart? What did he say when he bought Textron or Jewel Companies? Why did he always take his money in cash? What were the circumstances that led Pletscher to start copying Levine's trades?

If Pletscher's testimony were at odds with the bank's records or an earlier statement, the discrepancy had to be resolved. If Pletscher left out anything of substance, the omission could be used to attack his credibility later. Pletscher was cajoled and coaxed to recall every detail of his dealings with Levine. Meetings and telephone conversations, some nearly six years old, had to be reconstructed as accurately and completely as possible. It was essential that Pletscher remember Levine's exact words when the American first described why he wanted his mail held and why he had refused to provide bank officials with a telephone number.

Coupled with the records the bank had turned over, the testimony would form the basis for the SEC complaint against Levine and Meier. It also would be used by the U.S. Attorney's Office in New York to prepare criminal charges against Levine for obstruction of justice, the result of the cover-up attempt. Any mistake in Pletscher's testimony could be exploited by Levine's defense attorneys and boomerang on the government, Pletscher, and the bank. It could occur in pretrial hearings or at the eventual trial, when Pletscher would have to take the witness stand and repeat his version of events. Also, an outright lie by Pletscher during his sworn testimony could result in perjury charges against him that would not be covered by the agreement with the Justice Department.

By the end of the first day, Pletscher had undergone a rigorous and demanding ordeal and, despite the fact they were his own lawyers and they had explained their motives, he felt he had been handled roughly. They had covered less than a quarter of the material. By the time Pletscher returned to his room, he was so exhausted that he fell asleep immediately and slept until his wake-up call. It was his first night of sound sleep in more than a month.

On Thursday, Pitt and Rauch were joined by Michael Barnett and Claire Hepburn, who had come to advise their American counterparts on how much Pletscher could reveal about the client's activities at the bank without violating Bahamian law. Sherrill Caso accompanied the Bahamian lawyers to London to provide support for Pletscher, although she was not allowed to attend the questioning session.

Back in January, Pletscher had been searching bank files for material related to the case when he discovered the November 21 memo in which he had joined Meier, Coulson, and Fraysse in a written promise to support Meier's testimony about the cover-up story. Despite the careful wording, it appeared to represent written evidence of a conspiracy to change Meier's bank records and present a false story to the SEC. Moreover, the language implied that Pitt and Rauch had approved the deception, which was clearly not true. The memo was among the documents turned over to the SEC, and it certainly would be brought up by the government attorneys in the deposition. Pletscher was questioned carefully and at length by his lawyers about how it had come to be written.

Pletscher had difficulty remembering early events, but the details of the cover-up scheme were vivid in his mind, both because of their freshness and because they had troubled him so deeply. He could picture his hand dropping the passport photocopy into his office shredding machine and Meier following with the signature card. Relating them to Rauch and Pitt was another matter. His conscience was troubled by the disclosures involving Meier because he knew his testimony would form the basis for an SEC case against his friend as well as against Levine.

But since his agreement in February to testify in place of Meier, Pletscher had come to trust Pitt and Rauch, if not the system they represented. His reservations about testifying were deep-seated and personal, not a reflection of his relationship with the attorneys. During the two days of questioning, despite feeling bruised, his trust had deepened; he convinced himself that telling the full story was best for him and for Bank Leu. Yet nagging doubts remained about the impact on others and about whether he could stand up to the approaching encounter with the government lawyers.

That night, after a second full day of questioning, Pletscher and Caso went to dinner together and he spilled out his troubles.

"It's like a marathon, the strain and the demands on my memory," he told her. "I was so tired last night that I slept the entire night. This is one of the roughest times of my life. I tell you, at times I have felt like a complete idiot because I could not remember certain things. I'm told that no discrepancies are allowed, that I have to say things that will hurt people. But I don't want to hurt other people."

Caso is strong-willed and protective, and she had been a source of strength for Pletscher over the past weeks. The one bright spot in his life was planning for their wedding in May. She, too, had reservations about the course he was taking. Like Pletscher, she was not an American and she could see no illegality in the insider trading. Her chief concern, however, was the eventual impact of his actions on her future husband, personally and professionally. Those were the anxieties that intensified as she sat at dinner listening to his anguish and seeing the physical effects of his ordeal.

"Maybe Bernie was right in refusing to testify," she said. "Maybe this is not the right thing to do and it will hurt you in the end."

"I've asked myself many times why I'm doing this," he said. "But Harvey and Michael have convinced me that it's the right thing to do. It's best to cooperate and tell the truth. That's what's keeping me going."

By the time the two lawyers finished questioning him on Saturday, Pletscher had undergone a tedious and exhaustive four days of interrogation covering nearly six years and some of the most questionable actions of his life.

Not only was the banker now prepared for his encounter with the SEC, he had proven himself an excellent witness. Under expert prodding and with trading records and memos as reminders, Pletscher had demonstrated outstanding recall of the details and conversations that would convince the SEC they were on the verge of breaking a major insider trading case. Even his obvious emotional struggles over his disclosures would work to his benefit, illustrating that Bruno Pletscher was a man of conscience who had overcome honest misgivings to present a truthful portrait of a sordid affair.

The SEC lawyers were due to arrive the next day, and it would mark the start of a second round of informal questioning for Pletscher. Two days of informal talks had been arranged with the government attorneys. They could question Pletscher on an off-the-record basis, without administering an oath or bringing in a legal stenographer to record the session. Perhaps the government would obtain enough information in the informal session to make the deposition unnecessary or limit it. The preliminary session would provide an opportunity to set an accurate course for the formal testimony. It was the sort of secret session that never gets reported in the court record or press, but it would be a key to creating a smooth and orderly transcript for the actual deposition.

On Sunday afternoon, Paul Fischer, Leo Wang, and Peter Sonnenthal arrived at Fried, Frank's London office. Accompanying them was Charles Carberry, the Assistant U.S. Attorney who was gathering evidence for the anticipated criminal charges against Levine.

The agreement between Bank Leu and the SEC stipulated that the government could not ask any questions that might lead to the identity of the customer. The preliminary session was largely to make the formal testimony easier.

By this time, the government attorneys had reviewed the thousands of documents provided by Bank Leu, and the SEC attorneys recognized they were astride an investigation of major significance, perhaps the biggest insider trading scandal in history. In addition to the extent of the customer's trading, the government's case was important because it would demonstrate the agency's ability to penetrate a sophisticated attempt to deceive it and obstruct justice. Apart from those significant considerations, the attorneys knew that the insider was a major figure on Wall Street whose arrest would jolt the industry. All of the elements of a sensational and significant case were there, and they were eager to fill in the details through Pletscher's testimony.

As it turned out, the government attorneys were not going to be able to fill in all the details on the basis of the questions they had prepared from the documents alone. They simply didn't know enough to ask all of the right questions. After questioning him for four days, the bank's attorneys knew parts of Pletscher's story that the government never would have thought to explore, key elements that would have remained hidden without their assistance. The informal nature of the session allowed Pitt and Rauch to ask questions that filled important gaps with additional information, such as the letter from John Shad, chairman of the SEC, to the customer.

When he brandished the letter before Coulson and Pletscher in

December, Levine had not given them a copy. That meant that the letter was not in the documents the bank had turned over to the SEC, and the agency would have no way of knowing about it unless they were tipped to its existence during the questioning. The risk was that it would provide a strong clue to the customer's identity, but that danger was outweighed by the value of the letter as a means of convincing the SEC that they had a big player within their grasp—and one who had reveled in deceiving the agency.

So as Pletscher was describing various events in the cover-up and providing details about how the customer had boasted about fooling the SEC, Rauch said, "Bruno, tell them about the letter." And the attorneys learned that, at the height of the investigation, the chairman of their commission had written a neat little thank-you note to Moby Dick.

Throughout the questioning, Pletscher found himself nagged by the behavior of Leo Wang. It was the only problem during two days of informal talks, but it was beginning to loom as a serious impediment to the smooth progress of the meeting.

Paul Fischer, the senior SEC attorney, handled most of the questioning. He struck Pletscher as a fair and reasonable lawyer who was trying to obtain as much information as possible within the ground rules. Peter Sonnenthal was quiet. The few questions he asked were polite and intelligent. Surprisingly, Pletscher reacted most favorably toward Charles Carberry, the burly prosecutor who had recently become chief of the securities fraud unit at the U.S. Attorney's Office when Peter Romatowski left for private practice. Like Sonnenthal, Carberry said little. But when he did talk, Pletscher found his questions to be clear and straightforward. And, in Pletscher's eyes, he was the most humane and understanding of the government lawyers.

Leo Wang was tough and tenacious, which was within bounds. What disturbed Pletscher was what he viewed as Wang's excessive abrasiveness and disregard for the rules about not trying to trick him into disclosing the identity of the customer. He felt the brash government attorney twisted his answers, trying to push him further than he intended to go on several subjects. Despite Pletscher's outward stoicism, Pitt and Rauch observed their client's distress.

On Monday, the second day of the informal session and Pletscher's sixth consecutive day of interrogation, his discontent grew by the minute under Wang's questioning. He was bothered by the tone and the nature of the questions, not by the information they were causing him to reveal. He was so bothered that Pitt noticed the agitation and gently led his client from the room. "Bruno," he said soothingly in the hallway, "this has been a hell of an ordeal for you, and Wang's been on your case hard. Why don't you take a walk around the block and cool off?"

Pletscher left the building and briefly considered returning to his hotel. Inside the conference room, Rauch and Pitt emphatically told the government attorneys that there would be no badgering of their client, either in the informal session or in the deposition scheduled to begin the following day. When Pletscher returned, his temper had cooled but he remained frazzled and the session was called to an early halt.

As Pitt and Rauch had expected, the SEC still wanted its formal deposition. Indeed, the information provided by Pletscher on Sunday and Monday had made them more eager than ever to get his account into a sworn deposition that would be admissible as evidence.

On the morning of Tuesday, April 15, the conference room at Fried, Frank's London office was close to full. Carberry had returned to New York, but Fischer, Sonnenthal, and Wang remained. In addition to Pitt and Rauch, the bank was represented by Claire Hepburn and by David Hardison, the Fried, Frank associate who had been supervising the document copying in Nassau and who had helped prepare Pletscher for his testimony. Amy Jedlicka, a paralegal, was also present.

At 9:17 A.M., Fischer asked Pletscher the first recorded question, "Do you swear to tell the truth, the whole truth, and nothing but the truth?"

"I do," he answered firmly.

The first day's session lasted until nearly 5:00 P.M., with a short break for lunch and several brief interruptions while the separate groups of lawyers gathered in one corner of the room or another for discussions. The second session, on Wednesday, began at 9:25 A.M. and ended about 6:00 P.M. The questioning was formal, and the only interruptions by Pitt or Rauch this time were to stop Pletscher from answering a question or to provide an explanation for a point here or there. The customer was referred to carefully as "Mr. X," his nicknames left for sessions that were not destined to be transcribed and presented as evidence in court.

Fischer handled most of the questioning, a good strategy since Wang's attitude continued to irritate Pletscher. Since the interrogation was conducted in English, Pletscher had to pay careful attention to the questions in order to understand them and answer accurately. When he was questioned by Wang, his anger at the attorney clouded his concentration and his answers had to be repeated often.

Over the two days, Pletscher described the coded account opened by the customer and the photocopy of his passport and signature card that had been attached to the first file. He said he knew the customer was an American investment banker who lived in New York City. He outlined the methods by which the customer contacted the bank to place his buy and sell orders, and the cash withdrawals he carried away in plastic bags.

Even in discussing an element as dramatic as Levine's clandestine trips to Nassau, the language was controlled and formal.

"Did Mr. X indicate to you how he traveled to and from Nassau to pick up his cash withdrawals?" asked Wang.

"Mr. X indicated to me that on various occasions he travels to and from Nassau in various steps and quoted to us that he flies with different airlines; changes planes; never flies direct to Nassau;

always through different destinations; and mentioned at one point that he flew to Freeport first before he came to Nassau. He mentioned that at times he flew through Canada before coming down to Nassau, and he also mentioned that for some portions of his trips he even chartered a plane."

Pletscher described his own trading in eleven of the same take-over stocks, recalling how Meier had offered to let him in on the deal after he lost $3,700 on an options transaction. And he provided a detailed, step-by-step account of the cover-up, right down to shredding the two documents and lying to the lawyers, describing the customer's repeated boasting about how easily he had lied to the SEC to thwart past investigations and how his sources within the agency had kept him abreast of the current inquiry.

By Wednesday evening, it all seemed to be there—the investigation touched off by an anonymous letter written eleven months earlier was nearly at an end. The unnamed customer stood revealed as a criminal who had abused his position to collect $11.6 million in illegal profits and another $1 million in interest.

The next day, Pitt returned to Washington. Leo Wang remained in London for a few days of sightseeing. Pletscher and Caso accompanied Rauch to Zurich, where the lawyer and the banker provided a full report on the deposition to officials of the parent bank.

Their first night in Zurich, Pletscher took Caso, Rauch, and some of his friends out to dinner to celebrate the end of his ordeal. They went to his favorite restaurant, a small gourmet spot called Jacky's Stapferstube, where they ate what Pletscher boasted were the finest veal chops in all of Switzerland. Pletscher's spirits gradually were being restored. The fears for his and Caso's safety were subsiding. It would be useless for Levine to try to stop him now that his information was in the hands of the U.S. government. For the first time in months, Bruno Pletscher was eager to return to work and proceed with the career that he was certain his cooperation had assured. He was confident the most horrific period of his life was over. His only worries were a pleasure—planning his wedding less than a month away and arranging a honeymoon cruise in the Caribbean.

Elated with Pletscher's testimony, Fischer and Sonnenthal returned to Washington and briefed Sturc and Lynch on the fruits of their trip. It would be several days before the 201-page transcript of the deposition was available. But as the two lawyers read through their notes and described the testimony to their superiors, Lynch and Sturc recognized that the session had been a complete success. The detail was extraordinary and damning, and the case obviously was going to be a major step forward in the crusade against insider trading.

While three of the lawyers had been in London for the deposition, a fourth SEC attorney, Edward Harrington, had been continuing the analysis of the trading records provided by Bank Leu. The "Moby Dick" list provided by the bank was an enormous help, but Harrington's task was the drudge work of the case. He could not accept the bank's figures for anything, so he spent hours assembling the trading slips for purchases of stock in a particular company, matching the dates to public announcements of takeovers or other sensitive corporate transactions, and arriving at his own determination of the customer's profits. The original list of twenty-eight stocks had grown to forty, then fifty, and appeared to be settling out at fifty-four or fifty-five for inclusion in the SEC complaint against the customer, although he had traded in 114 stocks.

There would be no reason to include the forty-three losing stocks that the customer had picked. There were sixteen or seventeen stocks in which the customer had made a profit but his purchases could not be matched to any specific corporate event, a necessary requirement for insider trading violations. The success of the case would not rise or fall on whether the number of stocks in the final SEC list was fifty-four or seventy-one. The magnitude of the trading and the bottom-line profit of $11.6 million were sufficient to compel a dramatic reaction on Wall Street.

It was still too early for celebrating at SEC headquarters, however. The SEC had to begin the paperwork for an airtight case against the customer, based on the trading records and the gold mine of information provided by Pletscher. And, as significant and far riskier, Bank Leu still had to receive permission from the Bahamian authorities to divulge the name of their client. If the bank failed and the SEC were forced into court, the resolution could be months or even years away, and the unidentified customer would be alerted to the game afoot.

"There's still a lot to be done, and a major hurdle will be getting Bank Leu to disclose the identity of the customer definitively," cautioned Sturc.

But there was one piece of the puzzle that couldn't wait. As Wang and Sonnenthal had examined the trading records provided by Bank Leu prior to the deposition, Wang's earlier suspicions that the insider was Dennis Levine were strengthened by the involvement of his employers in many of the transactions. It also seemed likely to them from the pattern of purchases that, whoever the customer was, he was gathering information from at least one other person, and possibly several, which meant the case could extend beyond the single customer.

Wang had shared his suspicions about Levine with Sturc and Fischer and, the day after he returned from London, Fischer sent a young clerical worker to the SEC's library in the basement of the building. Check the discussions topics for the roundtable sessions for the last six months, he said. See if there was one that dealt with takeovers and, if there was, bring me a list of the investment bankers who participated.

The worker later returned with a list of investment bankers who had partcipated in a roundtable entitled "Recent Takeover Developments," held on November 26, 1985. One of the names on the list was Dennis Levine, managing director, Drexel Burnham Lambert.

21.

A Banking Relationship

The Water Club is an expensive seafood restaurant located on two stationary barges at the end of Thirtieth Street on the East River in Manhattan. When Levine had telephoned and invited Ilan Reich to lunch there on April 24, he had said he needed Reich's advice about an intriguing prospect.

"I've had a job offer from Ivan Boesky," Levine told his former confederate as they sat at a table overlooking the river. "He wants me to head his merchant banking operation and he's offered me a five-million-dollar signing bonus. It'd be the biggest signing bonus in Wall Street history. What do you think?"

As a merchant banker, Levine would not only advise corporations on takeover and acquisitions situations. He would assist in raising money for the ventures, earning even greater fees. Most of all, however, Levine loved the idea of setting Wall Street history with the signing bonus. When word of it spread, he thought, the fame would catapult him to the top of the heap in the investment banking world, over the likes of Tom Hill and Marty Siegel. Indeed, one of the reasons Levine told Reich he was entertaining the offer was to get out from under the shadow of Siegel at Drexel.

Just as Levine had feared in February, Siegel had ascended immediately to the top rung of the mergers and acquisitions unit at
Drexel. The blue-chip accounts once earmarked for Levine were
suddenly going to Siegel and it left Levine bitterly disappointed.
Levine was considering packing his bags and moving on, as he had
in the face of setbacks at Smith Barney and Shearson Lehman
Brothers.

"I'd be the biggest name in banking," he told Reich eagerly.
"You're one of the few people I'd trust with this news. I value your
judgment. Come on. What do you think?"

Reich's first thought had been that two men with egos as big as
those of Ivan Boesky and Dennis Levine wouldn't last long in the
same firm, and there was little doubt who would be leaving when
the inevitable clash took place. It was an opinion he kept to himself
as he advised Levine to weigh the great opportunity against the
possible risks in leaving a secure position as one of five managing
directors at Drexel Burnham.

"Well, nothing's firm," Levine said. "We're still negotiating and
it may not happen."

Although he did not mention it to Reich, Levine had also discussed the Boesky job with Wilkis at an earlier lunch in the same
restaurant, telling him the same story about a $5-million signing
bonus. He had told Wilkis that he could not decide whether to take
the offer and that his father had cautioned him against going to
work for Boesky. "My father tells me he's not a good guy," Levine
told Wilkis. "He says he's got a bad reputation."

What Levine did not tell either Reich or Wilkis was that the
enormous bonus was a means of concealing the payoff owed him
for the confidential information Levine had leaked to Boesky over
the past fourteen months.

Trading on Levine's inside tips had netted Boesky's affiliates
more than $50 million in profits since February 1985. Under their
formula, Levine's share stood at $2.4 million and he had not yet
collected a dime.

Because Boesky's arbitrage operation used investors' money, it was subject to stringent auditing requirements and the books were examined regularly by an outside accounting firm. Under no circumstances could he skim off $2.4 million to pay for Levine's tips, and he wasn't about to pay such a large sum out of his own money. So he and Levine had devised the hiring bonus as a way to use corporate funds and disguise the payoff. But the amount was in dispute. Levine insisted on $5 million, reasoning that he was already owed half that amount and there should be some real incentive for taking the job. Boesky was offering only $2 million total.

If the amount could be settled from Levine's point of view, the arrangement was ideal. Not only would he obtain the payoff Boesky owed him in legitimate money, he could profit two ways from his confidential information. First, the tips would be fed directly into Boesky's arbitrage operation and the payoff would be disguised as Levine's rightful share of the profits as a valued employee of the firm. With Boesky's enormous capital and Levine's golden sources, there was virtually no limit to the amount of money they could make on takeover stocks. The $10.5 million in Levine's Bank Leu account would be small change. Second, Levine could continue trading for his own foreign account.

In order to accomplish the second goal, he needed to get his money out of Bank Leu. He telephoned Pletscher repeatedly, insisting on arranging a meeting so that he could explain his proposal to take the funds elsewhere on what he claimed was a temporary basis. Pletscher continued to stall for time, urging Levine to wait until the end of the SEC inquiry.

Throughout the late winter and spring of 1986, Bob Wilkis noticed that Levine vacillated wildly over the course of the SEC inquiry. One day he would be all bluster and confidence, describing how forcefully he was demanding that the bank toe the line on the cover-up and threatening to withdraw his money from Bank Leu and start over at another bank. The next day, he might be morose and anxious. One night in April, Levine picked up Wilkis after work and they headed out to Long Island in Levine's Ferrari. As they screamed down the Long Island Expressway at 140 miles an hour, Levine looked over at Wilkis and said, "Bobby, I'm scared about this SEC thing." Wilkis thought Levine was going to crash the car and kill them both, but Levine soon regained his cool and began discussing the need for a contingency plan.

By early May 1986, Levine was fed up with the delays and determined to obtain his money. On May 6, he flew to the Cayman Islands, where Wilkis maintained his account, and went to its branch of Morgan Grenfell Ltd., the English merchant bank. Using the name "Robert Gold," he introduced himself to the bank's managing director, Brian Kieran, and said he wanted to open a trading account for his Panamanian company.

In a scenario similar to the one he had played out at Bank Leu almost exactly six years before, he said that he intended to trade actively in the United States stock markets and he would like to be able to telephone the bank collect to place his orders. He gave Kieran $5,000 in cash as an initial deposit and said his lawyer in Nassau would see that several million dollars was transferred into the account within a matter of days.

This bank's response was different, however. Kieran asked for a list of references for Mr. Gold and his company, International Gold Inc. He said it was standard policy at the bank before opening a corporate account. The request startled Levine but he promised that his lawyers would be in touch to provide any information required. He gave Kieran the name and telephone number of his attorneys and departed, leaving behind the $5,000 as an opening deposit.

The day Levine flew to the Cayman Islands, Michael Rauch and Harvey Pitt were in Nassau making final preparations for a meeting that would decide the course of the SEC inquiry and the fate of its quarry. At 3:00 P.M. on Wednesday, May 7, lawyers for the bank and the American government were slated to plead their case before Paul Adderly, the quixotic attorney general of the Bahamas.

The first disclosure of the Bank Leu investigation to Nassau authorities had come the previous week. The bank had delivered a cautiously worded letter to Adderly, which set forth the background of the case and detailed why the bank sought Adderly's permission to disclose the name of the customer involved to the SEC and Justice Department. As part of the care taken to avoid offending Adderly, the letter had been sent over the signature of Michael Barnett, the Nassau lawyer, and it requested an informal meeting to explain the situation further. In addition to the bank's lawyers, the meeting would be attended by Gary Lynch; Michael Mann, the SEC expert on international affairs; Lev Dobriansky, the American ambassador to the Bahamas; and a Justice Department lawyer.

On the morning of May 7, the SEC attorneys and the bank's lawyers met in Barnett's office to go over strategy for the meeting with Adderly. They discussed the points that each side would make and the order in which they would speak, and they attempted to think of answers to potentially difficult questions that Adderly might ask. They broke shortly before noon for lunch and agreed to meet at Adderly's office at 3:00 P.M.

The attorney general's office is in the seven-story post office building, a graceless structure of concrete and glass set on a hill overlooking the busy port of Nassau. The halls are awash in the sharp smell of disinfectant and the elevators provide a creaky ride to the third floor, where Adderly has his offices. A wooden planter delineates a small waiting area outside his modest office.

Paul Adderly is a small, trim man with graying hair and a booming voice. He rose to political prominence as a member of Prime Minister Lynden Pindling's independence movement in the late 1960s and early 1970s. He has been the nation's only attorney general since its independence from Great Britain in 1973.

As Pitt and Rauch walked into the anteroom shortly before 3:00

P.M., Barnett rushed up to them and said urgently: "I've been looking all over for you guys. We've got an emergency."

One of Adderly's deputies had just informed him that the attorney
general would not allow Pitt and Rauch to attend the meeting,
Barnett said. Adderly had decreed that he would not meet with any
American lawyers unless they worked for the government. He had
also refused to allow the Justice Department lawyer to attend. When
the unsuspecting Lynch and Mann arrived a few minutes later,
they found a livid Pitt pacing the linoleum hallway.

"The attorney general won't let us go to this meeting," Pitt told
Lynch. "It would be a breach of our understanding if you go without
us. You must get us into the meeting."

Lynch was unable to persuade the attorney general to change
his mind and he told Pitt that, even though he agreed that Pitt and
Rauch should be there, he would have to go to the meeting without
them.

Pitt then tried to get Barnett to persuade Adderly to change his
mind. The Bahamian lawyer also was unsuccessful. Pitt then told
Barnett that he should not go to the meeting.

"I can't refuse to go," said Barnett. "I've written a letter asking
for this meeting. And I have to continue practicing law on this
island."

The American lawyers were concerned over how the bank's side
would be presented if they were not at the meeting, but they agreed
that Barnett should go. As the others headed into Adderly's office,
the two Fried, Frank lawyers sat in the waiting area.

After several minutes, Pitt stood and said to Rauch: "I'm not
going to sit around here. He doesn't want to meet with us. I'm
going back to the bank." He packed his briefcase and headed toward
the elevator, with Rauch trailing behind.

On the steps outside the building, Rauch draped an arm across
Pitt's shoulders and said: "Look, Harvey, I know you're mad and
I'm mad, too. I'm mad at the attorney general and at Barnett and
at Lynch. But if something comes up and they come out and look

for us, we ought to be there. This is the most important event in this investigation from the bank's point of view. We ought to swallow our pride and go back up there."

Rauch prevailed and they returned to the attorney general's waiting room. A few minutes later, Barnett emerged from Adderly's office with a wide grin. "I've got great news," he said. "He's agreed. We can disclose the name. The attorney general wants to meet with you guys now."

Inside the office, Adderly explained that he had not allowed them into the meeting because he had no control over their actions. They were not responsible to him or to the American government. Rauch responded that they had been personally disappointed to be excluded. Pitt kept quiet.

As they emerged from the building, Lynch and Mann were waiting for them on the steps. The SEC attorneys were jubilant at the victory. The long shot had come in and, without spending a day in a United States or Bahamian court, the agency was going to get the name of the customer. But before they could provide the details of the victory to the two lawyers who had been excluded, Rauch chewed out both SEC attorneys for attending the meeting without them.

"Wait a minute," said Lynch. "Do you understand what terrific results we got? We got everything we wanted, for us and for you guys. This was a total victory."

Lynch went on to explain that Adderly had agreed the bank could disclose the name without fear of prosecution under the bank secrecy law. He said the attorney general had rendered a verbal opinion that, because the activities involved trading securities and not traditional banking practices, they were not covered by the secrecy law. In effect, they did not represent a banking relationship. It was an idea Mann had floated briefly that morning before the session. Now, according to Lynch, all Adderly needed was a quick letter clarifying a minor point and they were home free.

When Lynch suggested that Pitt and Rauch accompany them to Barnett's office to draft the letter, they refused. "We don't have anything to contribute," Rauch said. "We weren't at the meeting. Remember?"

Two hours later, Barnett called and asked Rauch and Pitt to review the letter before it was sent to Adderly. They agreed and he brought it over to the bank.

Before actually disclosing the name to the SEC, Pitt had insisted that Bank Leu receive a letter from Adderly outlining his position that the bank could reveal the name without fear of prosecution. When Barnett delivered the bank's clarification letter to a deputy attorney general, he was told that the formal letter granting Bank Leu permission would be available by Friday, May 9. Pitt told Lynch and Mann that they would have to wait until then to get the name.

The next morning, Dennis Levine telephoned the bank and threatened to disrupt the entire process.

Levine was rebuffed in his efforts to reach Pletscher and shunted off to Andrew Sweeting, a polished, mid-level bank employee who had spoken with Levine several times on the telephone in recent weeks as part of the effort to keep the customer out of contact with anyone he could press for a decision.

"I want to transfer ten million of my money to an account at a bank in the Cayman Islands," Levine told Sweeting.

With Pitt and Rauch standing over him, Sweeting rapidly scribbled notes of Levine's end of the conversation. Stall, the lawyers mouthed to him, stall. Sweeting responded by telling Levine that he did not know how to transfer money to another bank. Levine said he would call back with instructions or have his lawyers call and explain the process.

Suddenly the race with Levine was on again. The demand to transfer his money would have to be blunted without alarming him. Rauch and Pitt were still waiting for the letter from Adderly. They knew that they had to delay Levine until they got it and could disclose his name to the SEC. Then the responsibility for moving fast would rest with the government. Sweeting, a smooth-talking native of Nassau, was instructed on how to stall when Levine called back with the transfer instructions.

Later that same day, Levine telephoned again. "Here are the instructions. I've got the name of the bank and the account number."

"Well, we're going to need written instructions to transfer such a large sum of money to a foreign bank," responded Sweeting.

Levine sounded exasperated, but he had little choice: "Fine, I'll arrange for you to receive those instructions from my Bahamian lawyers."

The question became which would arrive first, the instructions or the letter from Adderly.

On Friday morning, the lawyers and the bank officials had another delicate task. They had to explain the situation to William Allen, the governor of the Central Bank of the Bahamas and the man who regulated all financial institutions in the islands. Permission from Adderly had cleared the way for revealing the name, but it was important for the bank's future that Allen not be angered.

Adolph Brendle, who was a member of the executive board of Bank Leu in Switzerland, had come to Nassau for the meeting. He accompanied Pitt, Rauch, Barnett, and Bruno Pletscher to the Central Bank offices on Friday morning. They explained the background of the case to Allen and told him Adderly had given the bank preliminary permission to disclose the client's name.

Allen said that he would not second-guess the attorney general about the legality of disclosing the name of the customer. But he was troubled by Bank Leu's involvement with a criminal customer. If banks are going to be given the safety and comfort of the secrecy laws, he explained, they must conduct themselves with a certain standard of integrity and professionalism. Allen was concerned that the standard had been breached by Bank Leu.

"The bank must be well managed and we must have assurances that you won't make the same mistake," he told the bank representatives.

Brendle, who had spent a decade in New York as an officer of another Swiss bank, was reassuring as he promised Allen that Bank Leu intended to be a law-abiding citizen of the banking community. He assured him that the proposed financial settlement with the SEC, which required the bank and some of its staff to return money, would not have any impact on the bank's customers or its solvency. Further, he said, Bernhard Meier, the portfolio manager who had handled most of the trading, had left Nassau. Meanwhile, the bank's board of directors would be reconstituted to provide firmer direction to its operations. But Brendle said the bank intended to keep Pletscher as general manager.

Bank Leu's offices are next door to the Central Bank and, as the lawyers and bank officials walked back, they were satisfied that the demands of the Bahamian government had been met. All that remained was to receive the official letter from Adderly—and to avoid a confrontation with Levine or his lawyers over the money transfer.

During lunch that day, Levine telephoned again and told Sweeting his lawyers would be sending over the written instructions immediately. If the letter from the lawyers arrived soon and the bank refused to transfer the funds, its lawyers were aware that Levine's attorneys could go into court that day and demand the transfer of the money.

About 5:30 P.M. a messenger delivered Adderly's letter to the bank. It was four paragraphs long and gave the bank permission to disclose the identity of its customer because the securities activities did not involve a "banking relationship" and the bank secrecy laws did not apply.

There was no time to waste celebrating the conquest of what had seemed, months ago, an insurmountable barrier. Pitt immediately telephoned Gary Lynch in Washington.

"We got the letter," he said. "Moby Dick is Dennis Levine, a managing director at Drexel Burnham Lambert."

Pitt warned Lynch that the SEC would have to move fast because Levine was trying to transfer his money out of Bank Leu. He assured Lynch that the bank would not voluntarily release a single penny, but he cautioned that the matter could wind up in a Bahamian court as soon as Monday.

A half hour later, the written instructions on transferring $10 million from the International Gold account to an account at Morgan Grenfell in the Cayman Islands arrived at Bank Leu. It was too late for Levine's lawyers to act that day. Pitt called the SEC and gave them the name of the bank and the account number to which Levine was trying to send his money.

About the time Pitt was placing his second call to the SEC, Levine was stepping out of a taxi outside the Gulf & Western building on Columbus Circle. He had been invited to an exclusive buffet dinner and advance screening of the new movie *Top Gun*, which was produced by the company's Paramount Pictures division. Levine had been invited to the posh affair because he had helped arrange Gulf & Western's acquisition of Esquire Inc. in the fall of 1983.

By the time Tom Cruise was piloting his navy jetfighter through the skies over California in *Top Gun*, SEC attorneys in Washington were already compiling the paperwork that would be needed for an emergency court hearing on Monday morning. The attempt by Levine to transfer his money had robbed the agency of any time to celebrate their victory, and the attorneys on the investigation worked late all three nights to get ready to go to court Monday morning against Levine and Bernie Meier.

As the SEC compiled its case against Levine, one of the examples the attorneys decided to use to demonstrate his insider trading involved the purchase of 15,200 shares of stock in Esquire Inc. in October 1983, before the announcement of Gulf & Western's acquisition attempt. He later sold the stock for a profit of $121,728.

With the disclosure of Levine's name to the SEC, Bruno Pletscher felt that he had drawn a line under his involvement with the sordid affair. And what better way to celebrate than with his wedding to

Sherrill Caso on Saturday, May 10. Pitt and Rauch stayed down for the ceremony, and one of their wedding gifts to the newlyweds was a copy of Herman Melville's novel *Moby Dick.*

On Monday morning, May 12, with John Sturc as the lead lawyer, the SEC received an order from U.S. District Court judge Richard Owen in New York that froze the $10.5 million remaining in Levine's bank account as well as his other assets. It was an emergency session that took place without Levine's knowledge.

The SEC civil complaint said Levine had reaped $12.6 million in profits and interest through illegal insider trading from 1980 until the end of 1985 through a financial institution in the Bahamas. The complaint listed fifty-four stocks in which the commission said Levine had earned a profit through insider information. The complaint also accused Bernhard Meier of violating United States securities laws and said the Swiss banker had earned $152,000 by following Levine on nineteen stock and option trades.

The complaint also outlined Levine's attempt to cover up his trading by persuading Meier to lie to the commission and destroy sensitive documents related to his account. What the complaint did not do was identify the bank where Levine held his accounts or mention the name of Bruno Pletscher.

Around noon that Monday, the SEC telephoned Frederick Joseph, the president and CEO of Drexel Burnham, and said the agency was looking for Dennis Levine to serve him with papers in a massive insider trading case. Joseph telephoned David Kay and told him, "They're going to arrest Dennis."

Levine was supposed to be talking with Ronald Perelman in the offices of Revlon in midtown about Perelman's latest acquisition effort, but when the anguished Kay called there he was told Levine had not showed up for the meeting. About an hour later, Levine called Kay from a pay telephone. He was distraught and his voice shook as he raged at the government.

"Yes, yes," he shouted. "I heard the SEC is looking for me. This is bullshit. They've been after me for months on a wild-goose chase. They're trying to ruin my life and destroy my career without even speaking to me first. I haven't done a thing wrong."

Kay managed to control his own reaction and offer Levine some good advice: "Listen, Dennis, you've gotta keep your mouth shut and go find a lawyer. I think you ought to talk to Joe Flom or Marty Lipton or Art Liman and then select one of them. You've gotta get yourself a lawyer."

Kay was deeply shaken as he hung up the telephone. He had been the driving force behind hiring Levine and suddenly Levine was in serious trouble.

Dennis Levine had planned to attend a charity ball for Mount Sinai Hospital at the Waldorf-Astoria that night. It was an annual black-tie affair that attracted the cream of the mergers and acquisitions community, including investment bankers and lawyers.

Instead, about 7:30 P.M. he went to the U.S. Attorney's Office in lower Manhattan to pick up a subpoena and a copy of the SEC complaint against him. When he arrived, he was handcuffed and arrested on criminal charges of obstruction of justice, securities violations, and tax evasion. He spent the night at the Metropolitan Correctional Center.

Early the next afternoon, Levine appeared in court wearing a navy blue suit, white shirt, yellow tie, and black Gucci loafers. His wife sat beside him, holding his hand and whispering occasionally as they waited for his case to be called. On the other side of Levine was his lawyer, Arthur Liman, a prominent white-collar defense attorney. They watched as federal magistrate Kathleen Roberts denied bail to two defendants in a drug case that immediately preceded Levine's.

After a hearing that lasted just seven minutes, Roberts freed Levine on a bail of $5 million. She said it could be secured by $100,000 in cash, his apartment at 1185 Park Avenue, and his shares in Drexel Burnham. As Levine walked out of court, a reporter noticed something was amiss: the French cuffs on his white shirt were not clasped together by cuff links.

22.

Cutting Deals

His arrest did not stop Dennis Levine from scheming. It only set the stage for the biggest trade of his life.

From the moment of Levine's arrest, the publicity was enormous, propelling the story off the business pages and onto the front pages and evenings news. The kid from Queens who made a million bucks a year and couldn't get enough was million-dollar copy. The crescendo of headlines rose when the SEC released a 201-page transcript of Bruno Pletscher's deposition. It was a story that seemed to have everything, from $100 bills in shopping bags and foreign-front companies to shredded documents and relentless pursuit by the SEC. And it seemed to confirm the public impression that the only moral guideposts on Wall Street were dollar signs.

In the executive corridors of Manhattan's investment houses, the scandal reverberated in an atmosphere of disbelief and anxiety over what the answer would be to the question on every Wall Street professional's mind: was anyone else involved?

On June 5, slightly more than three weeks after his arrest, Levine returned to court and pleaded guilty to four felony charges brought by the U.S. Attorney's Office. The charges were one count of securities fraud, for buying and selling the stock of Jewel Companies on the basis of inside information; two counts of income-tax evasion for failing to report his trading profits; and one count of perjury in connection with his testimony to the SEC and Leo Wang about Textron Inc. in the fall of 1984. The counts carried maximum penalties of twenty years in prison and $610,000 in fines, and sentencing was scheduled for later in the year.

He also settled the SEC charges, agreeing to pay $11.6 million, including the $10.5 frozen in his Bank Leu account, and accepting a permanent injunction barring him from the securities business for life. The SEC could have fined him up to $35 million. The government took his Ferrari, which had 3,847 miles on the odometer, but Levine got to keep his Park Avenue apartment, which was worth close to $1 million and had a mortgage of less than $250,000, his 1983 BMW, and about $100,000 in two accounts at Citibank.

Before entering his plea, Levine told Judge Gerard Goettel that he had obtained information about Chicago Pacific Corporation's bid for Textron Inc. in 1984 from another person, although he did not name that person. The disclosure confirmed the fears that Levine was implicating others as a result of his plea bargain.

In a clear voice, Levine told the judge: "To contest the charges against me on technical grounds would serve only to prolong the suffering of my family. It would also convey the wrong message. I have violated the law and I have remorse for my conduct, not excuses."

At a press conference after the plea, U.S. Attorney Rudolph Giuliani said, "We think Mr. Levine's cooperation will be very fruitful and very valuable to the government."

In Washington, Gary Lynch, the SEC enforcement director, said: "An integral part of our settlement was his agreement to cooperate with us. We've done very well."

Robert Wilkis

Bob Wilkis was at LaGuardia Airport waiting to board a plane for Omaha, Nebraska, on May 12 when he learned of the SEC case against Levine. Wilkis was headed for Omaha to lead a presentation by E. F. Hutton & Company to a corporate board of directors. He was told of the SEC suit against Levine by an executive recruiter who had been searching for a better job for Wilkis. At the time, Wilkis was considering competing offers from two Wall Street firms to become a managing director in mergers and acquisitions.

Wilkis went on to Nebraska. But the next day, after reading in the newspaper about Levine's subsequent arrest, he left the meeting early and returned to New York. When he got back that night, he telephoned Levine, who urged him to come to his apartment immediately. Arriving at Levine's apartment, Wilkis found Laurie Levine drawn and red-eyed. Dennis Levine, wearing a T-shirt and sweatpants, was sitting calmly in a chair as he said to Wilkis, "I have to focus on what's important."

Levine said he needed to line up someone who would claim to be the beneficial owner of his Swiss bank account. He asked if Wilkis would fly to the Cayman Islands and hire a lawyer to claim ownership of the account.

"Dennis, it's too late," said Wilkis. "It's too late."

On May 20, Levine and Wilkis met in the most inconspicuous location they could imagine—the garage in the Hell's Kitchen neighborhood of Manhattan where Wilkis kept his car. As they headed into the city traffic for a drive, Wilkis was amazed by Levine's sangfroid as he boasted, "This is the biggest insider trading scandal in history and it's all because of me." Approaching a newsstand, Levine asked Wilkis to pull over so he could hop out and buy a copy of *Newsweek*. "I hear I'm on the cover," he explained. Levine was disappointed. The cover showed several sets of hands reaching for a pile of cash beneath the headline GREED ON WALL STREET. Levine's photo was on page forty-five.

Wilkis had barely slept the previous week and his nerves were jangled. Urging him to calm down, Levine promised him there was no way the SEC and Justice Department could learn of Wilkis's involvement.

"You'll never get called in," vowed Levine. "I'm a stand-up guy and I'm going to fight this thing. I'll never give you up. Just stay cool and you'll be safe."

In the event the government did trace the scheme to Wilkis, however, Levine had a proposition. "Can you handle this?" he asked. "We're going to work out a story together."

If the government confronted him, Levine said, Wilkis should claim that he had accepted cash from Levine in exchange for inside information. There was to be no mention of Wilkis's trading or the secret bank account he had in the Cayman Islands. Wilkis would tell the government that he had used the money from Levine to pay for an apartment on Park Avenue that he had recently bought and other extravagances.

"You and I will go to jail together," said Levine. "We'll get a tan, play tennis, have a vacation from our wives. Then when we get out, we'll split the money in your Cayman account."

"Don't you know when to quit?" asked Wilkis, who had listened to the scheme in silent surprise. "I'm going to get a lawyer and turn myself in."

"Don't do that," Levine said sharply. "You don't need a lawyer. But if you do hire one, don't tell him the truth. Never tell your lawyers the truth."

The next day, Wilkis telephoned a Washington lawyer who had been recommended by a cousin. The lawyer named several New York attorneys who could represent Wilkis, and he offered a bit of advice: "Never talk to Dennis Levine again. He'll be walking around wired."

Wilkis hired Gary Naftalis, a former chief of the criminal division at the U.S. Attorney's Office in New York. Naftalis immediately told Wilkis he should surrender voluntarily and tell the government everything he knew about the scheme. Wilkis refused, saying, "I can't rat on anybody."

Over the next few days, Wilkis kept talking to Levine on the telephone and meeting with him. At 9:30 P.M. on June 2, Levine telephoned Wilkis at home. Using his considerable charm, he drew out Wilkis about his involvement in the insider trading ring. Wilkis still trusted Levine. Indeed, there was no reason to worry because Wilkis could tell from the jingle of coins and the operator's recorded request for more money that his friend was being careful and calling from a pay telephone.

What Wilkis had no way of knowing was that the telephone was set up in the U.S. Attorney's Office, and the sound of the coins and the prerecorded message were part of the elaborate ruse to lure Wilkis into divulging enough to corroborate Levine's claims while the call was recorded by the government. What Wilkis also did not know was that, after an adverse court ruling in the SEC case the previous week, Levine had decided to cooperate with the government.

Dennis Levine had made the biggest trade of his life: he agreed to give up the people who had been involved in his insider trading ring in the hopes of winning leniency for himself. Not only would Levine name his accomplices. He would actively help the investigators by persuading his cohorts to incriminate themselves in telephone conversations recorded by the government. And what better device for concluding the case than a telephone, the instrument that had played such an enormous role in Levine's career as an investment banker and as a criminal.

Three days after the recorded telephone call, Levine pleaded guilty to four felony charges. Robert Wilkis and his lawyer went to the U.S. Attorney's office to try to salvage the best deal possible. The government attorneys took a hard line. Wilkis hadn't come forward initially. And the government lawyers had listened for several days as Levine described Wilkis as the older, more sophisticated member of the ring.

In July, Wilkis settled the civil case brought against him by the

SEC, which charged that he received more than $3 million in profits by illegally trading on more than fifty takeover stocks from 1980 until late 1985. In the settlement, Wilkis agreed to turn over assets worth $3.3 million to the SEC, including all funds remaining in his secret trading account, $50,000 in cash he kept in his apartment, and virtually all of his other assets, except for $60,000 in cash.

On February 9, 1987, after pleading guilty to four felony charges, Wilkis appeared for sentencing before U.S. District Court judge Peter Leisure in New York. He faced up to twenty years in prison.

"I promise you I will never do anything against the law again," he said, trying to control his sobbing. "I beg this court to let me have another chance to make things right."

In imposing the sentence, Leisure said he was taking into account that Wilkis had emotional problems that allowed him to be recruited into the insider trading scheme by Levine, a man who has "a keen ability to exploit insecurities." He then sentenced Wilkis to a year and a day in prison and placed him on probation for five years.

Ilan Reich

A friend telephoned Ilan Reich in his law office on the afternoon of May 12 and asked if he had heard the news about Dennis Levine. When Reich asked what news, he learned the SEC had charged Levine with insider trading. That night Reich went to the charity ball at the Waldorf-Astoria, the one Levine had expected to attend, and he listened numbly as the room buzzed with gossip about the accusations against the Drexel Burnham managing director.

In the following weeks, Reich was anxious and depressed as rumors spread that Levine was naming names. When Levine called Reich in early July and tried to ask him about some of their insider deals, Reich said, "I don't know what you're talking about," and hung up.

A few days before, Reich had managed to find solace on a red-eye flight back from Los Angeles by writing down the facts against him on a yellow legal pad. There were no corroborative facts. He had never taken any money, so his name wasn't on any bank withdrawal slip or deposit form. He had never traded for himself. No one knew his name except Levine. In a contest of his word against Levine's, he would prevail.

The illusion was shattered on Tuesday, July 8, when the SEC served a subpoena on Wachtell, Lipton, demanding documents from many M&A deals over the past six years. At first, the firm's senior partners thought the subpoena was simply a fishing expedition in the wake of the Levine case, and Reich helped gather documents in response to the subpoena. But that Friday, Gary Lynch told Herbert Wachtell that the firm should get an outside lawyer for Reich because the inquiry was focused on him. As proof that it wasn't just Levine's word against that of the brilliant young lawyer, Lynch disclosed that Robert Wilkis had told the government that Levine had described Reich's involvement to him.

On Monday morning, Reich was confronted with the SEC accusations by four partners of the law firm. For two hours he denied everything and doodled madly on a legal pad. Then one of the lawyers told him that an accomplice had corroborated Levine's story about having a source at Wachtell, Lipton. The disclosure was something Reich had not counted on, and it destroyed his will to resist. He began to sob as he confessed his involvement, telling his partners how he had been seduced into the ring by Levine, given him tips on a dozen stocks, and never taken a dime for himself. It was a statement that could be used in court against him because his partners had made it clear they were not representing him.

The firm sent for Robert Morvillo, a highly respected former federal prosecutor who had represented another Wachtell, Lipton attorney, Carlo Florentino, in an earlier insider trading case. Morvillo listened to Reich's story and said he would cut the best deal he could for his young client. He also wanted a suicide watch put on Reich. Morvillo said he had never seen such a distraught person.

On October 9, Reich appeared in U.S. District Court in New York and pleaded guilty to two felony counts of fraud in connection with insider information he had passed to Levine. Each count carried a maximum of five years in prison. The felony conviction also meant that he was automatically disbarred from practicing law.

The same day, he signed a consent agreement with the SEC which said Reich leaked confidential information to Levine on at least twelve separate stock transactions that resulted in profits of $1.7 million for Levine. Although the government acknowledged that he had not received any money for the tips, Reich agreed to pay $485,000 to the government, virtually all of his assets.

On January 23, 1987, Reich appeared for sentencing before Judge Robert Sweet, who used the occasion to defend sending white-collar criminals to prison, telling Reich: "If this sentence involved just you and your family, the outcome would be that you have suffered quite enough for the tormented acts you committed. But unfortunately, the sentence involves all of us and the strength of the laws of our society. Simply stated, a breach of trust at this level with this effect requires a jail term as a deterrent, as a statement by our society that its rules must be obeyed and that personal integrity remain a paramount requirement of our society. You have, it is very sad to say, become a symbol of the sickness of our society and of that loss of integrity which cannot be condoned, whatever the cost."

Sweet then reflected on Reich's motives, acknowledging that the young lawyer was not motivated by greed or ambition, but by the desire for a special friendship with Levine: "Dennis Levine took you. He gave you that special feeling of belonging, as well as a sense of guilt, because you knew what you did was not right, but wrong."

Sweet said he hoped that Reich would someday be reinstated to practice law, concluding: "In imposing this sentence, I want to make it clear that if ever reinstatement to the bar is appropriate—and it is after a felony conviction—this is such a case. You will never, I am absolutely confident, betray your country's trust or the laws again."

Reich was then sentenced to a year and a day in prison and placed on probation for five years. He was given sixty days before starting his prison term so that he could be at home for the birth of his third child.

Bruno Pletscher

Two days after Levine's arrest, Bruno Pletscher sat in his office at Bank Leu making final arrangements before he left on Saturday for a two-week honeymoon cruise in the Caribbean. About midday, Adolph Brendle telephoned. The bank chairman said that Pletscher might have to go to New York the following week to testify against Levine at a court hearing because he was mounting an unexpected defense to the SEC case. Pletscher grew angry at the idea of interrupting his honeymoon, but his real anger was over the continuing intrusion of Dennis Levine into his life.

Brendle said the testimony could be important and they reached a compromise: Pletscher would begin his cruise as scheduled Saturday and telephone the bank Monday to see if his testimony would be required.

On Sunday night, however, Pletscher got a message aboard ship to telephone David Hardison, the young Fried, Frank lawyer who had assisted Pitt and Rauch. When he reached Hardison in Washington, he was relieved to hear that the government would be satisfied if Pletscher merely signed another set of statements about the case. On Monday, a Fried, Frank paralegal took a chartered jet to meet the ship at a Caribbean port. Pletscher signed the necessary papers and continued on his honeymoon, thinking the Levine affair was finally behind him.

The Bahamian government, however, was not content to let the matter rest. Largely because of the extraordinary publicity generated by the Levine case, and the black eye it had given offshore banking in Nassau, the Central Bank had to respond. It did so by pressuring Bank Leu International to remove Bruno Pletscher as its general manager and remove the entire bank board. The bank complied. At the same time, the attorney general's office leaked word through a local newspaper that it had opened a criminal investigation into the conduct of Pletscher and other bank employees.

Suddenly unemployed, facing possible criminal charges, and nearly broke after paying the SEC $46,000 in profits he had made copying Levine's trades, Pletscher had to leave the Bahamas. In August, he and his wife returned to Zurich, where he was told it would probably be better if he did not return to work at Bank Leu. For several weeks, Pletscher searched in vain for another job in banking. Finally, he accepted a sales position with a computer company and began a new career.

Bernhard Meier

Bernie Meier had been back in Switzerland for several months by the time the case broke. He never formally responded to the court case brought against him by the SEC, which charged that he violated United States securities laws in the buying and selling of stock in at least eighteen companies on the basis of confidential information obtained by Levine. Meier's illegal profits were placed at $152,000 by the SEC. A default judgment was entered against him in the summer of 1986 and, at press time, his lawyer was engaged in settlement discussions with the government. Like Pletscher, Meier no longer works for Bank Leu and has been unable to find a job in banking in Switzerland.

Ira Sokolow and David Brown

Ira Sokolow also received a call from Levine at his bogus pay telephone but, before Levine's guilty plea, Sokolow came forward and began negotiating an agreement to cooperate with the government. Sokolow, by that time a vice president in mergers and acquisitions at Shearson Lehman Brothers, was able to offer investigators a piece of the puzzle Levine hadn't been able to provide: the name of the source at Goldman, Sachs. He said he had received confidential information from his college friend, David Brown, and passed it to Levine.

The Justice Department said Sokolow tipped Levine to more than fifteen confidential transactions, including information he received from Brown. The transactions were among Levine's most profitable, including Nabisco; Levine's trading profits on the information totaled $7 million. In exchange, Levine had paid Sokolow about $125,000 in cash and Sokolow had passed on $27,500 to Brown.

On September 4, the two college friends appeared before Judge John Keenan. Each pleaded guilty to two felony charges of securities fraud and income-tax evasion. Each man faced a maximum of ten years in prison. Sokolow signed an agreement to pay the SEC a total of $210,000 in illegal profits and fines; Brown agreed to pay the SEC a total of $145,790 in profits and fines.

In a letter to guide Judge Keenan in sentencing Sokolow, Assistant U.S. Attorney Charles Carberry wrote about the ability to deter insider trading: "As in the case of Sokolow, rarely are the criminals acting out of economic need. People in the investment banking and securities industries are risk balancers. They balance the risk of getting caught and the consequences of apprehension versus the potential for easy money."

In November, Keenan sentenced Sokolow to a year and a day in prison. A few days later, the judge ordered Brown to spend weekends in jail until he had served a total of thirty days.

Randall Cecola

Randy Cecola was completing his first year at Harvard Business School when Levine was arrested. After his involvement was disclosed to the government by Levine and corroborated by Wilkis, Cecola agreed to plead guilty to a charge of tax evasion for failing to report his stock profits on his tax returns. He also signed a consent agreement with the SEC which required him to pay $21,800 in illegal profits and fines. The administration at Harvard suspended Cecola but granted him leave to reapply at a later date. On February 10, 1987, he was placed on probation for six years by a federal judge.

Ivan Boesky

Dennis Levine baited the hook and landed the little fish for the government, but for a time he was unable to deliver the biggest catch.

When federal prosecutors and SEC attorneys began to question Robert Wilkis in July, they became extremely interested in his description of Levine's relationship with Ivan Boesky. It appeared to Wilkis and his attorney, Gary Naftalis, that Levine had protected the arbitrager. At three interrogation sessions in July, the government lawyers pressed Wilkis for every scrap of information he could recall about Levine's dealings with Boesky. Wilkis described how Levine had told him about tipping Boesky on Houston Natural Gas and Nabisco; he recalled Levine's plan to go to work as president of Boesky's merchant banking operation. Then suddenly the attorneys stopped asking about Boesky; his name was not mentioned in any later sessions.

The information from Wilkis had provided the investigators with enough to corroborate Levine's tale of his confidential relationship with Boesky. With the help of Wilkis, the government had enough evidence to force Boesky to cooperate in an attempt to save himself from total financial ruin and possibly to lighten his prison term.

In the fall of 1986, Boesky allowed the government to monitor his telephone calls with a wide number of major financial figures on Wall Street. He also provided investigators with detailed accounts of his relationships with investment banks, particularly Drexel

Burnham and its junk-bond department. Among those he implicated was Martin Siegel.

On November 14, the SEC electrified the financial world with the announcement that Boesky had been caught in the Levine investigation. One of the richest and most visible figures on Wall Street had agreed to pay $100 million in penalties and returned profits, accept banishment from the securities industry for life, and plead guilty to a single, unspecified criminal charge that would carry a maximum jail term of five years.

The lawyer who negotiated much of the deal with the SEC and the Justice Department was one of Boesky's longtime corporate attorneys, Harvey Pitt. One of his partners during the negotiations was Michael Rauch.

In his SEC agreement, Boesky was charged with reaping profits of more than $50 million by using information from Levine to buy and sell stocks through his affiliated companies. The document also said that Levine had "cultivated" the relationship by initially providing Boesky with free tips before demanding money.

Boesky's bargain with the government was criticized as too lenient by some members of the financial community and some congressmen. Its very leniency, however, sent shivers of fear into the core of America's investment community because it signaled Boesky's full cooperation with the government's widening probe, a scandal dubbed "Wall Street's Watergate" by *Time* magazine. The fears seemed justified in the days following the announcement as word spread that Wall Street was awash in subpoenas, even though a subpoena represents no allegation or evidence of wrongdoing. Among the recipients were Drexel Burnham Lambert and its junk-bond king, Michael Milken, along with some of the nation's leading corporate raiders.

Breaking up Levine's operation had pushed the SEC's crackdown on insider trading onto the front pages. But following the trail to Boesky had touched off the biggest Wall Street scandal since the Great Crash. Aside from the minor complaints about the terms of the agreement with Boesky, the SEC was awash in praise, and its newfound power promised to provide the agency with leverage over the financial community for months.

But the high praise turned to bitter complaints a few days later when it was disclosed that Boesky had been allowed to sell off $440 million worth of holdings, mostly in takeover stocks, before the announcement of his cooperation, which sent the price of most takeover stocks plummeting, at least for a matter of days. John Shad, the SEC chairman, was forced to explain to Congress that Boesky had been permitted to sell in advance of the announcement to avoid a panic in the markets, but many critics viewed it as the ultimate insider transaction.

Boesky's cooperation carried the scandal across the Atlantic. He told the SEC about his secret role in the manipulation of stock prices by Guinness PLC, the giant English liquor and brewing company, during a takeover bid for Distillers in early 1986. The SEC passed the information on to its counterpart in Great Britain and, on December 1, the British government announced a major investigation of Guinness and other elements of the securities industry in London.

As part of that inquiry, the Guinness board of directors disclosed in January 1987 that Bank Leu of Zurich had played a central role in an illegal program of stock purchases designed to drive up the Guinness stock price during the $3.8-billion battle for control of Distillers.

Martin Siegel

Marty Siegel was spending the afternoon of November 14, 1986, in the Park Avenue office of Martin Lipton, the prominent takeover lawyer. Along with being principal architects of many corporate defenses, the two men were close personal friends. About mid-afternoon a federal marshal walked into the office and handed a subpoena to a startled Siegel. When Siegel opened the document and read that it covered his dealings with Ivan Boesky, his shock turned to anguish and he began to sob.

Siegel decided very quickly to plead guilty and, although he continued to work at Drexel Burnham, he stopped playing an active role in transactions. He sold his cedar-and-glass home on the Connecticut shore and moved his family away from the New York area.

On February 13, 1987, a Friday, the private end to Siegel's career became a public one. Flanked by two attorneys and dressed in an expensive gray suit, he appeared in federal court and pleaded guilty to one count of conspiracy to violate securities laws and one count of tax evasion for failing to declare the payoffs from Boesky on his tax return. Under his agreement with the SEC, Siegel paid $9 million to settle the civil charges, although he had received only $700,000 from Boesky. Siegel also provided the government with the names of three more Wall Street professionals and claimed they had participated with him in a scheme to make illegal stock profits.

It was almost noon on a clear, cold Friday when a dark blue car carrying Dennis Levine and his wife pulled up outside the tiny federal courthouse in White Plains, New York. More than seventy-five reporters, photographers, and television camera crews swarmed around the car as it came to a halt. For ten minutes, the Levines remained trapped inside, unable to open the doors in the frenzied crush. Finally, Levine and his wife pushed their way out of the car and through the throng on the sidewalk, striding into the courthouse, grim-faced and silent.

Judge Goettel had been transferred from Manhattan to the tiny branch court forty-five minutes north of New York City in January, and on February 20, 1987, the reporters had trekked up to cover the sentencing. United States marshals barred the journalists' entry to the building until moments before the sentencing, so they waited outside, stamping their freezing feet, sipping coffee, and grumbling about the last revenge of Dennis Levine.

For all the drama of financial power and corruption that had set the stage for that afternoon, the proceedings themselves were a bland anticlimax. No voices were raised in the name of mercy or justice. No emotions were expressed. It might have been a sentencing for a petty thief, except for the reporters, pens poised over notebooks, who lined the rows of blond wood pews, and the handful of television sketch artists who sat in the jury box.

Levine's wife, Laurie, wearing an expensive gray dress, sat in the second row of benches with her father-in-law and other family members. Levine sat at the defendant's table, flanked by his attorneys, Arthur Liman and Martin Flumenbaum.

Liman opened the hearing by asking Goettel for leniency as a result of his client's "forthright" cooperation, which he said had come despite the stigma of being labeled an informant and despite a death threat (which turned out to be a crank call). Liman read off the names of those whose convictions or plea agreements with the government were the result of that cooperation: "Boesky, Wilkis, Sokolow, Reich, Brown, and Cecola."

And he appealed to Goettel to recognize the punishment already suffered by Levine: "He's broke. He's bankrupt. Everything is gone. That's the least of it. What he has endured is a form of banishment. He is an outcast, a leper like I've never seen. Dennis Levine's name will always be remembered, Your Honor, as a synonym for this offense."

When the judge asked if he had anything to say, Levine rose and faced him. He wore a gray pinstriped suit, crisp white shirt, red-striped tie, and gold-rimmed glasses. His pudgy face was expressionless and his voice was flat as he delivered the following plea in about ninety seconds:

"Last June when I pleaded guilty before Your Honor, I was automatically sentenced to a life of disgrace and humiliation. I have disappointed my wife, my children, my father, my brothers, my family, my friends, my colleagues. I abused the system I believe in and I will never forgive myself. I'm truly sorry and ashamed, not only for my past criminal behavior, but for all the anguish and humiliation and embarrassment I caused my family, mostly because it's been their love and support that has sustained me throughout this very difficult period. Over the last ten months, Your Honor, I have been very hard on myself. I assure you that I have learned my lesson. I swear in this court that I will never violate the law again and I beg you to allow me, to give me a chance to put the pieces of my life back together, to help my family get through this, to try and become a contributing member of the community again. Thank you."

There is no easy yardstick for measuring the value of cooperation in a criminal case. A draft of federal sentencing guidelines completed in 1986 said a judge should reduce a sentence by a maximum of 40 percent as a result of a defendant's cooperation. The figure was eliminated as too restrictive in a later version and it was left solely within the discretion of the sentencing judge to calculate the value of cooperation.

"I have concluded that the offense, standing alone, is such as to warrant a sentence of five to ten years' imprisonment," Goettel said as Levine stood alongside his attorneys. "Against that we have to put the fact that he pled guilty and he has cooperated and that his cooperation here has been truly extraordinary. Through the information he has provided, an entire nest of vipers on Wall Street has been exposed.

"Now, there are those who say that persons who cooperate like this and become informers are doing so simply to save their own skins and that they should not be afforded any consideration because of it," Goettel continued. "I think, obviously, they are doing it to save their own skins, but if you don't reward that sort of behavior you won't get that kind of cooperation in the future."

The U.S. Attorney's Office was prohibited from making a recommendation on sentencing as a result of the plea bargain struck with Levine the previous May. As a result, Goettel said, the only guidance he received in determining the sentence was a six-page letter from Assistant U.S. Attorney Charles Carberry which offered the barest outline of Levine's crimes and a brief summary of his cooperation.

Satisfied that he had explained his dilemma, the judge eyed the packed courtroom one last time and delivered the sentence: two years in prison and a fine of $362,000, which the judge said he doubted Levine would ever be able to pay.

There was a momentary hush as everyone strained to pick up some visible or audible sign of emotion from the man in the gray pinstriped suit. There was none. Levine walked quickly to the side of the courtroom, looked in brief confusion at the crowd of reporters now on their feet and blocking the public exit, and then left through the judge's private door, followed by his wife and attorneys.

Near the back of the courtroom sat Elsa Wilkis. She had not learned of her husband's involvement in Levine's ring until June 1986. After struggling for months to help her husband cope with his pain and anguish, she had needed to see for herself whether there would be any justice for the man she blamed for it all. Watching Levine slip out the rear door, she had the distinct sense that he was suppressing a smirk. And one of Dennis Levine's favorite sayings came to mind. She could almost hear him say the words: "I'm not a banker. I'm a thespian."

Epilogue

The Morning After

One question seems to hang over the story of Dennis Levine: is he a clever, greedy anomaly or does he embody the decline and fall of business ethics?

In the first days following his arrest, Dennis Levine was viewed in the narrowest of terms by Wall Street. He was a cunning scoundrel who had betrayed the trust of his employers and clients to enrich himself. Soon he moved up a notch, becoming a symbol for the materialism and cynicism of the new generation of professionals on Wall Street, the young men and women just out of business school or law school for whom more did not seem to be enough. The joke was that the Yuppies had become Yippies—Young Indicted Professionals. This image of unbridled avarice was bolstered in late May 1986 when five men in their twenties, including a corporate lawyer and three Wall Street professionals, were indicted for sharing confidential information about takeover bids to buy and sell stocks and further their careers.

There also was an uglier, more disturbing undercurrent to the reaction. Levine and many others caught up in the scandal are Jewish, and ethnic jokes and disparaging remarks about Jews were often heard on Wall Street. The rustlings of anti-Semitism, reminiscent of the attitude of the financial establishment a century before, raised concerns among Jews and others about a potential backlash. Even more than the attempt to attach all blame for the scandal to the industry's young professionals, the anti-Semitism represented a distasteful and misguided diversion into irrelevancies that was part and parcel of Wall Street's refusal to recognize the real issues.

Eventually, as the true dimensions of the scandal became known, Wall Street had no choice except to face a harsher reality: the problem was not relegated to a few individuals, nor could it be restricted to an unethical generation. The integrity of the profession itself came under scrutiny, and slowly the perception that Levine & Co. represented the ethical anemia of a generation gave way to far deeper concerns about the vertiginous drop in standards of honesty and ethics in the American financial community. While the emphasis was on investment banking, the central role of that profession in the business arena and the involvement of lawyers and arbitragers made the crisis far broader.

Wall Street is not overrun by sly fast-buck artists; the majority of those who work there are decent and honest. But the magnitude of the insider trading scandal exposed institutional failures that maligned the honesty of an entire sector of the American economy.

One victim was the long-held notion that Wall Street could regulate itself—that a professional's word was his bond. Despite the fact that the Merrill Lynch compliance department set the scandal in motion by responding properly to an anonymous letter, there was ample evidence that what *Fortune* magazine called the "profit-at-any-price malaise" had eroded the ability and motivation of the industry to police itself. Voices were raised in Congress and on the Street for stricter regulation by the Securities and Exchange Commission. Harvey Pitt was asked by a Senate committee to lead a blue-ribbon inquiry into whether new laws were needed to protect the public.

Calls for tighter regulation and new laws are well and good, but they beg the critical point. Symbolized by his extra-long telephone extension cord at Lehman Brothers, part of Levine's job was tapping the gossip network flourishing among investment bankers, lawyers, raiders, and arbitragers. Throughout his career, Levine was rewarded for his ability to develop information that no one who knew him could have believed was the result of his brilliant analysis of stock prices or financial data. Protection from the rampant greed of a Dennis Levine is only partly the province of laws and regulators; the bulk of the burden rests with the financial community, and so does the bulk of the blame for the demise of integrity. Levine not only existed but thrived because too many of his colleagues chose to look the other way in a business climate where the size of the fee dwarfed long-range considerations such as the well-being of the client.

Assessing the meaning of the scandal in *The New York Review of Books* on March 12, 1987, Felix Rohatyn of Lazard Frères warned that "a cancer has been spreading in our industry. . . . The cancer is greed." He went on to emphasize the broader issue of the decline of ethics and integrity, saying: "Too much money is coming together with too many young people who have little or no institutional memory, or sense of tradition, and who are under enormous pressure to perform in the glare of Hollywood-like publicity. The combination makes for speculative excesses at best, illegality at worst. Insider trading is only one result."

No system yet invented can provide complete assurance that everyone will behave ethically. But it is the responsibility of Wall Street's wise men to assure that, at the very least, the atmosphere rewards ethical and honest behavior and does not tolerate unscrupulous actions, even if these fall short of blatant illegality.

The purging of Levine, Boesky, and their ilk might yet have a profound effect on the way Wall Street conducts its business. Throughout the history of the United States, there have been periods of financial excesses. The Robber Barons of the nineteenth century did not get their names because they behaved like Boy Scouts, and the Great Crash of 1929 was the result of the speculative orgy fueled by Wall Street. Each of these periods has been followed by a cycle of reform, and perhaps another is due.

The answer to the question "What is Dennis Levine?" is this: he is indeed clever and greedy, but he is no anomaly. He is Wall Street's worst nightmare come true, and he came true because of Wall Street's failure to instill any sense of ethics or standards or tradition in a whole generation of its employees. This institutional failure occurred at a time when the frenetic pace of mergers and acquisitions demanded greater care and caution, not less. Too many young graduates of business school and law school were viewed as fodder in the war for enormous profits to pay the vast overhead and inflated bonuses of the senior partners at some of the most respected firms on Wall Street.

The most stringent system of ethics and the highest standards would not have stopped Levine. He scuttled into his career with a predisposition toward crime. But unwavering insistence on adherence to codes of ethical conduct would have stopped him somewhere along the line, rather than rewarding him with promotions and ever-larger salaries and ultimately transforming him into a star. And those he dragged into his web of illegality and excess might have been spared if there had been some alternative voice insisting on ethical behavior. Instead, all eyes were focused on the bottom line, and in the cutthroat world of investment banking in the 1980s—plagued by eroding standards of behavior and marred by the absence of an institutional conscience—crossing the line into illegality was a step taken too easily.

Author's Notes

This is a true story, and every name, date, episode, and conversation are real.

The primary source of factual material was hundreds of hours of interviews with people who have firsthand knowledge of the subject matter. In many cases, more than one participant in an event was interviewed. Those interviews were augmented with thousands of pages of documents, ranging from government files to the handwritten notes of some of the participants.

Under the federal Freedom of Information Act, thousands of pages of documents were made available from the files of the United States Securities and Exchange Commission regarding Case No. HO-1743, the investigation of Bank Leu International Ltd. and, ultimately, Dennis Levine. Among those documents were the complete trading records of Dennis Levine, Bruno Pletscher and Bernhard Meier at Bank Leu, memos and notes written by bank personnel following meetings with Levine, and internal Bank Leu reports and correspondence. In addition, the SEC files contained Levine's personal appointment calendars, telephone logs, and travel records; internal documents from Drexel Burnham Lambert; the Merrill Lynch trading records of Brian Campbell, Carlos Zubillaga, and Max Hofer; Campbell's sworn testimony to the SEC; notes taken by SEC attorneys from interviews with other people involved in the investigation; and hundreds of other documents.

The complete records of the civil and criminal proceedings against Levine, Robert Wilkis, Ilan Reich, Ira Sokolow, David Brown, Randall Cecola, Ivan Boesky, and Martin Siegel, along with the civil case file against Bernhard Meier, were also available. The court records contained the transcript of Pletscher's deposition in London. This book drew on voluminous additional material—the report of the court-appointed receivers who reconstructed Levine's spending between January 1, 1980, and May 12, 1986, court records from other SEC cases, and archive material from the SEC. In addition, background material was drawn from hundreds of magazine and newspaper articles as well as from many books. Every effort was made to verify material in these sources. Particularly informative was the work of *Wall Street Journal* reporters James Stewart and Daniel Hertzberg.

References to weather are drawn from the records of the National Weather Service and back issues of Bahamian newspapers. Physical descriptions of settings are nearly all the result of the author's firsthand observations.

The book is written in a narrative style that attempts to place the reader as close as possible to the major events. As a result of this form, it was necessary to reconstruct conversations without interrupting the narrative flow to attribute the sources. Every conversation was reconstructed as precisely as possible from a variety of sources, and each conversation reflects the essence of what was actually said. Often, however, the conversations do not represent the exact words spoken by each participant. Rather, techniques developed during the author's fourteen years as a reporter were employed to obtain the most accurate reconstruction possible. In addition to the recollection of participants, the conversations are based on contemporaneous notes taken by participants, memos written after conversations, the knowledge of other people involved in the conversations, and sworn testimony contained in court records. In nearly every instance, the dialogue represents the best recollection of at least one participant in the conversation. A few conversations, however, were reconstructed on the basis of information supplied by people who were not present but were reliably informed about what was said.

Following are some of the sources of information in greater detail.

Chapter 1

The physical descriptions are based on a visit to Nassau. The description of Levine's appearance and the occurrences at Bank Leu are based on interviews with Bruno Pletscher and memos written for the bank's files by Jean-Pierre Fraysse following each meeting. Information regarding Levine's previous Swiss account came from the report of the court-appointed receivers and from information Levine supplied to Robert Wilkis. All empirical information throughout the book on Levine's securities transactions is drawn from SEC documents, the actual trading records now in SEC files, or the trading analysis prepared by the bank and labeled PROFITS MOBY DICK.

Chapter 2

Several people who knew Dennis Levine as a youth and young man were interviewed, including two of his professors at Bernard Baruch College, Jack Francis and Leonard Lakin. Additional material about his years at Smith Barney came from interviews with people who knew him during that time, and from the firm's personnel records for Levine, which are contained in court files.

Some of the material about Levine's background was drawn from newspaper and magazine articles, including a series of articles in the *Chicago Tribune* on June 15, 16, and 17, 1986, and an excellent article in the *Washington Post* on May 22, 1986.

Chapter 3

The history of investment banking in America is recounted in great detail in two excellent books, *Competition in the Investment Banking Industry*, by Samuel L. Hayes III, A. Michael Spence, and David Van Praag Marks (Cambridge, Mass.: Harvard University Press, 1983), and *Investment Banking and Diligence*, by Joseph Auerbach and Samuel L. Hayes III (Cambridge, Mass.: Harvard Business School Press, 1986). In addition,

Hayes, the Jacob Schiff Professor of Investment Banking at Harvard Business School, wrote two influential articles for the *Harvard Business Review* about changes in investment banking, and those articles provided solid factual information. Hayes also was interviewed extensively, as were others familiar with the investment banking business.

Chapters 4–9

These chapters rely extensively on interviews with the participants in the various deals as well as court records and SEC documents. The story of Ilan Reich's relationship with Levine was first told in an article entitled "Death of a Career," which appeared in the December 1986 issue of *The American Lawyer*. It was written by Steven Brill, the editor of the magazine. The author of this book spent many hours interviewing Reich and reviewing the facts with him.

The history of Lehman Brothers and the story of the forces that led to its acquisition by Shearson American Express are recounted dramatically in Ken Auletta's book *Greed and Glory on Wall Street: The Fall of the House of Lehman* (New York: Random House, 1986).

One of the most accurate and complete early articles tracing Levine's career was contained in the *Wall Street Journal* on May 15, 1986.

Many of Levine's encounters with Bank Leu personnel are described in detail in Pletscher's deposition before the SEC. Pletscher expanded on those instances and added much more in interviews with the author at his home outside Zurich and in subsequent telephone calls.

Some material came from the many lawsuits filed against Levine and others following the SEC's disclosures. One example is some of the material about the Litton-Itek transaction described in Chapter 7.

An example of the *modus operandi* employed throughout the book is the Crown Zellerbach deal described in Chapter 9. The crucial lunch at Sir James Goldsmith's townhouse at which Levine "went gray" was described in detail in the sworn testimony of Roland Franklin. The information was then expanded by interviewing two participants in the lunch. An analysis of the takeover bid for Crown Zellerbach is contained in an internal Drexel document. Goldsmith's background was described in a *Wall Street Journal* article on November 21, 1986.

Chapter 10

Material about Ivan Boesky came from many interviews, SEC papers filed in the case against him, and dozens of lengthy newspaper and magazine articles, including two excellent profiles of Boesky—an August 6, 1984, piece in *Fortune* magazine by Gwen Kinkhead, and a December 1984 story in the *Atlantic Monthly* by Connie Bruck. The analysis of Boesky's earnings draws on many sources, including an article in the December 15, 1986, edition of *Forbes*.

Boesky's dealings with Levine are described in the SEC lawsuit against Boesky, and the arbitrager's relationship with Martin Siegel is outlined in the SEC lawsuit against Siegel. In addition, the description of Siegel's relationship with Boesky relies extensively on an article in the *Wall Street Journal* on February 17, 1987. A government lawyer and another attorney familiar with the case verified the accuracy of the substance of the article in separate interviews with the author.

Chapter 11

Former and present attorneys at Merrill Lynch & Company described the events that followed the receipt of the anonymous letter regarding Carlos Zubillaga and Max Hofer. Brian Campbell's sworn testimony before the SEC provided additional information.

The history of the two precedent-setting cases involving Swiss banks is drawn from interviews, court files, and newspaper articles.

Chapters 12–16

Many of the seminal events in these chapters were first mentioned in Pletscher's deposition: some were described in considerable detail in that document. Each of them, however, was fleshed out through interviews with at least one of the participants or the recollections of at least one person who was reliably informed about what transpired.

The travel and expense records from Levine's tenure at Drexel Burnham provided details about such events as his June 1985 vacation in France and his purchase of champagne to celebrate the Pantry Pride–Revlon transaction.

A transcript of the SEC roundtable discussion on takeovers is contained in the agency's archives.

Chapters 17–20

At the instruction of their lawyers, Pletscher and Richard Coulson kept detailed notes of their meetings with Levine from the time the bank changed its strategy for dealing with the SEC. Copies of these notes are contained in SEC files and were used to reconstruct many of the conversations that occurred in late 1985 and in 1986. In some cases, the notes were used to refresh Pletscher's memory.

Details about the recapitalization of FMC are contained in a lawsuit filed in federal court in Chicago.

Although Levine hinted at many junctures that he had one or more sources within the SEC, lawyers for the agency said no evidence was found that Levine was receiving information from any government employee. He was probably relying on Wall Street gossip.

Levine's "genius plan" to resume trading, first mentioned in Pletscher's deposition, was described in interviews with Pletscher and others. A clearer explanation of how it would have worked is not possible because of Levine's silence and because there is some doubt that Levine actually understood what he was discussing.

The March 19, 1986, agreement between the SEC and Bank Leu International is contained in SEC files along with the attachment describing the customer.

The letters exchanged between the SEC and the U.S. Customs Service are in SEC files.

A copy of the letter from Levine's Nassau lawyers to the bank concerning the possibility of a lawsuit is contained in SEC files.

The events leading up to the formal deposition in London were first described by Pletscher in an interview and later confirmed by Harvey Pitt and Michael Rauch in separate interviews.

Chapter 21

Levine's job negotiations with Boesky were first mentioned in an interview with Reich and confirmed by Wilkis. A third party agreed that the talks occurred and that the dispute involved how much signing bonus Levine would receive.

Paul Adderly, attorney general of the Bahamas, was interviewed about the May 7 meeting and his subsequent letter to Bank Leu.

Levine's appointment calendar noted that he would attend the *Top Gun* screening on May 9, and a Paramount employee confirmed that his name was on the invitation list. His appointment calendar also noted that Levine was scheduled to attend the Mount Sinai charity ball on May 12.

Chapter 22

Wilkis described the government reaction to his information about the relationship between Boesky and Levine, and Wilkis's attorney, Gary Naftalis, felt that the government agencies appeared not to have known about it. However, attorneys for the Justice Department and SEC refused to discuss the matter.

Transcripts from the sentencings of the various defendants were used to verify quotes taken down by the author and by other reporters who attended the sentencings.

Adderly confirmed in December 1986 that his office was conducting a criminal inquiry into the activities at Bank Leu.

Index